INDIAN

SOCIAL JUSTICE

INDIAN
SOCIAL JUSTICE
A CASE FOR REVIEW

L. M. KHANNA

PARTRIDGE

A Penguin Random House Company

To order additional copies of this book, contact
Partridge India
000 800 10062 62
orders.india@partridgepublishing.com

www.partridgepublishing.com/india

Dedicated to the

People of India

CONTENTS

Clarification

In this manuscript, American spellings have been followed throughout except in extracts and quotations taken from different sources, in which the original spellings are retained. The quotations in the text are in inverted commas, single or double depending upon their length. A few older references from internet are either not available now or have been shifted to the Archives. A few important ones are mentioned. One article on untouchables was a paper published by the American Congress Library and the other was an unpublished article written by Dr Ambedkar, a part of which, the editor said, was not even corrected. The third was the original 2008 Judgment of the Supreme Court of India in *Ashok Kumar Thakur v. Union of India* Case No. 265/2006, which was downloaded from the Supreme Court website soon after its delivery in April 2008. The four different judgments had no pages, only paragraphs which were numbered separately for each judgment. The judgment was published in *A.I.R.* Supreme Court 2008 Supplement 1 in early 2009. It can also be obtained from the Court. It is also available in *Supreme Today* 2008 Volume 3 published by Vikas Books Unlimited. Both can be correlated with the original downloaded judgment or the latter obtained directly. Most references are from the judgment of Chief Justice K.G. Balakrishnan and a few from Justice Dr. Arijit Pasayat and Justice Dalveer Bhandari. In 2005, an Expert Group on Equality of Opportunity was set up under the chairmanship of Prof. N. R. Madhva Menon by the Sachar Committee appointed by Government of India. The Group's report was put up on the Internet and has been quoted in Chapter 9 of this book. It is a part of the Sachar Committee Report and can be accessed with it.

Abbreviations

Other Backward Classes	OBC
Scheduled Castes	SC
Schedules Tribes	ST
2008 Judgment of the Supreme Court of India	Judgment 2008

PREFACE

In 1979, the Central Government constituted the Second Backward Classes Commission, 'to investigate the conditions of socially and educationally backward classes,' to take steps for their advancement' and 'to examine the desirability for provision for reservation of appointments or posts in favour of such backward class of citizens which are not adequately represented in public services."[1] As there was no consensus on the acceptance of this report, it remained unimplemented for ten years.

1990 was a tumultuous period in the history of India. The country was ruled by a minority Indian Government, which was on the verge of collapse. In a desperate effort to save itself, when the government accepted the recommendations of the Second Backward Classes Commission, it was followed by widespread protests in which many students lost their lives. Ultimately, the matter reached the Supreme Court in the form of *Indra Sawhney and Others vs. Union of India* case, which was heard by a Special Bench of nine judges.

In 1992, the court gave a divided verdict in which the majority judgment described the Scheduled Castes as outcastes and Panchama; and the rest of backward class of citizens as Shudra. In a scathing attack on the Hindu religion, the court observed that the constitution makers were men of vision. They were aware that the Hindu religion, the way it was being practiced, lacked in egalitarian ethos and although the Shudras were 'no better but better than Panchama', due to social stigma attached to them, they had no deliverance except, perhaps, death. A relatively small section of Hindu community, under the label of Scheduled Castes was certainly depressed and some of them were also untouchable, but, it was difficult to accept that, because the Backward Classes Commission had described them as Shudra, socially and educationally backward classes, or backward class of citizens other than Scheduled Castes, with 52 percent of total population of India,

---

1   A.I.R. Supreme Court 1993: 507: 12

were in any way comparable or similar in their backwardness to Scheduled Castes, To justify their lower status, the respondents blamed their lowly and menial hereditary occupations, which, they claimed, they had been forced to follow for thousands of years.

The acceptance of the term Panchama for the first time in the judicial history of India gave a new legal meaning to the Hindu social structure. Invented in the early 19th century, Panchama, which meant fifth Varna, had a highly contentious history. The British gave up its use after a trial in one or two censuses in the 19th century. Though the term remained in circulation in a few circles, the *Hindu Law* enacted in 1837 and the British courts, till they left India in 1947, continued to treat the lowest castes as Shudras. Not to speak of Panchama and Shudra, even on the definition of caste there has been no consensus. Similarly, it is also questionable to attribute one's actual position in society to nexus between caste and hereditary occupation. So is the division of society into different races of Aryans, Dravidians and Aborigines. Aboriginals are controversial category; existence of Dravidians is unproven, and the theory of Aryan invasion of India and Aryans making serfs and slaves of the other two categories has few, if any, takers. Despite that, all social ills in Indian society were attributed to racial discrimination and the matter was taken to the United Nations in the early 21st century.

On the legal side, too, there has been no unanimity and different Benches of the Supreme Court have held different opinions. In 1992, for instance, the Supreme Court overturned a vital opinion of the same court held for thirty years. The new direction, too, is not un-debatable. Equation of caste and class is another issue. Creamy layer, the way it is implemented, has aggravated inequalities. The theory of compensatory discrimination, to compensate backward classes for centuries of atrocities committed by ancestors of the forward castes is popular, but unproven. Equality of opportunity and its application are other problems. Therefore, despite more than six decades of reservations, most families and individuals among the backward classes have failed to gain. The better off among backward classes refuse to wean off and continue to capture majority of reserved seat and the really poor and the illiterate are left high and dry. Governments succumb to blackmail because of the political fallout. To stick to real causes of backwardness like poverty and illiteracy, thus, is not easy in the present caste and religion stuck political society.

The Hindu social structure even in the best of times has been misrepresented and controversial. Therefore, it was not surprising that the notions of past two hundred years should influence the court decisions in the post-colonial era. It is only due to the last 3-4 decades of untiring researches of the British, the American, the European, the French, the Japanese, the Indians and the other historians, historiographers, sociologists and one lone lawyer, Marc Galanter, that there is a change in the perceptions of Hindu society and the backward classes. These studies have reopened the whole issue of caste-structured social justice. As the matter is of considerable importance to the Indian nation, I have quoted these authors and their publications, wherever necessary. No issue of social justice in India can be complete without citing Dr B. R. Ambedkar from his own writings. Wikipedia, the free encyclopedia, the British Encyclopedia and Ultimate Reference Book, besides other encyclopedias, have provided valuable material. The wide literature on the Internet has also been of assistance. Therefore, there is no claim to original or primary research on my part. This book is not an academic treatise on religion, sociology, history, race, law, genetics, and politics. The aim is to collect Information from all known and reliable sources and produce it in the form of a *case presentation* before the Indian people and the ultimate arbiter—the Apex Court, by a citizen of India who sincerely believes that in its search for social justice, the nation has strayed due to pressures, distortions, religious and political ambitions of the colonial rulers and the equally unceasing politicization of inequalities in the post-independence India. It would be my endeavor to critically review the past ideas and concepts that are intimately related to the judicial proceedings in relation to backward classes and their uplift in India, and report the current knowledge and events of last a few decades, which have convincingly challenged the, so far, entrenched hypotheses.

Acknowledgement

Without the literature quoted from the various authors and the other sources mentioned above and cited in this book, this presentation would not have been possible. Finally, I am grateful to the staff of the Partridge Publishing India, A Penguin Random House Company, for their patience and help which I received from the first day onwards in publishing this difficult book.

Relevant Articles of the Indian Constitution

Note: During the British times there were three types of backward classes: depressed classes, backward tribes and backward classes. Depressed classes became Scheduled Castes, backward tribes Scheduled Tribes and backward classes, Other Backward Classes. After the independence Other Backward Classes were called socially and educationally backward classes in Article 15(4); and backward class of citizen in Article 16(4). The final category is backwardness due to simple poverty and illiteracy, the category of socio-economic backwardness, known in rest of the world, but, caught in the web of caste, disregarded in India, even by the courts.

Relevant articles of the Indian Constitution concerned with the backward classes are reproduced from the judgment in *Indra Sawhney and Others* v. *Union of India* case[2] for the convenience of the reader. Clause 5 of Article, 15 which was enacted later, was down loaded from the Internet.

Article 14

Equality before law: The State shall not deny to any person equality before the law or the equal protection of the laws within the territory of India.

Comment: It is a fundamental right. It is said to include right to equality, including equality before law, prohibition of discrimination on grounds of religion, race, caste, gender or place of birth, and equality of opportunity in matters of employment, abolition of untouchability and abolition of titles.

Article 340

The President may by order appoint a Commission consisting of such persons as he thinks fit to investigate the conditions of the socially and educationally backward classes within the territory of India and the difficulties under which they labour and to make recommendations as to the steps that should be taken by the Union or any State to remove such difficulties and to improve their condition.

---

2   *A.I.R.* Supreme Court 1993: 503-505

Article 15

Deals with reservation in educational institutions with bar on discrimination on grounds of religion, race, caste, sex, or place of birth:

1. The State shall *not* discriminate against any citizen on grounds only of religion, caste, sex, place of birth or any of them.
2. No citizen shall, on grounds of religion, race, sex, place of birth or any of them, be subject to disability, restriction or condition with regard to access to shops, public restaurants . . . use of wells, tanks . . .
3. Nothing in this article shall prevent the State from making special provision for women and children.
4. Nothing in this article shall prevent the State from making any special provision for the advancement of *any* socially and educationally backward classes of citizens, or for the Scheduled Castes and the Scheduled Tribes.
5. Nothing in this article or in sub-clause (g) of clause (1) of article 19 shall prevent the State from making any special provision, by law, for the advancement of any socially and educationally backward classes of citizens or for the Scheduled Castes or the Scheduled Tribes in so far as such special provisions relate to their admission to educational institutions including private educational institutions, whether aided or unaided by the State, other than the minority educational institutions referred to in clause (1) of article 30.

Article 16

Deals with equality of opportunity in matters of employment and reservations in services under the State:

1. There shall be equality of opportunity for all matters relating to employment or appointment to any office under the State.
2. No citizen shall, on grounds only of religion, race, caste, sex, descent, place of birth, residence or any of them, be eligible for, or discriminated against in respect of, any employment or office under the State.

3. Nothing in this Article shall prevent Parliament from making any
   law, prescribing, in regard to a class or classes of employment or
   appointments to an office under the Government . . ."

4. Nothing in this Article shall prevent the State from making any
   provision for the reservation of appointments or posts in favour of
   any backward class of citizens which, in the opinion of the State, is
   not adequately represented in services under the State.

Comment: The Constitution provides equality of opportunity in
employment and prohibits discrimination against any backward citizen on
grounds of his/her caste, religion, race, etc., but permits reservations in favor
of *any* backward *class* of citizens which in the opinion of the State is not
adequately represented in its services. In Draft Article 10(3), the precursor
of Article 16(4), there was no mention of 'backward' before 'class of citizens'.
Ambedkar added 'backward' before class of citizens before 1950 and the
Apex Court added 'socially' before backward class of citizens and added
Scheduled Castes and Scheduled Tribes in clause 4 on its own in 1992.

Article 341: Scheduled Castes

1. The President may with respect to any State or Union territory, and
   where it is a State, after consultation with the Governor thereof, by
   public notification specify the castes, races or tribes or parts of or
   groups within castes, races or tribes which shall for the purposes of
   this Constitution be deemed to be Scheduled Castes in relation to
   that State or Union territory, as the case may be.

2. Parliament may by law include in or exclude from the list of
   Scheduled Castes specified in a notification issued under clause (1)
   any caste, race or tribe or part of or group within any caste, race or
   tribe, but save as aforesaid a notification issued under the said clause
   shall not be varied by any subsequent notification.

Article 342: Scheduled Tribes

1. The President may with respect to any State or Union territory, and
   where it is a State, after consultation with the Governor thereof, by
   public notification, specify the tribes or tribal communities or part

of or groups within tribes or tribal communities which shall for the purposes of this Constitution be deemed to be Scheduled Tribes in relation to that State or Union territory, as the case may be.

2. Parliament may by law include in or exclude from the list of Scheduled Tribes specified in a notification issued under clause (1) any tribe or tribal community or part of or group within any tribe or tribal community, but save as aforesaid a notification issued under the said clause shall not be varied by any subsequent notification.

Article 335

The claims of the members of the Scheduled Castes and the Scheduled Tribes shall be taken into consideration, consistently with the maintenance of efficiency of administration, in the making of appointments to services and posts in connection with the affairs of the Union or of a State.

INTRODUCTION

It seems to be rule of wisdom never to rely on memory alone . . .
but to bring the past for judgment into the thousand-eyed present
and live ever in a new day.

(Ralf Waldo Emerson)

Social justice depends upon two factors, how accurately a social structure is perceived and how relevant are social laws. There was nothing wrong with the social laws enacted by the constitution makers. The problem is with the perception of social structure inherited from the colonial times, and the interpretation of laws to justify it. Enough literature has appeared during the last three to four decades to challenge the colonial perceptions and based on them the local propaganda, which have unduly influenced the people's psyche. In *The Preamble of Indian Constitution,* justice has three distinct forms: social, economic, and political, secured through various provisions of Fundamental Rights and Directive Principles. Social justice denotes equal treatment of all citizens without any distinction based on caste, color, race, religion, sex, and region. Economic justice means non-discrimination between people on account of economic factors. It involves the elimination of glaring inequalities in wealth, income, and property. A combination of social justice and economic justice denotes what is called 'distributive justice'. Political justice implies that all citizens should have equal political rights and equal voice in the Government.

The British identified certain sections of Hindu society who were victims of a peculiar idea of purity and pollution, gave them various names, but ultimately called them Scheduled Castes. They gave them reservations in legislatures, educational institutions and services. Post-colonial Indian governments followed the same, but also added backward tribes as Scheduled Tribes who were, again, mostly Hindus. The third category, the other backward classes, was expected to be from all section of society, but got embroiled in controversy. Despite the constitution using the word classes, caste was introduced even in the last category.

A dissenting judge in *Indra Sawhney and Others* v. *Union of India case* (popularly called the Mandal case after the name of the chairman of the Second Backward Classes Commission) aptly wrote, "The Mandal Report invents castes even for non-Hindus. The obsession with caste and the desire to apply the same yardstick to all Indians impelled the Commission to identify backward classes among non-Hindus also by the exclusive test of caste regardless of the fact that caste is anathema to Christianity, Islam and Sikhism."[3]

In 2001, the population of Muslims was 140 million, that of Christians 25 million, and that of Sikhs about 20 million. The literacy rate among Hindus, Muslims, Christians, and Sikhs was 65 percent, 59 percent, 80 percent, and 69 percent and work participation was 40.4 percent, 31.3 percent, 39.7 percent, and 37.75 percent, respectively. Figures for the 2011 census are not available. A recent survey published in 2013, however, shows much improvement in the condition of Muslims. They only lack in participation in government jobs by a few percent, but there is an increase in percentage in self-employment. Therefore, barring the Scheduled Castes and to an extent the Scheduled Tribes, criteria for identification of backward classes in rest of the population should have been either specific to each community or common for all communities, including Hindus. There was little excuse for not having common criteria in the twentieth century. The constitution also intended the same, but after 1951, the State and the courts, while interpreting, converted classes into castes.

When Justice Krishna Iyer of the Supreme Court saw that even the courts have related inequalities in society to caste and caste system, he wrote in his judgment in the case of N.M. Thomas in 1976 that in addition to caste and caste system, conception of equality was not a constitutional abstraction distant from everyday experience in India's long history, or a foreign notion imported from Western political theory, but was rooted in the nation's past. He suggested, "India's past would need to be rewritten to emphasize that equality is indeed part of Indian history, and that the constitution reflects the realization of ideals that were not brought from abroad but instead grew from Indian national experience."[4]

---

[3]   *A.I.R.* Supreme Court 1993: 722: 622: (vii)
[4]   Krishna Iyer, A.I.R. 1976 S.C. in N.M. Thomas: 529

According to Sasha Riser-Kositsky from University of Pennsylvania, earlier Europeans insisted upon the essentially religious character of caste and denied its political configurations on the excuse of 'science' and the British transformed it from a loose, discriminatory hierarchy in which the main differences between castes were political into an officially structured and State-sanctioned hierarchy. This "lack of British understanding of the caste system, and their misdirected efforts to reform it, has important ramifications which continue to influence the social climate in India today."[5]

If there is no clarity on the definition of caste, there is also no clarity on the definition of backward classes. The Supreme Court acknowledged on more than one occasion that determination of socially backward classes was very complex and it would require re-evaluation with the progress in knowledge. Another judicial source says that a general definition of social justice is hard to arrive at and even harder to implement. One concept demands people have equal rights and opportunities; others demand an even playing field. But what is just or fair and what defines equal? Who should be responsible for making sure that the society is a just and fair place? Should it be legislature or the moral fabric of society? Because the previous judgments did not speak with one voice, in 1991 the Constitution Bench hearing the Mandal case referred it to a Special Bench of nine judges to finally settle the issues. When the judgment was delivered in 1992, it was hoped that it would be the last word on the subject, but the anthropology on which the majority judgment relied upon was highly debatable. In 2008, the issue of reservation in postgraduate institutions again came up before the Supreme Court, but the court once again restricted itself to the constitutionality of the newly introduced clause 5 in Article 15, which provides reservation in postgraduate studies. On the social side, things were even more complex. There was no unanimity even on the structure of society. New terms coined in the nineteenth and the twentieth centuries played havoc with the Hindu social structure. Equation of caste with class was another problem. There was only an impression, not any tangible proof of thousands of years of backwardness or centuries of nexus between caste and occupation. Recognizing the changing perceptions of social structure, the Supreme Court observed in the case of *Balaji*, "An elaborate investigation and collection of data and examining the said data in a rational

---

5   Sasha Riser-Kositsky, 4916 *Penn History Review*, Vol. 17, Iss. 1 (2009), Art. 3—as quoted in Wikipedia

and scientific way" was necessary to determine socially and educationally backward classes. (Page 166) This is not a book of law, but because it deals with that portion of Hindu Law, which was the brainchild of the colonial period and adopted by free India as Law of Caste, it was bound to influence the court judgments. It cannot be accepted in 2014 and should be reviewed in the light of change in perceptions.

Writing about India's missing historians, Mihir Bose quotes R. C. Majumdar, the doyen of Indian history, "One of the gravest defects of Indian culture that defies rational explanation, is the aversion of Indians to writing history. When it comes to evidence of what life was like in the ancient times there are no accounts by Indian writers."[6] Even the subject of positive discrimination in favor of lower castes, with no parallel elsewhere, was little examined by Indians.[7] Therefore, what is now called the history of India is a construction of 'the British Imperial mind and its administrators'[8] (Marshal, 1970).

In ancient times, society was divided into two different ways—Varnas and Jatis. Varnas were four and Jatis many. The English word 'caste' was derived from the Spanish and Portuguese word *casta*. According to Wikipedia, the Spanish version of the word *casta* means a clan or lineage while that of the Portuguese 'many in-marrying hereditary Hindu social groups'. The British adopted the later version and converted Varnas into primary castes and Jatis into sub-castes. In fact, Varnas had nothing to do with Jatis, and endogamy was not practiced at the level of Jatis as a whole, but in smaller sub-units. Time has shown that the Spanish version of clan - or kin-based families would have been in tune with the functional unit in which the Hindu society has operated for centuries.

Writing in *The Hindu* on 30 June 2008, historian Upinder Singh states that Indian history in the eighteenth and the nineteenth centuries was dominated by 'Orientalists' or Indologists, who translated the ancient texts with the help of 'native informants'. They judged the ancient religious and social institutions from a Western point of view and painted the Indian society 'as static, and its political system despotic, over the centuries' and confused race, religion, and ethnicity with one other. In the late nineteenth century and in the first half of twentieth century, another set of historians

---

[6]   As quoted by Mihir Bose, 2007: India's Missing Historians. *History Today*, Vol. 57, Iss. 9

[7]   Ibid.

[8]   British Historiography: http://eprints.hec.gov.pk/2590/

appeared who were called nationalist historians. They insisted on the cultural role of development by 'exalting' the Vedic age and Gupta period and refuted that India was ever despotic, but maintained the idea of Hindu, Muslim, and British parts of Indian history. The author thinks that many stories in history have still to be written and gender, family, and household should form a part of larger social history. Although family, class and Varna, were different bases of social identity than Jati, they were 'intersected and changed'.[9] Therefore, the former three, too, must be revalued and applied in their original sense.

The nomenclature confusion started in the nineteenth century when the British planted a fifth Varna of Panchama on the existing four Varnas of Hindu social structure, coined the terms outcastes, outcasts, outcaste Hindus, pariah, and out of pail for the lowest castes, and attempted to have a threefold division of Hindu society. The aim was to detach a large chunk of population from the mainstream Hindus by the use of the above terms and create a non-existent fifth Varna separate from the original four. Dissatisfied with the original term 'outcaste' and to show that the lowest castes were a part of Hindu society, in 1931 the census commissioner converted outcastes into exterior castes. In 1992, Fuller repeated the colonial version of caste, but with the difference that he replaced castes with classes. He says, "Hindu society has been divided into four Varna, or classes, a convention which had its origins in the Rig Veda, the first and most important set of hymns in Hindu scripture which dates back to 1500-1000 BC. At the top of the hierarchy are the Brahmins, or priests, followed by the Kshatriyas, or warriors. The Vaishyas, the merchants, the farmers and the artisans, constitute the third class. At the bottom are the Shudras, the class responsible for serving the three higher groups. Finally, the untouchables fall completely outside of this system. It is for this reason that the untouchables have also been termed Avarna (no class)."[10] The word 'classes' used for Varnas are sufficient to say that such classes of people could be identified in every section of society, including in different castes. Avarna were those who did not believe in Varna classification, and they could be anyone, even a Brahmin. It was ridiculous to compare them with untouchables. Many

---

[9]   Extracted by Naginder Singh from his book *A History of Ancient and Early Medieval India*: Pearson Longman

[10]   C.J. Fuller, 1992: *The Camphor Flame: Popular Hinduism and Society in India.* Princeton: Princeton University Press: 12. And http://www.ambedkar.org/News/ reservationinindia.pdf

highly regarded groups like Yogis and spiritual teachers in India did not believe in Varna classification. Even untouchables had castes, by which is meant Jatis. That was why they were called Scheduled Castes. The term caste *system* was coined to depict a 'complex whole formed from related parts' and to justify conversion of Jatis into sub-castes of Varnas. Caste as a 'system' was a British invention for divide and rule. Simon Commission wrote in 1929:

> Separate electorate would no doubt be the safest method of securing the return of an adequate number of persons who enjoy the confidence of the Depressed Classes, but we are averse from stereotyping between the Depressed Classes and the remainder of the Hindus by such a step which we consider would introduce a new and serious bar to their ultimate political amalgamation with others.[11]

The Simon Commission was not only against showing depressed classes separate from their parent community, but also favored their political amalgamation with other Hindus. Racial division of India and its society was challenged even in the nineteenth century. A Pakistani-American sociologist gives another version, "As for *Hinduism,* the hierarchical principles of the Brahmanical social order have always been contested from within Hindu society, suggesting that equality has been and continues to be both valued and practiced."[12] Wikipedia quotes sociologists Kevin Reilly, Stephen Kaufman, and Angela Bodino, who were critical of casteism, but also stated that casteism in India was presently "not apartheid and untouchables, as well as tribal people and members of the lowest castes in India benefit from broad affirmative action programmes and are enjoying greater political power". Caste is often thought of as an ancient fact of Hindu life, but various contemporary scholars have argued that the caste 'system' was constructed during the British times.[13]

Ambedkar had warned even as early as in 1917 that 'castes divided people, only to disintegrate and cause myriad divisions which isolated

---

[11]   John Simon, 1930: India and the Simon Report: A Talk. New York: Coward-McCann, Inc. And http://www.ambedkar.org/News/reservationinindia.pdf

[12]   Ayesha Jalal in Democracy and Authoritarianism in Contemporary South Asia. Cambridge: Cambridge University Press (26 May 1995)

[13]   http://en.wikipedia.org/wiki/Caste_system_in_India

people and caused confusion.' He gave the example of the Brahmin class, which, he said, was 'split into well over 1,400 sub-castes.' This, he said, was supported by 'census data collected by colonial ethnographers in British India'.[14]. In a message to Gandhi, Ambedkar observed in 1933:

> The Outcaste is a by-product of the Caste system. There will be outcastes as long as there are castes. Nothing can emancipate the out-caste except the destruction of the Caste system. Nothing can help to save Hindus and ensure their survival in the coming struggle except the purging of the Hindu Faith of this odious and vicious dogma.[15]

The appearance of backward classes was not a benign affair. In the beginning of the twentieth century, all non-Brahmin Hindus in the 'Dravidian' South were described as Shudras. Coming from some South Indian States, they combined and called themselves *Backward Hindus*. These Backward Hindus revolted against a small group of 'Aryan' Brahmins who were more educated and better represented in services under the State. A 'non-Brahmin manifesto' was released in 1917 to protect the interests of backward classes in the fields of education, employment, and politics. 'The move was led by members of *upper* castes of Velalas, Reddys, Kamas, Velmas and Nairs and their supporters from these and upper trading castes.'[16] In 1920 when all and sundry started to join Backward Hindus, the British divided the existing backward classes into *depressed classes* and Backward Hindus or simply Backward Classes. Gradually, the movement of Backward Hindus spread to other parts of India, especially the then Bihar and United Provinces. In 1930, the Starte Committee classified *backward classes* into depressed classes, 'Aboriginal' and Hilly Tribes, and renamed the last category as Other Backward Classes and Intermediate Classes. This was a definition of backward classes, not of the Hindu community, as construed later. When the non-Hindus were also included among the Other Backward Classes, the question cropped up whether backward classes

---

[14] B.R. Ambedkar, 1917. *Castes in India: Their Mechanism, Genesis and Development* and http://en.wikipedia.org/wiki/Caste_system_in_India

[15] B.R. Ambedkar (February, 1933). 'A note to Gandhi'. *Harijan* 3. Quoted in http://en.wikipedia.org/wiki/Caste_system_in_India

[16] Radhakrishnan P, 1996: 113 quoting from Andre Beteille, 1969

of each community should be viewed in their own community sense or in the general sense applicable to all communities.

In 1936, depressed classes were converted into Scheduled Castes whose population was 14 percent of the total population of India. Schedule means a list, not a particular status, though now the term is politicized and used more or less as a type of people rather than a collection of variously situated castes. After the independence, the Aboriginal and Hilly tribes, mostly identified as criminal tribes by the British, were labeled Scheduled Tribes. According to Wikipedia, the concept of 'original inhabitant' or Aborigines is directly related to the initial peopling of India, which, due to the debate on topics such as the Indo-Aryan migration hypothesis, has been a contentious area of research and discourse. Some anthropologists hypothesize that the region was settled by multiple human migrations over tens of millennia ago, which makes it even harder to select certain groups as being truly aboriginal. The Bhils and Gonds are frequently classified as Australoid groups. Most anthropologists and geneticists agree that Caucasoids, which included the Dravidians and the Indo-Aryans, and the Mongoloids (Sino-Tibetans), immigrated into India after the Australoid. Nagas, described by Ambedkar are probably the same groups. The Bhil Rebellion against Mughal authority of 1632 and the Bhil-Gond Insurrection of 1643 were both crushed by the Mughal soldiers. During the British period many of the tribal population was reduced to bonded laborers due to Jagirdari system and zamindari system. Though they do not have castes and have different names, there is no unanimity on their separate origin. Recent genetic research, on the other hand, suggests that for thousands of years India has been a mixed society and the hill tribes might be the progenitors of the caste societies in the plains. To call them aborigines and criminal tribes might itself be criminal.

According to the 1951 census, Scheduled Castes comprised 15 percent and Scheduled Tribes 7.5 percent of the total population. Besides being poor and illiterate, the main grouse of the backward classes other than SC and ST was that they had no or little representation in Government services. These Other Backward Classes were re-designated socially and educationally backward classes after the independence, and Article 340 was enacted to appoint a commission to suggest ways and means to uplift the socially and educationally backward classes. To offset their low representation in Government services, the backward class of citizens was granted reservations under clause 4 of Article 16 of the Constitution. As both Articles 340 and 16(4) did not mention Scheduled Castes and Scheduled Tribes before 1992, the courts took socially and educationally backward classes under Article

340 and the backward class of citizens in Article 16(4) as the same as Other Backward Classes.

In 1951, the Supreme Court held that reservations in educational institutions for Other Backward Classes on the basis of religion and caste were unconstitutional, but in the same year, the State amended the Constitution, added clause 4 to Article 15, renamed Other Backward Classes as socially and educationally backward classes, and added Scheduled Castes and Scheduled Tribes in addition. The First Backward Classes Commission was appointed in 1953 to give them reservations in educational institutions, but due to differences in opinion on caste based reservations, in 1995 it was not implemented. In 1961 the Central Government left the matter to the States with the advice to apply economic criteria than go by caste.[17] In the early 1960s in the case of *Balaji*, the Supreme Court approved reservation in educational institutions under Article 15(4).

In 1979, the Second Backward Classes Commission (Mandal Commission) was appointed to recommend reservations in service under the State. It submitted its Report in 1980. It calculated the population of OBCs from 1931 census as 52 percent of the total population and called them Shudras for the first time. The Supreme Court accepted the same in 1992 and, by including Scheduled Castes and Scheduled Tribes, legally converted 75 percent of total population of India into backward and discriminated castes. Out of Other Backward Classes, 43.70 percent were Hindus and 8.60 percent non-Hindus. Backward Hindus, Backward Classes, Other Backward Classes, socially and educationally backward classes, backward class of citizens, Intermediate Classes, and the new titles of socially backward classes and Shudra given to the same classes in 1992 further added to the confusion. In the same year, the Court accepted the title of Panchama for Scheduled Castes for the first time in the judicial history of free India and gave a new legal twist to the Hindu social structure. Finally, it accepted the Government's plea and gave reservations to backward class of citizens or Other Backward Classes with the stipulation that total reservations for all categories of backward classes would not exceed 50 percent of the total seats available in services under the State. It rejected reservation in promotions as well as 10 percent reservations for poor among the forward castes.

In the meantime, two more categories claimed to be discriminated. One was of women whose population was 1 to 2 percent below the 50 percent

---

[17] A.I.R. 1993 Supreme Court: 506-507

mark. The other alleged 'discriminated' category was roughly 16 to 18 percent population of minorities, but mainly Muslims. Even if the overlap is taken into account and adjusted, their inclusion would still raise the population of the discriminated, the backward, and the ostracized to 90 to 92 percent of the total population. Then there was a large population of poor and illiterate which was left un-redressed because it could not boast of being Shudra. Uplift of backward classes in India has not taken place for altruistic reasons. Caste, religion, race, politics, religious expansionism, administrative requirements of colonial rulers, alienation of backward classes, dithering of national leaders on basic issues such as temple entry and separate dining, vote bank politics before and after the independence, and lack of consensus on the meaning of 'backward', 'caste', and discrimination have all played a role in causing the present conundrum. Since the independence many Apex Court judgments have been delivered, but they have not been able to resolve the issue of social identity of the backward classes. Articles 15 and 16 prohibit discrimination on the basis of *only* caste and *only* religion, yet on one pretext or the other, reservations for Other Backward Class*es* were converted into reservations for backward *castes* and in one or two States for whole religious community. Forward and backward classes are misnomers for the alleged lower and the upper castes, for in every caste and community there are elements that are socioeconomically forward and elements which are socioeconomically backward. There is, therefore, little justification to continue reservations for whole castes and in some States for a religious community as a whole.

The Supreme Court acknowledged the 'overriding importance of income' in determining 'status, facilities and opportunities' on many occasions, but when the question arose of reservations on economic grounds in the *Indra Sawhney and Others* v. *Union of India* case the Court decreed that 'a backward class cannot be determined only and exclusively with reference to economic criterion' and reservations in services of the State were exclusively meant for Shudra, Scheduled Castes and Scheduled Tribes and similar classes among the minorities.[18] Therefore, unless the controversy on the definition of Shudras is settled, the social identity not only of Other Backward Classes but also of Scheduled Castes and Scheduled Tribes cannot be resolved. The Court's ruling that "the backwardness contemplated in Article 16(4) is mainly social backwardness and it would not be correct to say that backwardness

---

[18]   *A.I.R.* Supreme Court 1993: Page 562: Para: 90

under Article 16(4) should be both social and educational",[19] as in the case of Article 15(4), has further complicated the matter.

The argument that reservations were not given to Shudras on the basis of *only* caste but also on the intertwined economic and educational backwardness may be true, but it is also true that the alleged upper castes with the same economic and educational backwardness were denied reservation only because they were from the upper castes. If poverty and occupation could turn a backward caste into a backward class and reservations were permissible to such a backward class, would not denial of reservations in the presence of the same factors in the case of an alleged forward caste be discrimination on account of *only* caste? Regarding denial of reservations, the courts are silent. Where the constitution specifically stipulated reservations for backward *classes*, even there the State converted them into reservations for backward castes.

The first Central Backward Classes Commission in the 1950s was wound up because of the difference of opinion among the members and because its chairman wrote to the President that caste-based reservations would not be in the interest of the country. In 1979, when the Central Government appointed the Second Backward Commission under the chairmanship of B. P. Mandal, it opted for caste-based reservations and changed the whole scenario. The 52 percent socially and educationally backward classes it identified in the total population were backward and discriminated due to their caste factor, which was current in the case of Hindus, and the past in the case of non-Hindus. The composition of Other Backward Classes on the basis of *classes* would have been different. One could argue that once castes and tribes as Scheduled *Castes* and Scheduled *Tribes* were covered, there could be no rationale for the Constitution to go back to them again and that reservations under Article 15(4) and 16(4) were enacted in the constitution for those who were victims of the prevailing widespread socioeconomic inequality, but the intense propaganda to the contrary eclipsed that. The governments avoid these issues due to political considerations, and the courts acquiesce before the popularized versions due to lack of enough challenge by the petitioners.

According to the Mandal Commission cited by the Court, any Hindus who did not belong to twice-born (Dwij) Varnas were considered socially backward. This was unacceptable, because twice born are not one category and Varnas distinguish individuals, not categorize groups like castes and

---

[19]   Ibid.: 486

communities. Among the non-Hindus, one was socially backward if one was either a convert from those who were socially backward among Hindus or, if not a convert, his/her parental income was below the poverty line which was less than Rs.71 per month per person at that time. An educationally backward person was one whose father and grandfather had not studied beyond the primary level. Strangely, these tests of social and educational backwardness were accepted by Union of India as evidence of thousands of years of social and educational backwardness. Petitioners criticized these criteria and respondents supported them. The Court explained the matter by giving it a different direction.[20] Such criteria along with some others equally vague could not be accepted as proof of more than half of India's population as socially backward and discriminated Shudras, not to speak of a testimony of centuries of backwardness.

The judgment in the Mandal case was a divided judgment. Justice T. K. Thommen ruled that reservations were exclusively meant for "Harijans, the Girijans, the Adivasis, the Dalits or those most unfortunately referred to in the past as the 'untouchables or the 'outcastes' by reason of their being born in what was wrongly regarded as low castes and associated with what was wrongly treated as demeaning occupations . . ."[21] He further added that it was for the State to prove that such backwardness also existed among Other Backward Classes, and even if it did, the 'overriding condition' would be a 'predetermined economic level'. There was nothing to suggest that socially and educationally backward classes were similarly backward as Harijans and Girijans who became Scheduled Castes and Scheduled Tribes. Predetermined economic level was crucial. In 1960, the Central Government had also advised the States to use economic criteria. Pre-1990 lists were made mainly on economic grounds. After the submission of the Mandal Commission's Report, the then Home and Defense Minister admitted in 1983 that the 'problem that confronts Government' was to 'arrive at a satisfactory definition of backward classes and bring about an acceptance of the same by all the States concerned'.[22]

There are two types of backwardness-ascription-oriented and achievement-oriented. The dictionary meaning of the word ascription in sociology is 'arbitrary placement (as at birth) in a particular social status.' In the pre-industrial Western societies, it was described as 'occupation and

---

[20]   Ibid.: 580-581: 118A, 119-120
[21]   Ibid.: 698: 554—Justice T.K. Thommen
[22]   *A.I.R.* Supreme Court 1993: 512, 514: 20

individual was one' or there was nexus (connection) between occupation and individual. Mr. Barber almost always was a barber. In India, this 'occupation and individual was one' was converted for unknown reason into 'occupation and caste was one' or that there was nexus between caste and occupation and all members of a barber caste had the social status of their traditional or hereditary occupation. In a graphic manner, the Supreme Court explained this in 1992, "In rural India, caste occupation nexus is true even today . . . it does not matter if he has gone abroad . . . if he has earned money . . . may not follow that occupation . . . the label remains."[23] The other type of backwardness was due to the low achieved social status due to poverty, lack of education, and low occupation, a feature of most modern societies. The question before the court was which applied to Other Backward Classes. In 1992, the majority views favored ascription-oriented backwardness.

However, in a dissenting observation Justice Thommen rejected the theory of nexus between caste and occupation by saying that reservations could not be given "because of their caste and occupation which are incidental facts of history", but they could be given on account of "their backwardness and disability stemming from identified past and continuing inequities and discrimination".[24] In the case of the latter, he was not alone. There are many similar opinions. However, what the learned judge meant by 'identified past' was not clarified. The nexus between caste and occupation will be elaborated in due course.

Despite the numerous literatures, there is no one description of caste on which the people would not emotionally contest. The Varnas do not depend on birth, but depend on *gunas* or qualities.[25] Adi Shankara did not even admit the reality of the world, including the creation of castes. He interpreted the Upanishad to mean that the Viraj only projected the four castes (English version of Varnas in translation) but did not really create them and implied that Varna did not have any reality, only an empirical or behavioral reality that enabled people to carry out their dharmas (duties) in this world.[26]

[23] Ibid.: 553: 82
[24] Ibid.: 699
[25] Textual Sources for the Study of Hinduism (Textual Sources for the Study of Religion) by Wendy Doniger O'Flaherty (Editor, Translator). Bhartiya Vidiya Bhavan: 31, 32
[26] Rajendra Prasad, *A Conceptual-Analytic Study of Classical Indian Philosophy of Morals*, Centre for Studies in Civilizations (Delhi, India), Project of History of Indian Science, Philosophy, and Culture. Sub Project: Consciousness, Science, Society, Value, and Yoga: 337

Dumont also stated that "the terms *varna* (theoretical classification based on occupation) and *jāti* (caste) are two distinct concepts. While Varna is the idealised four-part division . . . jāti (community) refers to the thousands of actual endogamous groups prevalent across the subcontinent. A Jati may be divided into exogamous groups based on same *gotras*. The classical authors scarcely speak of anything other than the varnas; even Indologists sometimes confuse the two".[27] The presence of people with different *gotras* in which endogamy is prohibited does not support the theory of endogamy in caste as a whole. Caste is also not homogenous in terms of income, education, and occupations. It is surprising that these opinions did not receive the recognition they deserved.

According to Harold Gould, activities like continuous contact with 'blood, death, and dirt', singly or in combination, may make 'unclean' castes and the rest 'clean castes', but the basic distinction in rural India remain between the land-owning, cultivating castes, who dominate the social order, and the landless craft and menial castes, who are subordinate within the 'system'. The same cultivating castes constitute a major part of Other Backward Classes in the post-1947 India and, yet, claim to be backward for thousands of years.

In a significant comment, Wikipedia says, "Caste is commonly thought of as an ancient fact of Hindu life, but various contemporary scholars have argued that the caste system was constructed by the British colonial regime." Another opinion says, "Although we do not subscribe to the view that the British invented caste or religious community identities in India, it is clear that British policies of enumeration, and divide and rule, did much to harden these identities in the seventy or eighty years before Independence."[28] Basham suggests that Jati system in its modern form developed very late.[29] In an interesting comment, Wikipedia also says, "The Indian government officially recognizes historically discriminated lowest castes of India such as untouchables and Shudras under Scheduled Castes, and certain economically backward castes as Other Backward Castes."[30]

---

[27]   Louis Dumont, 1980: *Homo Hierarchicus: The Caste System and Its Implications*. Chicago: University of Chicago Press, 66-67

[28]   Reinventing India: Liberalization, Hindu Nationalism and Popular Democracy authored by Stuart Corbridge, John Harriss

[29]   A.L. Basham, 1967. The Wonder That Was India. Grove Press: New York, 148; Sidgwick and Jackson, Understanding Caste, Mankind Quarterly, Vol. 34 (1993), 117-123

[30]   Wikipedia on Caste System as above: Talk page and Christopher Jaffrelot, 2006:

The problem is with Other Backward Classes who are not 'historically discriminated' and whom the Mandal Commission did not recognize as economically backward classes and called them Shudras. Ironically, the Supreme Court consented. If OBCs had been recognized and treated as economically backward classes, at least by the Court, there would have been no need to write this book.

The nineteenth and the twentieth centuries colonial versions of caste have come under severe criticism in recent decades. Niels Brimnes[31] from Aarhus University reports that historians frequently view caste as a great barrier in modernization of Indian society and describe the *essence* of a distinct Indian civilization as the high position of Brahmans, commensality, relationship of pollution with untouchability, hierarchy, and nexus between caste and occupation. Dumont's notion that the ruling principle of Indian society was the principle of *hierarchy* which could be expressed as 'opposition between pure and impure' and that *caste system* was the social manifestation of this abstract principle was another issue. Dumont considered the principle of hierarchy as 'religious 'and implied that the king and State had always been 'weak' compared to the Brahman in the Indian history. Therefore, the task of 'historians of India' he said, was not to look for 'historical change', but to search for '*fundamental constants*' in Indian civilization. These constants were called by others' 'essences'. On the contrary, Nicholas Dirks and Susan Bayly in two separate monographs challenged both the notions. In the 1980s under the influence of Edward Said, the historiographers had already begun to question the origin and authenticity of the alleged '*timeless traditions*' invented by the colonial state, which later culminated in Dumont's *essentialist view* of caste. Bernard Cohn summed up the 'constructivist position' *as* a concept which reduced the 'vastly complex codes and their associated meanings' to a few metonyms. A metonym is a figure of speech which depicts an attribute of something as the thing itself. The British not only determined what they called 'rules and orders' but also interpreted them as the 'Indian rules and customs' to ensure that the Indians conformed to these constructions.[32] Thus, an age-old essence of

---

'The Impact of Affirmative Action in India: More Political than Socioeconomic'. *India Review,* Vol. 5, Iss. 2, 173-189

[31]   Niels Brimnes, Aarhus University, 2002: Caste between Essentialism and Constructivism: http://eurasia.nias.ku.dk/nytt/2002-4/caste.htm. Seen on Internet in January 2012

[32]   Ibid

Indian society, i.e. separation of Varna and Jati, was constructed into the colonial version of caste or caste system in which Varnas became castes and Jatis their sub-castes. This was the fundamental flaw in the understanding of caste in the Law of Caste in the Hindu Law enacted by the British, which continued as such after independence and percolated in the court judgments in the form of watertight compartments.

In 2001, Nicholas B. Dirks contradicted the essentialist view and stated, 'Caste as we know it today is not in fact some unchanged survival of ancient India, not some single system that reflects a core civilizational value, not a basic expression of Indian tradition.'[33] And although it existed before colonialism, 'it was thoroughly reconfigured by British rule'. He even suggested that caste was 'a conscious design of British colonial policy' invented to facilitate colonial rule.[34] Another Chicago-based historian Ronald Inden remarked that caste, thus, became one of the four major essences constructed by Westerners to 'control' India by 'denying it a history of its own'.[35]

Susan Bayly observed in 1997 that the Western constructions of caste had a considerable effect on Indian life, particularly when they found support from the Indians themselves. In 1999, however, she tried to find a middle path between the essentialism of Dumont and the constructivism of Dirks and stated that although caste had been a real and active part of Indian life for many centuries and not a mere self-serving Orientalist fiction, it 'was both consolidated and its importance enhanced under colonial rule'.[36] The British might not have invented caste, but, according to her, they certainly transformed the pre-colonial caste into a colonial version under their rule. Luckily, there is increasing awareness of the difference between Varna and Jati in social sciences. Varnas divided the society on the basis of traits and activities, while Jatis were more political than social formations and have remained so even now.

The constructions of colonial period had no pre-colonial precedence. A fifth Varna of Panchama constructed in 1807 had no equivalent in the Hindu social structure. The British imported racial theory from Europe

---

[33]   Nicholas Dirks, 2001: 5

[34]   Ibid.: 249

[35]   Niels Brimnes, Aarhus University, 2002: Caste between Essentialism and Constructivism: http://eurasia.nias.ku.dk/nytt/2002-4/caste.htm. Seen on Internet in January 2012

[36]   Ibid.

in the nineteenth century to divide India into three races of Aryans, Dravidians, and Aborigines, which is under heavy cloud and with it the threefold division of the Hindu society. The three economic classes in which the whole world was divided were neglected after independence in the pursuit of caste-based backward classes. Therefore, there is need to have another look at the colonial notions and explore how the society was conceived in ancient times, how it got misrepresented subsequently and how it is functioning now. There was no system like caste system; there were only Jatis read as castes. One of the aims of this book is to bring out how the British used caste, race, and subterfuge to fragment a dynamic society and a country in the search of God, glory, and gold. Yet, it was not an insignificant number of the British who went against the official versions.

Free India did no better than the colonial rulers. It defeated the constitutional goal of a casteless society and perpetuated the English term 'caste' without defining it. Worse, it adopted the British 'Law of Caste' in *Hindu Law* without a second look. Social justice has two considerations: non-legal and legal. Non-legal issues involve religion, social anthropology, history and historiography, race, class, and politics. This includes the functional unit of social stratification in which the Hindu society has functioned for centuries. Its importance has started to emerge only in recent times. Legal considerations include constitutional provisions, but their interpretations depend heavily upon the perceptual considerations.

Another crucial issue is of discontinuation of reservations which were initially meant for ten years. Because the courts are hesitant to take it up and the Parliaments refuse to discuss it for fear of political fallout, it has the potential of continuing forever. Justice Thommen aptly addressed the incongruity in his minority view in 1992, which is extracted as under:

> At the same time reservation is not the end in itself. It is a means to achieve equality . . . (It) must be consistent with the objective in view. Reservation must not outlast its constitutional objective, and must not allow a vested interest to develop and perpetuate itself . . . Every reservation founded on benign discrimination . . . must necessarily be a transient passage to that end. It is temporary in concept, limited in duration, conditional in application and specific in object.[37]

---

[37] *Judgements Today*, 1992: 361: 258: J.: 682: 485

The socioeconomic and educational status and social standing of castes or caste clusters are changing and their members are not collectively backward as a whole—a necessary condition laid down by the Supreme Court for giving reservations. Continuing revision of a highly ambiguous 'creamy layer' has further increased intra-caste inequalities, making it impossible for the remaining backward sections to gain from reservation. Scores of castes may not be even 50 percent backward and yet they continue to be among the backward classes.

The excuse that one cannot give with one hand and then take away with the other hand, with the highest respect, is specious. The aim of a benevolent State is to see every hand shares the benefits. If demand is more than the remedial resources, the measure has to be small and not a constantly enlarging financial limit of creamy layer. Reservation is an extreme measure and should remain available only to those who are in extremes of difficulties, even among the backward classes. After that, they have to be on their own or helped by the State through a modified affirmative action, where and when required. The imprecision of caste was not new in 1992. The courts had more or less, openly or by implication, continued to read four Varnas as primary castes, relate centuries of backwardness to a nexus between caste and occupation, and treat caste as class, but the legal acceptance of the controversial version of five Varnas altered the ancient Hindu social structure irretrievably.

In 2006, when the Parliament passed the 93rd Amendment of the Constitution and added clause (5) in Article 15 to provide reservations in institutions of higher education run by the State, it created a pandemonium. Finally, the matter landed up in the Supreme Court via Writ Petition 265 of 2006 in the form of *Ashok Kumar Thakur* v. *Union of India* and related cases. On 17 May 2007 a two-judge Bench of the Apex Court referred the cases to a larger Bench not only to decide the validity of the 93rd amendment and 'OBC quota law' but also to determine:

(1.) Whether caste-based reservation was permissible under Article 15 of the Constitution; if yes, what were the criteria *for identification* of the 'classes' sought to be given benefit of reservation.

(2.) Whether caste-based reservation was inherently divisive and incompatible with the unity and integrity of the nation.

(3.) Whether substitution of the expression 'socially and educationally backward classes' by 'socially and economically backward classes' would fulfill the constitutional intentions and objectives?

When the judgment was delivered by the Constitution Bench in 2008, barring in an indirect way, these issues were barely touched upon and once again left to the 'future generations'. Even the parameter of educational backwardness, crossing which no one could be educationally backward for the purpose of future reservations, was left unqualified. Reservations in promotions to higher echelons of administrations in services under Article 16(4) were rejected by the Supreme Court in 1992, but restored in 1995 for Scheduled Castes and Scheduled Tribes by amending the constitution and enacting Article 15(4A). Subsequently, the Court restricted reservations by invoking conditions contained in Article 35 of the constitution

In 2012 a new Bill was introduced to amend the Constitution to bypass its Article 35 (See Preface) and allow reservation in promotions to Scheduled castes and Scheduled tribes with effect from 1995. The Bill is still to be passed by the parliament. The resistance to discontinuation of reservations in those who have recovered have affected adversely even the lower echelons of scheduled castes and scheduled tribes. At the same time, would such out of turn promotions not curtail the individual rights of those who are equally or better qualified and also senior in services? Justice Altamas Kabir, the former chief justice of India, remarked, "The personal liberty of an individual is the most precious and prized right guaranteed under the Constitution."[38] Though he observed this in the context of preventive detention, the constitutional guarantee of the right to personal liberty of an individual to pursue one's legitimate goal and occupation could not be limited to only one aspect. Group rights must be balanced by the Apex Court with individual rights, when governments try to curb the latter in pursuit of vote banks. Even among group rights, there should be provision for individual rights, for all members are not similarly situated.

The above contentious issues have been highlighted with the hope that it would raise a debate and the matter would ultimately reach the Supreme Court in one form or the other, for whatever was entangled in the Supreme Court has to be disentangled in the same Court. Therefore, before the State legally deprives someone and his/her family from their constitutional right to admission in educational institutions and services under the State, it must be obliged not only to give specific reasons for doing that, but also produce unimpeachable evidence of continuing discrimination of those who are still being discriminated and of those who continue to discriminate. Comparative reduced participation in educational institutions and less

---

[38] *Mail Today*, 10 September 2012

representation in services is not unnatural in a vast population like that of India, and can not only vary with time, but also be due to either or both external and internal factors.

The reader might consider an important stipulation at this stage. In Chapter IV of the Mandal Commission's Report, which will be discussed separately in due course, the Commission cites some extremely depressed classes or Scheduled Castes to justify reservation for socially and educationally backward classes / backward class of citizens by calling the latter Shudra. This produced severe psychological reaction on the nation, including the judges. It also raises a number of questions.

First, are classes mentioned in Articles 15(4) and 16(4) interchangeable with castes and on what grounds? *Second,* are farmers, cattle raisers, artisans and others like Yadavs, Ahirs, Gujjars, gavalas and hundreds of others in the North, and Lingyats, Okkilogas, Reddy's and others in similar occupations in the South, engaged in menial and stigmatizing occupations, or kept away from the society? *Third,* did they ever had to walk, or still walk at a certain distance from Brahmin or to hide themselves to avoid polluting others, as shown in Chapter 1V of the Mandal Report? Finally, why did the dissenting member of the Mandal Commission record in its report that most socially and educationally backward classes lived in harmony with the, so called, upper castes?

CHAPTER 1

EMERGENCE OF BACKWARD CLASSES AND POLITICS

Emergence of backward classes in India was not an innocuous or straightforward process. There were both internal and external factors. Internal factors were intense poverty, illiteracy, a complicated social structure with its multiple interpretations, conservatism in society, disaffection of the lowest classes, and conversion of the notion of purity and pollution into untouchability. External factors were centuries of subjugation, appearance of foreign religions and their expansionism, creation of an all-India class of untouchables and another of backward tribes on racial grounds, manufacture of debatable nomenclature for the lowest section of society and the application of racial theories to divide castes and the country by colonial rulers. The British not only mutilated the Hindu social structure but also made its mutilation a permanent feature of the Hindu Law enacted by them. The post-independence India adopted the same Law of Caste in the Hindu Law and gave it a fresh legal status.

In 1947 almost 80-90 percent Indian population was poor and illiterate. Free India enacted a number of laws to uplift the backward classes, but there was a curious hesitation on the part of the constitution makers to define the nature of backwardness and explain the terms they used in the various articles of the constitution. The matter was further aggravated when the courts, too, could not convincingly interpret the nature of backwardness and the structure of the society. Both adopted the insufficient, often contrived, colonial terminologies. In a recent article on caste system, an author commented on the Internet, "The religious theories explain how four Varnas were formed, but they do not explain how Jats (Jatis or castes) *in* each Varna or the Untouchable were founded." This existing misgiving is an important cause for the present situation. *Jatis* had never been *in* or part of Varnas since the ancient times. There are many theories on the origin of

Jatis, but each is more suspect than the other. Varna formation had little to do with Jatis. Even the British time process of identification of Scheduled Castes by the Governor, which was also adopted for Scheduled Tribes by free India, was more subjective and political, than objective. Poverty as the primary disability, which is the commonest cause of backwardness throughout the world, and which is almost always associated with illiteracy and low social position in society, was rejected as the primary cause of backwardness in India.

Sir Herbert Risley was the census commissioner for the 1901 census. He was the key figure in creating untouchability from the notion of 'purity and pollution' and a class of untouchables on racial basis. Up to the mid-nineteenth century, there were no designated groups among the population that could be identified as different races. Later, when the theory was imported from Europe, Hindu castes were divided into Aryans, Dravidians, and Aborigines instead of populations, as done in Europe, and the country into Aryan North and Dravidian South. Despite the rejection of racial terms, they remain in use even today.

An eminent historian A. L. Basham wrote in *The Wonder That Was India*, "India was a cheerful land, who's people, each finding a niche in a complex and slowly evolving system, reached a higher level of kindness and gentleness in their mutual relations than any other nation of antiquity, before the Muslims came to India."[39] This was hardly the description of a people who treated a large majority of its population as serfs, slaves, and untouchable or who worshipped Buddha as an incarnation of God, but hated his followers. Nevertheless, when politics took over, it became a fashion to blame the ancient past for the loss of control over capital and the accompanying inequalities seen in the present-day India.

Politics of Caste and Race in Colonial Period

Before the 1901 census, racial theory had already divided the population into Aryans, Dravidians, and Aborigines, but when Risley found that castes, meaning Jatis, could not be classified by their rank, he decided from the outset not to classify them by status and embarked on ethnography on the theory that physical differences between forward and backward castes were due to their different racial origins. In a few decades, when it was found

---

[39]   Basham: as quoted by Morton Klass, 1993

that there were no physical anthropological differences among Chamars and Brahmins in any given area, not only his ethnography but also his classification based on linguistic terminology was rejected. In 1931, J.J. Hutton, the British Census Commissioner, was petrified to see the list which Risley had drawn up according to their 'rank' on the basis of 'his admirable theory of relative nasal index'. Risley failed in his proposed ethnography, 'but his effort gave rise to a deluge of representations with highly complex histories, asking for recognition'.[40] By introducing caste in census operations, Risley imposed caste and endogamy on an exogamous society where marriages were prohibited only among the people from the same *gotras*. Therefore, in 1947 no authentic figures were available to show the supposed hierarchical position of any caste and none exists even now. Time proved that even the description of Hindu society as a *hierarchical race* was unfounded.

Risley's next contribution was his opposition to parliamentary government. In 1905, he scuttled the demand of a Swadeshi (of Indian origin) movement for political reforms. In 1909, the Morley—Minto award suggested a separate electorate for Muslims. Risley's new anthropology did not hinder nationalism, but he was able to contain the nationalist movement that had erupted with the partition of Bengal on communal grounds. In 1910, the British used full State machinery in an attempt to impart untouchables a different racial identity in the form of a separate electorate and also encouraged a separatist movement in South India by labeling peninsular India as a Dravidian country. G.S. Ghurye was, perhaps, the first serious scholar who commented that politicization of caste was 'not merely a natural growth of the traditional institution but a *conscious design* of the British colonial policy', premeditated for the 'safety of the British dominion in India'. He blamed Risley for politicizing caste and attempt to distinguish castes in the form of different races.[41] It is ironic that after the independence, even the Indian successors of the colonial regime adopted the colonial policy.

Hocart was the first British social anthropologist who distinguished between an 'impure' Brahman and a 'pure' Brahman or a Brahmin by *caste* and a Brahman by *attributes*, but his work remained unrecognized till his death in the late 1930s. In 1993, Declan Quigley resurrected Hocart's work

---

[40]   Risley, quoted by Dirks: 234

[41]   G.S. Ghurye, 1932: *Caste and Race in India*: Bombay. Popular Prakasham: 5th edn., 1969: 157

and brought out its importance in his book *Interpretation of Caste*. However, the first European to show the distinction between a Brahmin priest and a Brahman by attributes was the German Indologist Herman Oldenburg. He wrote in 1916, "As this speculation is building up . . . about the concept of the world, there comes up the class of Sramna which was higher and differently placed in the social life of Upanishidic period, away from the castes of the men of the world. While the Brahmans also appeared to be involved in the worldly life as other castes, the Sramanohood is rooted in knowledge and mystic contemplation, at least in striving for it".[42] The model of Brahman and Brahmanism of colonial period gave an adverse connotation to the history and religion of ancient India. The same was with other Varnas which divided the Indian society on the basis of traits and function.

The first attempt to fragment the country and the society in the colonial period started with the invention of a fifth Varna of Panchama. The *second* attempt was made in the mid-nineteenth century by importing three races of Aryan, Dravidian, and Aborigines and attaching them to castes and regions. The *third* attempt was made in the 1901 census when depressed castes were renamed 'untouchables'. Untouchables were not a single homogeneous racial category in the whole country, as Risley made out in the 1901 census. Ultimately, the British regime 'conceptualized' the lowest classes "under the rubric of untouchability . . . not as a congeries of depressed groups, but as a stratum of all India dimension with shared characteristics".[43] Untouchability as a term went beyond the original concept of impurity or pollution and gave the latter a sinister meaning. While quoting the Mandal judgment in 2008 (see chapter 8), even the Supreme Court admitted that physical untouchability was confined only to scavengers and the rest of the Scheduled Castes were only depressed.

O'Malley was another prominent census commissioner. He wrote in 1932: "'Untouchability was a name of *recent* origin applied to persons of the lowest classes of Hindu society, referred to as 'depressed classes' and sometimes also called *outcastes* and *outcaste Hindus*." The term *outcast* (without 'e'), he stated, was a misnomer, for 'the untouchables had castes just as other Hindus' and an 'untouchable belonging to higher caste could be out casted if he accepted food from those of a still lower caste'[44] (emphasis added). The *fourth* attempt was made when the Minto—Morley Committee

---

[42]   H. Oldenberg, 1963: 116-117

[43]   Marc Galanter, 1984: 25

[44]   L.S.S.S. O'Malley, 1932: Reprint 1974: 137-140

in 1909 introduced a separate electorate on grounds of religion. Mahatma Gandhi and the Congress Party opposed it, but the Muslim League with the connivance of British administrators carried the day. Marc Galanter, the eminent lawyer and author, states that the proposal of the census commissioner in 1911 to separate depressed classes from the mainstream Hindu community, to which the Muslim League readily agreed, was an 'unacceptable proposition'. The *fifth* attempt divided India into Aryan North and Dravidian South and Hindus on the basis of worship of Shiva, which was depicted as the god of the local Dravidians, and of Indra, the god of invading Aryans. The British could not admit the existence of a uniform religious system that welcomed all schools of thought and did not think redemption lay only through a particular prophet or a particular seer. The *sixth* attempt was the exclusion of 30 percent of the population of Sikh depressed classes from the Hindu Scheduled Castes, showing that Sikhs were different from Hindus. Mazhabi Sikhs or previous 'untouchable' were included among Scheduled Castes in 1956 by free India.[45]

The *next* attempt was an artificial division of the majority community in *Hindu Law* into (1) those who were 100 percent Hindus and (2) those that were less than that, not to speak of encouragement of denial of temple entry in the name of 'custom and tradition'. The last attempt was made when the word 'Dalit' was coined indigenously and adopted in the 1940s to build up vote banks. It caused further confusion. One definition identifies Dalits with untouchables or *Achhyut*; another says it is used in the manner 'nigger' was used by Americans. Another brings in *Panchama* ("fifth" Varna);[46] still another says, Dalits include 'people as leather-workers, scavengers, tanners, flayers, cobblers, agricultural laborers, municipal cleaners, gymnasts, drum beaters, folk musicians and street handicraft persons, and like the upper castes, Dalits also include various castes or Jatis.' Dalit Panthers, a party affiliated to Republican Party, in their 1972 manifesto described Dalit as 'a member of Scheduled Castes and Scheduled Tribes' and included "neo-Buddhist, the working-people, the land-less and poor peasants, women, and all those who are being exploited politically, economically, and in the name of religion". Noted Dalit Laureate Gangadhar Pantawane has his own view: "Dalit is not a caste; Dalit is a symbol of change and revolution. The Dalit believes in humanism. He rejects existence of god, rebirth, and soul, sacred books that

---

45   Galanter Marc, 1984: 305
46   http://en.wikipedia.org/wiki/Dalit

teach discrimination, fate, and heaven because these make him a slave."[47] Then there are Christians and Muslims who claim that despite having converted decades and centuries ago and not included among the depressed classes by the British, their communities nevertheless treat many of them as *Dalits*.

An official paper of the American Congress Library published on the Internet a few years ago stated about untouchability: "Traditionally, the 'Untouchable' were those whose occupations and habits of life involved polluting activities, of which the most important were (1) taking life for a living, a category that included, for example, fishermen, (2) killing or disposing of dead cattle or working with their hides for a living, (3) pursuing *activities* that brought the participant into contact with emissions of the human body, such as feces, urine, sweat, and spittle, a category that included such occupational groups as sweepers and washer men, and (4) eating the flesh of cattle or of domestic pigs and chickens, a category into which most of the primitive tribes of India fell." The causes of social unacceptability were polluting activities and habits of life, not a person as such or his particular caste, which had no relation to his habits or occupation.[48]

An individual's activities, behaviors, and traits determined one's Varna, not one's birth, Jati or occupation. An artificial creation of twice-born and once-born *castes*, instead of *persons*, distorted the social structure. According to Marriot, it is misleading to think that twice-born are "one recognizable group ranked on single ascending scale of precedence. Instead they represent a set of divergent and incompatible social ideals around which claims of standing may not be organized. Nor are groups belonging to same *Varna* rated as equal".[49]

However, the real problem started in the early twentieth century when, despite the repeated entreaties of Ambedkar to fight against the bar on temple entry, the Indian National Congress ignored his pleas under an ill-conceived apprehension of delay of its nationalist agenda of freedom from colonial rule. This gave the British enough time to project caste as 'a sign of Indian civilization, at best the object of relentless colonial critique, at worst a general trope for barbarism'.[50]

---

[47]   Ibid.
[48]   http://www.nacdor.org/TEXT%20FILES/Dalit.htm. The reference seems to have been sent to Archives
[49]   Marriot as quoted by Galanter, 1984: 11
[50]   Dirks: 232

Politics of Temple Entry

Jytotiba Phule appeared on the political map of India in 1850s as an opponent of Brahmins and a champion of backward classes. He belonged to Mali caste, a Shudra caste, one of the low castes. Untouchables came on the scene only in 1901. He and his wife Savitribai Phule were pioneers of women's education in India. His remarkable influence was apparent in fields like education, agriculture caste system, women and widow upliftment and removal of untouchability. He was one of the prominent social reformers of the nineteenth century India. He led the movement against the prevailing caste-restrictions. He revolted against the domination of the Brahmins and for the rights of peasants and the people of other low-castes. Jyotiba Phule was believed to be the first Hindu to start an orphanage for the unfortunate children. He was mostly known for his efforts to educate women and the lower castes as well as the masses. Jyotiba believed that enlightenment of the women and lower caste people was the only solution to combat the social evils. Therefore, in 1848, he along with his wife started a school for the girls. He was blamed for vitiating the norms and regulations of the society, and many accused him of acting on behalf of the Christian missionaries, but Jyotiba was firm and continued the movement with the help of some Brahmin friends, who extended their support to make the movement successful. In 1873, Jyotiba Phule formed the Satya Shodhak Samaj (Society of Seekers of Truth). The purpose of the organization was to liberate the people of lower-castes from the suppression of the Brahmins. In 1868, in order to give the lower-caste people more powers Jyotiba decided to construct a common bathing tank outside his house. He also wished to dine with all, regardless of their caste. He combined in him both the 'elite based conservative trend and a more genuine mass-based radicalism'.[51] If his elitist trend made him to claim a Kshatriya status for the Marathas, who left him in 1930 to join the Indian National Congress, his 'mass-based intolerance' made him to attack the entire caste system and Brahmin hegemony, which, he attributed to the indulgence of the Peshwas and the administrative requirements of the British colonial regime. Phule with his English education was an unrelenting adversary of 'Brahmanism', but nevertheless fought against attempts to separate depressed classes from their parent community in 1911 and despite his hatred for Brahmins, did not convert. Ambedkar's

---

51   Gail Omvedt: Cultural Revolt in a Colonial Society: The Non-Brahman Movement in Western India, 1873-1930. Scientific Socialist Education Trust, 1976: 2

description of Mahatma Phule as the greatest Shudra not only tells his own social identity but also the identity of all the lowest castes.[52]

E. V. Ramaswamy Naiker and Ambedkar did not come to Indian National Congress to criticize Hindu community. In fact, they were very respectful of Mahatma Gandhi till events took a different turn. Both of them wanted the Mahatma to act expeditiously against restriction to temple entry, but he and the Congress were more interested in freedom from the British Raj. After two decades of procrastination, when the Indian National Congress Party woke up in 1924 and passed a resolution which stated that 'temple entry was the birthright of all Hindus including the lowest castes', it had already incurred the ire of Ambedkar and EVR. In addition, it provided an excuse to the Muslim League and the British to treat the Congress mostly as Hindu Party. They held on to the same position up to the end of the British rule till in 1947 an independent State of Pakistan was born.

EVR, who was born in 1879 and got English education, entered Indian politics as an ardent supporter of Gandhi and joined the Indian National Congress. He went to prison in 1921 for taking part in the non-cooperation movement. He spoke against the restrictions in entry to temples and adopted the 'Gandhian principles enthusiastically'. He waged an aggressive war against the established order and, in response to a call from the movement, destroyed his own 'promissory notes and mortgage documents' worth 50,000 rupees, which was a fortune in those days. His original aim was a 'casteless society' and freedom from the clutches of 'Brahmanical Hinduism'. He was against Varna classification of people which, he said, divided the society. He wanted untouchability to be an offence and advocated abolition of '*purohit system*' and supported inter-caste, intra-caste, and widow marriages.[53]

Unfortunately, EVR and Ambedkar gave too much importance to Varna classification. It was only a classification of individuals among human beings, which was far more theoretical than usable in practice. Formal acceptance or rejection of four Varnas had no effect on the existence of the learned, the fighters, the agriculturists, the businessmen and the artisans, or those in services. When his pet issue of temple entry was not combined with the other national issues, under the pretext that it was an internal matter of the Hindus, EVR was disillusioned. Matters became worse and EVR left the Congress in a rage in 1925 and declared that his political agenda henceforth would be 'no god; no religion; no Gandhi; no Congress; and no Brahmins'.

52   Ibid.: 21 and http://www.culturalindia.net/reformers/jyotiba-phule.htm
53   Debi Chatterjee. 2004: 31-35

In 1916, his Justice Party, which had come up in South India, 'successfully mobilized non-Brahmin opinion and pushed through the first communal legislation demanding non-Brahman participation in government services'. EVR, however, remained critical of Congress and hateful of Brahmins. He blamed Gandhi for not taking a more active part in the social uplift of depressed classes and stated that 'Gandhian constructive principles' were abandoned in the pursuit of fraudulent unity and to establish a 'Gandhi Mutt'. 'Since madness is characteristic of all Mahatmas, our own is no exception to the general rule.'[54]

In his view, by upholding the fourfold Varna, Gandhi represented a conservative outlook. The future proved that EVR was mistaken, but the damage had been done. Probably, no one pointed out to him that the British had given up placing Jatis into 'Varna pigeonholes' and social scientists regarded Varnas to be theoretical in nature and never found them on the ground. EVR resented the word *Shudra* for the lowest castes, which, according to him, meant 'sons of prostitutes'. Chances of rapprochement disappeared when EVR insisted on 'destruction of Indian National Congress, Hinduism and Brahmanism'. He wrote that Gandhi was not interested in the abolition of untouchability and 'reform religion and society' and, therefore, 'we are, sadly enough, forced to confront and oppose the Mahatma'.[55] Few knew that the Brahminic domination did not exist even in ancient times, and though some sages, not necessarily Brahmins, might have been the advisers, it was the king and the kinghood that were supreme.

Unlike Ambedkar, EVR's struggle revolved around both constitutional and extra-constitutional methods. To curb 'Brahminic' hegemony, he supported 'proportionate communal representation', which produced cleavages in the society and defeated the principles of equal opportunity and equality of all citizens before the law. His proposal was community centric, not individual sensitive. Caste-based reservations have drowned the differences between individuals and families and encouraged caste politics. Only a few thrive at the expense of large sections of backward classes.

While EVR wanted the State to rectify things, Ambedkar, since he himself was a lawyer, wanted constitutional guarantees. The events of the next sixty years belied his fear that the state power would pass into the

---

[54]   Sumit Sarkar, 1997: *Writing Social History*: 390 Oxford University Press India; Also in Google Books 1998

[55]   Ibid.

hands of the 'hostile Hindu Brahminical community'. Till recently, political power laid in the hands of regional parties and the balance of power with the religious minorities. Both EVR and Ambedkar were critical of Hindu community, Indian National Congress, and the Mahatma for supporting Varna classification. Further cracks developed on the issue of 'communal representation' for backward classes.[56] Gradually, the break became complete, and in 1926, EVR launched his 'self-respect movement' and persisted with his core demand of right to temple entry throughout his career. In the 1930s, he embraced communism and 'preached against Brahmins and Britons as agents of world capitalism'. To him, nationalism was 'an atavistic desire' which showed the Hindu priest on a more durable and contemporary foundation.[57] In 1944, he established Dravida Kazhigham-the name derived from his pet theme that all South Indians were Dravidians and victims of Aryan Brahmins. In 1944, Ambedkar differed and stated that India was one country and 'not a sub-continent'. By 1948, Ambedkar had rejected the notion of Aryan invasion of India and as a consequence the theory of Aryan conquest of Dravidisthan. The European racial theory had convinced EVR that the Aryans and the Dravidians differed both racially and linguistically.

EVR allied with the ruling DMK to enact a law to do away with the practice of hereditary priests and pave the way for persons of all castes to take up the priesthood, but the Supreme Court held the new law unconstitutional on the grounds that "any State action which permits defilement or pollution of the image by the touch of an Archaka not authorized by Agamas would violently interfere with the religious faith and practices of the Hindu worshipper in a vital aspect and would therefore be prima facie invalid under the Constitution".[58] The Court had relied on historian P. V. Kane's controversial interpretation of Brahma Purana that religious freedom 'had to be decided . . . with reference to doctrines of particular religion', but without critically examining the doctrine itself. Kane's interpretation was lopsided and against the basics of Hindu faith in which Dharma and Adharma depended upon the conditions, demands, and exigencies of place and time (Dasa and Kala)[59] Policies, dogmas, traditions, and customs are not fundamentals of religions that cannot be changed or do not become redundant with passage

56   Debi Chatterjee: 71-72
57   V. Geetha and S.V. Rajadurai: *Towards a Non-Brahmin Millennium*. Bombay: Popular Prakasham, 1998
58   Ibid.
59   R.S. Sharma, 1982: 186 and Pandharinath Prabhu, 1936

of time. It was an outmoded decision. Otherwise, too, a progressive step was reversed without giving due consideration to changed times.

Although EVR was preoccupied with matters of caste throughout his life, his position on 'untouchables' always remained that of 'Shudra'. He barely addressed rights or concerns of untouchables separately from those of Shudras.[60] Unlike Ambedkar, EVR was not interested in politics. Therefore, there was little communication between the two. Ambedkar's concern was to project depressed classes as an oppressed and disenfranchised minority, and to curb Brahminic hegemony. To achieve this, he advocated proportionate communal representation. He also agreed with Risley that caste was invented to prevent miscegenation, when he stated in 1916 that exclusion was achieved 'when through a closed door policy' the priestly class 'became a caste' and the others followed.[61] Another anomaly occurred when the British administrators used the expression 'community' for caste and created hundreds or thousands of communities among Hindus, six communities among Christians, but left the Muslims as one community.[62] The whole classification was mischievous, divisive and political.

The differences between Ambedkar and Gandhi increased when Ambedkar claimed that he was not 'quarreling with Hindus and Hinduism' because of 'imperfections of their social conduct', but 'his quarrel was . . . over their ideals'. He refused to support Gandhi's advocacy on banning discrimination in temple entry, which he vehemently supported earlier, for that could 'destroy the basis of the claim of untouchables to be treated as separate from Hindus'. Therefore, he came away from the 'Temple Entry Bill,' arguing that although he had supported in the past, 'temple entry was (now) a side issue'. Finally, he wrote that he had no interest in joining Congress on the issue of temple entry if they did not join him in his effort 'to 'destroy the caste system itself'.[63] He would have been aghast to see his followers fighting for indefinite perpetuation of caste. Politics has no ideals!

When Ambedkar shifted his stand on removal of ban on temple entry and wrote that the Hindus did not regard the existence of these classes (untouchables) as a matter of shame and 'did not enquire and atone for their

---

60   Dirks: 265
61   *A.I.R.* Supreme Court 1993: 550: 76 quoting Ambedkar
62   Ibid.: 549
63   Geetha and Rajadurai: 1998: *Towards a Non-Brahmin Millennium*. Bombay: Popular Prakasham

growth',[64] it was not out of conviction, but to avoid supporting the Congress on the issue. After a tiff with Gandhi at the Round Table Conference on a separate electorate for Harijans, when things were resolved amicably in the end, Ambedkar told Gandhi that India needed him. Gandhi on his part also valued him and after independence told Nehru to appoint him as the first law minister of India. When Ambedkar resigned in 1951 due to opposition to his draft of Hindu Code Bill, which sought to expound gender equality in the laws of inheritance, marriage, and economy, it was not for an unjust cause. It was, however surprising that Ambedkar refused to recognize that the Brahmins were themselves subservient to the king and his cohorts and that he had himself acknowledged that in the fight between the Shudras and the Brahmins the latter were the losers. Finally, he embraced Buddhism, a religion nearest to the Hindu religion, on 14 October 1956 at Deekshabhoomi in Nagpur and took twenty-two vows. He died two months later on 6 December 1956.

Gail Omvedt, an American-born and naturalized Indian sociologist and human rights activist, comments that Ambedkar's Buddhism was ostensibly different from that of those who accepted it as faith, went for refuge, and accepted the canon. Ambedkar's Buddhism did not accept the scriptures of the Theravada, the Mahayana, or the Vajrayana in totality. His followers do not believe that a person's conditions at birth are the result of previous karma—a necessary belief in traditional Buddhism.[65] In 1990, Ambedkar was posthumously awarded India's highest award of Bharat Ratna. History would have been different if his and EVR's demand for removal of ban on temple entry was pursued and not delayed unnecessarily. Time has shown that it was equally important, if not more, than other national issues of that time. While Ambedkar and EVR criticized Congress and Gandhi for, what they called, their 'anti-backward classes' attitude, the others blamed both of them for weakening 'the ideological charter of the anti-colonial form of nationalism'. Ambedkar was blamed even for siding with the colonial rulers. But the stories converge as well. And in this convergence, they also remind us that 'the most pernicious inheritance of colonialism' was not 'the colonial rule' but the ideologies it constructed to frustrate the building up of a national community. Its impact is visible more than sixty years after

---

[64]   Ambedkar, 1948: *The Untouchables*: Shravasti: x-xii

[65]   Gail Omvedt: quoted by Christopher S. Queen and Sallie B. King, 1996: *Engaged Buddhism: Buddhist Liberation Movements in Asia*. New York: 47ff. u.A.— en.wikipedia.org/wiki/Dalit_Buddhist_movement

the cessation of direct colonial rule. Its result is that despite the present State being relentlessly threatened by communities that exercise collective control over production and distribution, the oppression is still attributed to the so-called Brahmanic fold of Hindu civilization. Legal equitation of caste on class has further aggravated the prevailing confusion. While Gandhi and Ambedkar struggled throughout their life time over definition of caste and ultimate authority of Hinduism, the social anthropologists and historians have no less battled for 400 years over the confusion created by the European term 'caste'.

Gandhi and Ambedkar agreed on the ritual exclusion of untouchables, but differed on the crucial societal exclusion. Gandhi advocated removal of untouchability from within the Hindu fold, while Ambedkar, who 'was committed to politicize caste', advocated conversion and stated that although he was born a Hindu he would not die as one. But by saying he was born a Hindu, he conceded that the depressed classes or the untouchables were indeed Hindus and had always been an integral part of Hindu society and attempts to show them outside the Hindu society by concocting different terms like outcastes, pariah, out of pail, and a fifth Varna of Panchama were political and motivated. His conversion was an individual issue.

Calling some people as traditionally disadvantaged groups in Indian society was a ploy of the British administrators and its clergy to show them as almost permanently disadvantaged without having to give any proof. The traditions which made them disadvantaged for centuries were never told. Similarly, whether the untouchables (were) a mix of caste groups or as outcastes, outside the caste system and Hindu society were all misconceived and political. It was difficult even to imagine 'what constituted an untouchable caste' in 'Madras and Bombay Presidencies and Central India' and what in 'the northern and eastern India where the identities were less clear'. Despite mixing of ritual with societal exclusion, no class or caste of untouchables could be typified or specified when ordinary socioeconomic differences were not considered crucial in identifying depressed classes. Therefore, unless we settle the issue of Shudra, which was unnecessarily complicated during the colonial rule, we cannot settle the issues of untouchability and untouchables. In the nineteenth century, enough attempts were made to include Panchama in census operations, but officially and judicially, the lowest classes remained Shudras and the term Panchama had to be given up. The total population of the four occupational groups which were traditionally associated with impurity and pollution and described by Abe Dubois in 1804 and Risley in 1901 as Chamars, Doms, washer men who

washed clothes soiled with menstrual blood, and scavengers who carried
night soil[66] could not have been 14 percent of the total population projected
in the 1931 census. The Simon Commission's admission in 1929, that the
connection between theoretical untouchability and practical disabilities
was less close and that the number of those who were denied equal rights
in the matter of schools, water and the like was less than the total given
for the depressed classes in those areas, was enough to show that the actual
population of depressed classes might have been much less than what was
shown in 1931 census.[67] By bloating the population of untouchables to 14
percent of the total population of India, identifying depressed classes with
unrelated criteria and collecting all of them in a list or schedule in 1936,
the colonial State left the actual identity of real untouchables unclear and
undetermined.

After the independence, the issue of untouchables and untouchability
was further magnified. In a 1958 judgment cited by Marc Galanter, the
Supreme Court noted that the word 'untouchability' under Article 17 (that
abolished untouchability in any form) often referred to untouchables as
"beyond the pail of caste system… on the ground of birth in certain castes".
The Court did not explain the historical development that were blamed or
the meaning of beyond the pail. Marc Galanter found that beyond the pail
of caste system was a disingenuous and impractical formulation and that
the lowest castes were 'within the traditional system of reciprocal rights and
duties'.[68] When such terms could confuse social scientists, legal luminaries,
and even courts, an ordinary villager, even an educated one, could not
have known how to distinguish whether one was in pail or out of pail or
outcast, outcaste, or exterior caste or a pariah or a Panchama. 'Historic
developments' is another phrase which covers so much and yet says so little.
Did history start with Aborigines, Dravidians, and Aryans of which no trace
was visible even in medieval India or when Indian civilization was at its peak
or did it when Muslims came to India or when, as Quigley surmises, caste
became an 'Orientalist construct'? Those who use these terms innocently
or on purpose have to answer.

Repeated invasions, the rise and fall of Buddhism and arrival of Muslims
and Europeans could not have left the society unaffected. The events of these
periods were far more important to contemporary India than the coming of

---

66   Abe Dubois in 1804 as quoted by Klass in 1993 and Risley from 1901 Census
67   Galanter M.: 1984: 125
68   Ibid.

Aryan barbarians, for even if they had come from outside, they were trained in agriculture, shipping, and other arts by the uncivilized 'Dravidian slaves and serfs' and 'uncouth, primitive and uncultured Aborigines', till they were absorbed beyond recognition. Walker's statement that "we do not know who Aryans were and where they came from" was more honest.[69] The recent genetic findings settle the issue convincingly. There were no Aryans, Dravidians, and Aborigines. There was only a mixed population, which had been present for 40,000 years since the Ancestral North Indians came and mixed with the Ancestral South Indians to produce a mixture that no longer resembled either of them (Section on race and class).

Though caste as Jati had always been a part of Hindu society in India, it did not become institutionalized into Government organizations until the arrival of British colonizers. The removal of the boundaries between civil society and political society meant that caste now played a huge role in the political arena and also influenced other Government-run institutions such as police and the judicial system. Sir Herbert Risley, in 1901, was the first person to have turned India into an ethnographic state, but in the end ethnography was rejected. The irony is that despite the awareness in social sciences circles, the recent findings have not percolated down to general populace, sadly even to legal profession. Far more people are poor, illiterate, and socially backward due to events of the last 1,200 years. Statements like 'even as the details of the evolution of the caste system remain obscure, it may be said with a measure of certainty that the system grew out of process of conflict and interaction between these new arrivals and earlier non-Aryan residents of the region'[70] appear ludicrous in the twenty-first century.

Emergence and Politics of Other Backward Classes

The simmering against the preponderance of Brahmins in educational institutions turned into an organized movement led by a small elite group of small rulers, land holders, industrialists, agriculturists, and professional classes in 1910.[71] In 1917, a 'non-Brahmin manifesto' was released to protect the interests of backward classes in the fields of education, employment, and politics. 'The move was led by members of *upper* castes of Velalars, Reddys,

---

[69]   Ibid.; B. Walker, 1995: 299-300
[70]   Chatterjee, 2004: 3-4
[71]   Beteille, 1969: 176

Kamas, Velmas and Nairs and supporters from upper trading castes.'[72] The expression 'upper castes' used by Andre Beteille for these OBCs says a lot in an area of the country which boasts of 97 percent population of discriminated Shudra. In 1919, twenty-eight out of ninety-eight seats in Madras Legislature were reserved for non-Brahmins. The principle was later extended to new appointments in all departments under the Government. Despite the motto of 'equal opportunities' for all, the beneficiaries were mostly 'forward' non-Brahmins, whose ascendancy began in 1920s and reached its peak in 1950.[73] The other places where backward class movement took hold were Uttar Pradesh and Bihar—the two most backward States in the country. Rajputs and Thakurs, who described themselves as Kshatriyas, Brahmins, and some merchants and trader castes, described as forward castes, were excluded from the backward classes. Associated denominators for backwardness, however, remained intense poverty, illiteracy, low occupations, and exploitation.

In 1925, a Government resolution in Bombay defined backward classes as 'all except Brahmans, Prabhus, Parsis, Banias and Christians,' and the Hartog Committee defined backward classes as 'educationally backward' and included depressed classes, Aboriginal hilly tribes, and criminal tribes among them.[74] Till then, there was no definite ideology to identify depressed classes and backward tribes, but it did seem that caste was not the primary concern, educational backwardness was more important an issue and the depressed classes were one of the important beneficiaries.

In 1950, the Madras High Court held the Government Order (GO) of giving reservation to Backward Hindus void. Despite the claim that they were the discriminated Dravidians and possibly Shudra, a seven judges Bench of the Supreme Court in a landmark judgment upheld the high court decision in 1951.[75] This was reversed in the same year by amending the constitution and adding clause (4) to Article 15. Later, in 1950s, the Central Government appointed First Backward Classes Commission under Kaka Kalelkar to identify socially and educationally backward classes, but it had to be wound up due to difference of opinion among its members. The chairman reported to the President that reservations on the basis of caste

72   Radhakrishnan P, 1996: 113-14
73   Beteille as quoted by Radhakrishnan, 1996: 114
74   Roy Burman, 1992: 3
75   Radhakrishnan, 1996: 116-122

would harm the nation. The Central Government left the matter to State Governments in 1961 with advice to follow economic criteria.

The Second Backward Classes Commission under B. P. Mandal was constituted in 1979 for the uplift of socially and educationally backward classes, the same as Other Backward Classes. The Mandal Commission's Report was put into cold storage because of lack of consensus on the use of Shudra or because the British Government and its courts had used the Shudra identity for the Scheduled Castes for more than a century and the Indian Constitution and the succeeding governments and courts avoided it altogether. Since 1990, when the hotchpotch coalition Government of V. P. Singh resurrected the Report as a last-ditch effort to save itself, the nation has been left in a quandary.

Up to 1947, the term 'Backward Classes' had not acquired a 'definite meaning at all India level' nor did the British deploy it at national level. The first uncertainty started in 1946 when Jawaharlal Nehru "resolved to provide safeguards for minorities, backward and tribal areas, and depressed and other backward classes", and the term 'backward' began to mean the following:

(i)   More inclusive group of those who need special treatment and
(ii) A stratum higher than the untouchables but, nonetheless, depressed.[76]

Both groups were part of depressed classes. In 1929, while appearing before the Frachise Commission, G.S. Pal from United Provinces, presented a list of depressed Classes and told Ambedkar that it contained both untouchable and a stratum higher. (Marc Galanter 1984) Probably, taking cue from this, Nehru described them as 'inclusive group' that required special treatment and the second detonation of 'stratum higher', but nonetheless depressed. The behavioral tendencies like beef eating had already been recognized as a cause of pollution or 'untouchability'. In 2008, even the Supreme Court described a part of Scheduled Castes as not untouchable, but nonetheless depressed (chapter 8). Thus, Scheduled Castes included and still include both untouchables and not untouchable, but depressed - the same as 'stratum higher than the untouchables'.

After the independence, a large number of dissatisfied and uncompromising groups of population in the South and in Uttar Pradesh

---

[76]   Galanter: 159

and Bihar in the North, who were earlier tenants, became the owner-cultivators of lands after the land reforms of 1950. Terming the displacement of landowners by *middle farmers* as one of the most significant developments of post-independent India, Meenakshi Jain chided the British administrators for calling the lowest castes Shudras, but admitted in 1996, 'The middle farmers today constitute the most powerful group in the countryside economically as well as politically', yet 'the Upper Shudras have not shared power with Lower Shudras who form 40 percent of backward caste population'. Upper Shudras of North India included 'such economically powerful and politically aggressive groups as Jats, Kurmis, and Koiris, while the Lower Shudra included the humble Hajam, Kumbhar, Lohar, Teli, Dhanuk and Mallah'.[77] She gave no reasons for accepting 'economically powerful and politically aggressive groups' of 'upper' Shudras as backward and discriminated. Instead, she quoted Srinivas, who had stated, "The term Shudra spans such a wide cultural and structural arc as to be meaningless. They are at one extreme the *dominant, land owning peasant castes* which wield power and authority over local Vaishyas and Brahmins, whereas on the other extreme are *poor Untouchable groups* just above the pollution line" (emphasis added). Till 1983, the share of Lower Shudras in government posts was only 7 percent.[78] In the Bihar Assembly in March 1985, 41 percent of its members were Yadavs, when their percentage of population was a mere 11 percent. In Uttar Pradesh, the dominant castes are Jats, but they are also facing competition from Yadavs. In Haryana, Ahirs, Gujars, Yadavs, and Jats are among the better placed communities. Jain concluded, 'The determination of backward castes to seize power together with internal contradictions and struggle within their alliance system' has created dissentions between 'Upper Shudras and Lower Shudras and among Jats, Yadavs and Kurmis of the former group'.[79]

A similar situation existed in the South. In order to placate similar large, powerful, and politically active groups in the South, 25 percent reservations were given under the Madras Educational Rules to Backward Hindus and some converts to Christianity, but it failed to satisfy them. Vanniyars, who had earlier claimed to be Kshatriyas, were particularly active in demanding reservations. In 1969, DMK Government under Karunanidhi increased the quota of reservation to 31 percent, but refused to apply income

---

[77] Ibid.: 136-138
[78] Meenakshi Jain: 135-160
[79] Ibid.

limit recommended by the Backward Classes Commission. In 1979, the AIDMK Government of M. G. Ramachandran tried to implement the income limit clause, but made a hasty retreat in the following year. In 1982, a new commission appointed under Supreme Court's directions gave its recommendations, but it created controversy. In 1989, the Congress Government succumbed to the pressure of the powerful Vanniyars with a population of 12 percent and set aside 20 percent reservation out of a total of 50 percent for a mere 39 out of a total of 201 affected communities.[80] Kuppuswamy found that Vokkilogas and Lingyats of Karnataka, Reddys and Kamas of Andhra Pradesh, Nayars and Eshovas of Kerala, and Vallalas and Nadars of Kerala in the South though were not as highly educated as advanced castes; they were nevertheless powerful landowners and traditional headmen. Today, they are financially well off and occupy high positions in social and political fields. In the early 1990s, their representation in government jobs was relatively low, but in the caste hierarchy, they were next only to Brahmins. Yet they have developed vested interest in remaining backward. The real sufferers are the economically and educationally 'weak' backward classes 'who have not been able to combine with scheduled castes to fight back the advanced castes'.[81]

In *People of India*, which was a study undertaken by the Anthropological Survey of India in the 1980s and published their findings in the 1990s, P. S. Singh, its former Director General, rejects any racial difference between the higher and lower castes on the grounds of physical anthropological and biological parameters. He attributes the high position of Brahmins, Rajputs, Kshatriyas, Kyasthas, and Banias to 'higher position in socio-ritual hierarchy, better control over land and non-communal relations with others'. Singh too divides middle castes into two categories of Middle A and Middle B, owing to wide difference in their socioeconomic status.[82] In the case of tribal, he says, 'Tribal have their own notion . . . they have no stigma due to caste factor and majority are avarnas.'[83] He calls Panchama *'a non-existent fifth Varna'* (all emphasis added).

M.N. Srinivas commented that Shudras are 'vast majority of non-Brahminical castes which have little in common' and 'ranking of castes on economic and political considerations would produce stratification different

---

80   Radhakrishnan, 1996: 121-131
81   B. Kuppuswamy, 1990: 251 Social Change in India Jain Book Depot Delhi
82   Singh: Vol. 1: 78-80
83   Ibid.: 25

from that based on ritual considerations'.[84] The terms non-Brahminical and Shudras do not mean only the lowest. They appear to support the view in Puranas which stated that in the Age of Kali only Brahmins and Shudra would survive. It meant, barring Brahmins, both forward and backward castes or Jatis and the people composing them would exist among Shudras. Therefore, not only Shudras need clarification, but also middle classes which are described as powerful landowners and traditional headmen. Obviously, they cannot be called backward and discriminated, as is being done even today. The confusion caused in colonial times and after the independence in the genesis and application of middle or intermediate classes will be taken up in the later chapters.

Social justice is a strange story of tit for tat where present generations have to do reparation for the alleged follies of their past generations, though their ancestors cannot be traced beyond a few generations. In a telling report to the Mandal Commission, Tata Institute criticized the states for not adopting common criteria to identify backward classes. The institute also pulled up the states for manipulating a constitutional provision that 'provided protective discrimination for the socially and educationally backward classes and Scheduled Castes and Scheduled Tribes'. The Registrar General of India found the same situation five years after the Mandal case judgment and criticized the State Governments for not following uniform criteria. When such differences were pointed out to the Mandal Commission, it observed, "It is no doubt true that the major benefits of reservations and other welfare measures will be cornered by the more advanced sections of the backward communities. But is this not a universal phenomenon?" The commission forgot that it was appointed to prevent this universal phenomenon. There is no point in blaming China for supplying arms to Naxalites if we cannot reign in the commissions appointed to redress the poor and the illiterate, unless of course they are following the political agenda of their appointees.

In a recent article, *History From Below, Caste Politics in Recent Times—A New Trend,*[85] published on the Internet, its author, Partha Chatterjee, makes some interesting observations. The following account is based on this article. Thirty years ago, there were two main contending schools of historians dealing with modern historiography. One group was based at Cambridge University. Its argument was that in a bid for power some 'Indian elites', on the pretext of 'Indian nationalism', used the 'traditional bonds of caste and communal ties to mobilize the masses' against the British rule. The other

---

[84]   M.N. Srinivas, 1991: 30-31
[85]   Partha Chatterjee: http://mondediplo.com/2006/03/14india

group was of 'Indian nationalist historians' who believed that the material conditions of colonial exploitation created the ground for an alliance of different classes in Indian society under a 'nationalist leadership', which could enthuse and organize 'the masses to join the struggle for national freedom'. The targeted groups were different in both the cases.

A third group of historians, continues Chatterjee, appeared in 1980s and specialized in what they called "subaltern studies". Inspired by the 'Italian Marxist Antonio Gramsci', these historians denounced both the Cambridge and the nationalist schools which represented 'either colonial or nationalist elitism'. According to this group, 'nationalism' was wholly a product of elite action, which gave no opportunity to subaltern classes (rural peasants and urban workers) to undertake 'independent political action'. Since the 1980s, modern Indian history has been mostly confined to these three approaches. The first phase of subaltern studies was a strong critique of bourgeois-nationalist politics and was dominated by peasant revolt, but in 1987 and 1989, the approach changed and it was acknowledged that the 'subaltern histories were fragmentary, disconnected and incomplete' and 'subaltern consciousness' was itself split. Therefore, there was a 'move from feudalism or agrarianism toward capitalism, industrialization, secularization, rationalization, or modern ideas and practices'.

However, the latest approach has changed and moved toward political alliances between castes at the middle and bottom rungs and the alleged oppressed groups such as tribal and religious minorities. In this, even the major political parties are involved. The minorities, for example, enjoy more constitutional safeguards than the majority, and their backwardness is not due to external oppression but internal factors. Yet the commissions and the committees appointed for their benefit ignore the latter. The result is that it is difficult to find the oppressor majority. In the Mandal Report, the commission found the population of forward castes or oppressor groups to be less than 18 percent of total population, but now even among them some have struggled for backward class status and got it in some states. They are now demanding the same at the central level. Under the circumstances, it might have been simpler to identify forward castes and groups and declare the rest of Indian population backward and discriminated!

Another example of politicizing caste was the *Dalit Convention's Resolution under Communist Forum* held at New Delhi on 22 February 2006, published on the Internet. It repeated the same old story of "reactionary varna and caste system, the notorious text Manusmriti; the stories of Shambuka in the Ramayana; and of Ekalavya in the Mahabharata" as the classic testimonies of the 'non-egalitarian nature of Hindu society', as if these people still exist or the Manusmriti is still the law of the land. Some people cannot help quoting incidences and names for propaganda which, in private, they dismiss as fiction. The convention misconstrued the meaning of 'Varnas' even in 2006. The use of the political expression Dalit—of meaning of which even the erudite are puzzled—was also not innocent. The National Commission for Scheduled Castes recently asked the State Governments not to use the 'unconstitutional' word 'Dalit' in official documents. The appropriate and notified word in Article 341 of the Constitution was 'Scheduled Castes'. Acting upon the order, the Chhattisgarh Government directed the district collectors and its departments not to use 'Dalit' word in official documents.[86]

The CPI (M)'s updated 'Programme in 2000', however, summarizes the caste equation with some justification. 'That the bourgeois-landlord system has also failed to put an end to caste oppression' is true, but 'all Dalits are even now' subjected to untouchability is untrue. This is no longer true even of scavengers. An odd incidence is glamorized or blown out of proportion. The only remaining problems are the denial of temple entry in a few famous but highly orthodox temples and the attitude of some conservatives. Unfortunately, the State and the courts, too, tend to look the other way due to, what they call tradition and custom.

When the communists argue that some caste leaders from 'bourgeois political parties' take advantage of polarization on caste lines for narrow electoral gains and prevent building up of common movement of the oppressed sections of *all* castes, to which may now be added religions, and ignore the basic class issues of land, wages and fight against landlordism, they are not wrong. However, when the same Communist parties support the same caste-based political parties which perpetuate caste and oppose the implementation of abolition of caste enjoined in the Directive Principles of the Constitution, their protests appear hollow. In more than two decades of rule in West Bengal and during the first tenure of the rule of United Progressive Alliance, which depended upon their support for survival, communists did nothing to force abolition of caste. Opportunistic and stagnant political parties do not create revolutions.

Caste as a Jati has always been a part of Hindu society, but its institutionalization occurred after the arrival of the British colonizers.

---

[86] *Express India.* 18 January 2008. Retrieved 27 September 2008. Also http://en.wikipedia.org/wiki/Dalit

Today, caste not only plays an enormous role in the political arena but also influences other government-run institutions. Gender, too, plays a significant role in the power dynamics of caste politics at Panchayat, State, and now also at national level. Caste alone may not determine the voting behaviors, but it does play a significant role. André Béteille comments that if there is one thing that is common among the experts in the media is their preoccupation with caste and the part they play in electoral politics. They do not let caste to die down or disappear from the political scene. India has changed in many ways since independence, but the hopes of earlier Indian leaders that a country of so many castes and communities would change into 'a nation of citizens with the adoption of a new republican constitution' has not been realized.[87] Therefore, one cannot but agree with Béteille when he says that it would be a pity if we continue to allow the media to reinforce caste consciousness and 'to persuade us that caste is India's destiny'.[88] Only a few decades ago, matrimonial advertisements in the newspapers did not mention castes, which have become the rule today.

Minority Backward Classes are another problem. According to Wikipedia, Dalit theology is a branch of Christian theology that emerged in India in the 1980s. Dalit theology opposes indigenization movements in India, while Christian liturgy seems to reinforce the traditional caste hierarchies. Therefore, many Catholics complained against the discrimination by the members of the Catholic Church. While addressing the bishops of Madras, Mylapore, Madurai, Cuddalore, and Pondicherry in the late 2003, Pope John Paul II criticized caste discrimination in the Roman Catholic Church.[89] Conversion was meant to emancipate 'Dalits' from untouchability, not to subject them to caste discrimination after conversion.

In 1992, the Supreme Court especially mentioned Christians and Muslims for inclusion among backward classes.[90] If despite the Court's ruling the Christian Backward Classes did not get reservation under Articles 15(4) and 16(4), it is certainly a case for probe and proper redress, but if they are not availing reservations on their own, especially in South India, then why this complaint now? They cannot apply the word 'Dalit' to every type

---

[87] Beteille: *Hindu*: article published on 12 February 2012
[88] Ibid.
[89] http://en.wikipedia.org/wiki/Caste_system_among_Indian_Christians
[90] *A.I.R.* Supreme Court 1993: 554-555

of backwardness, which neither the Apex Court nor recently the Sachar Committee did.

Writing in an article 'Beyond Minority Reports—Identity politics deepens social prejudices', Andre Béteille traces the history of enactment of Constitution in which both Nehru and Ambedkar gave preference to individual rights over group rights. He says, "The positive response of the Sachar Committee report was an endorsement of Ambedkar's view that it would be wrong to ignore the existence of minorities. But what about his view, that it would be wrong for the minorities to perpetuate themselves?" He warns, "Minority right is a powerful sword but it would do well to remember that, in our present political circumstances, it is a double edged sword."[91]

On the legality of 4.5 percent reservations separately for minorities out of the 27 percent reservation for OBCs, the Andhra Pradesh High Court ruled on 28 May 2012, "We must, therefore, hold that Muslims, Christians, Sikhs, Buddhists and Zoroastrians (Parsis) do not form a homogeneous group but a heterogeneous group." Noting the words, 'belonging to minorities' or 'for minorities', the Court observed that these indicate that 'the sub-quota was carved out only on the religious lines' and not on any other intelligible bases. The Bench, therefore, directed. "We have, therefore, no option but to set aside the carving out of a sub-quota of 4.5 percent in favor of backward classes belonging to minorities out of the 27 percent reservation for OBCs."[92] The matter has now reached the Supreme Court. It is time to examine the social structures of communities other than Hindus to discover the specific reasons for their backwardness. Either this should be done or, preferably, there should be common criteria for all communities. The time has come to have a re-look at caste-based reservations, not to speak of starting reservations on the basis of religion, majority or minority.

Summary

The British not only divided the country on the basis of caste, race, and religion but also region. We are still suffering from the after-effects. The role of Indians, too, was not helpful. By declining to support EVR and Ambedkar in the fight against restriction on *temple entry*, the Indian National Congress and Mahatma Gandhi not only failed to affect a welcome social change, but

---

91   *Times of India*, 12 October 2009
92   *Indian Express*, 29 May 2012

also failed to contain a social evil. Caste and religion politics is ruining the country. Sachar Committee's recommendation to create a National Data Bank (NDB) to maintain relevant data pertaining to socioeconomic and educational status will be useful only if poverty and illiteracy are dealt with without bringing in caste, religion, sex, or region, as envisaged by Nehru, Ambedkar, and the Indian Constitution.

As the backwardness of all backward classes is traced to societies of ancient India, it becomes crucial to start from the Vedic period, but here, too, there is no unanimity. Yet one has to start from somewhere. Rather than enter into controversies, it would be prudent to take refuge in the views of Dr Ambedkar on the Vedic and the following periods and on appearance of Shudras and untouchables. His views might be acceptable to most, especially the backward classes.

CHAPTER 2

BHIMRAO AMBEDKAR—REVISITED[93]

Shudras

Starting from a humble origin and educated by an upper caste ruler of a State, Ambedkar rose to be the first law minister and chairman of the Drafting Committee of the Constitution and become one of the its main architects. The Supreme Court clarified in the Mandal case that though the opinions expressed by the members of the Constituent Assembly on the meaning of 'backward' in Article 16(4) were 'not binding upon the Court', 'the speech of Dr Ambedkar stands on a different footing' and its taking into account 'was unavoidable'.[94] Ambedkar rubbished the prevalent view that Dravidians came to India and made Aborigines untouchables and Aryans came and made Dravidians slaves and serfs. His views on a number of diverse terminologies such as Aarya, Dasa, Dasyus, Nagas, Rakhshasas, and Mlecchas described in the Vedas and other scriptures did not coincide with colonial time interpretations. He had no objections to the cosmogony of Purusha Sukta as such, but was highly critical of that part which said that Shudras came out from the feet of the Creator.

He discussed Shudras and untouchables in Volume 7 of his *Writings and Speeches* re-published by the Education Department of Government of Maharashtra in 1990, but without mentioning a fifth Varna of Panchama. His views on the supposed *historic* injustices and inequalities in the Vedic period in his book would be of considerable interest. Throughout his life, he was concerned with the uplift of depressed classes, the untouchables,

---

93   Volume 7 of *Writings and Speeches* of Dr Ambedkar mostly of pre-1950 compiled and re-published by the Education Department of Government of Maharashtra in 1990

94   *Judgements Today*, 1992: 636-637: 786

who later became Scheduled Castes. He did not even define the word 'backward' in backward class of citizens in Article 16(4) and left the definition of backward class of citizens to the Supreme Court. Therefore, when he protested against the ill treatment of Shudras in Manusmriti, he protested against the discrimination committed against the lowest castes, the depressed classes, whom Risley converted into untouchables in 1901 and the British Government into Scheduled Castes in 1936. Ambedkar did not distinguish untouchables from Shudras, when he described Phule as the greatest Shudra.

Ambedkar was not a Sanskrit scholar on his own admission. His opinions were influenced by the social and political views of his times and aggravated by the cold shoulder shown to him by the Indian National Congress. In the first three chapters of *Riddle of Shudras*, Ambedkar describes what he calls the 'Brahminical' Theory of the Origin of Shudras and the Brahminical Theory of the Status of Shudra.' He found 'Brahminical speculations' of four classes of Brahmins, Kshatriyas, Vaishyas, and Shudras in ancient literature illogical. He believed that the allegory of Purusha Shukta was superadded in the Vedas and was responsible for the wretched condition of the Shudra.[95] He struggled all his life for the uplift of Shudras and to protest against their ill treatment in the Manusmriti. When he burnt hundreds of its volumes in public in 1927, he was agitating for the uplift of depressed classes, not Backward Hindus or Other Backward Classes. Untouchables, he said, appeared much later than 400 A.D. He stated that the 'imposition of disabilities in the Manusmriti and similar literature would not have been so atrocious' if the disabled had been free to outgrow those conditions. What was atrocious was that breach of these conditions was also regarded as a crime involving dire punishment. This not only sought to impose disabilities but also made them permanent.[96] This observation raises identification issues. *First,* who were the Shudras in ancient times and how were they defined and identified? *Second,* who are the present-day Shudras and on what evidence they are said to be progeny of the same Shudras who were mentioned in the scriptures? In 2008, the Chief Justice of India distinguished between the *social acceptability* of scavengers and the rest of the lowest castes or Scheduled Castes, who were only *depressed.* Among

---

[95]   Ambedkar, 1990: Vol. 7: 65-68: *Writings and Speeches*, published by Government of Maharashtra
[96]   Ibid.

scavengers, too, only those were 'untouchables' who carried human excreta and lived away from the main community.

As more than 90 percent population lived in the rural areas and almost all used open spaces, the population of sweepers was small and did not have to carry human night soil. In the semi-urban areas, too, separate latrines could not be possible in relatively small hutments. Large cities were few in those days. India was not unique in having scavengers. As recently as the late nineteenth century, sewerage systems in parts of the highly industrialized United Kingdom were so inadequate that streets were engulfed in foul smell and water-borne diseases. Diseases like cholera and typhoid were common occurrences. The issue here is not so much of the sewage carriage or disposal, but the need of it and the people required to do the work. In ancient India which was ahead in sewage disposal than most civilizations of early times, manual carrying of human night soil must be exceedingly rare and the people to do that very few. The claim that sweepers carried human excreta for thousands of years and were considerable in number is untenable.

Till the middle of the twentieth century, the main job of scavengers in rural areas was to clean areas like streets and pick up cattle dung which when dried provided fuel for the poor. In India, proper clothing, gloves, and other facilities are not provided even to those who are in Government service. Cleaning is a vocation, provided it is given dignity and carried out with adequate protective gear. For this one cannot blame Manu, in whose time such people would be very few, if at all any. 'Chandalas' were the first known people to live away from the people, but they were hunters, not scavengers. Purity and pollution had many reasons. Physical segregation was uncommon and that also for a specific period. Ambedkar's statement that not only the Brahminic writers 'do not give any clue' as to who the Shudra were and how they came to be the fourth Varna but also the Western writers do not have 'a definite theory about the origin of the Shudra'[97] is more realistic. The disinformation started when the society was divided on racial basis into Aryans, Dravidians, and Aborigines in the nineteenth century. Today, few would believe in the racial theory, but Dr Ambedkar was unconvinced even then that ancient India was a land of primitive people and that it was conquered 2,000 years before the birth of Christ by hordes of chariot-riding Indo-Europeans. He did not think the word 'Varna' meant 'color' or 'complexion'. He criticized Western and westernized Indian writers for giving different racial cover to the upper and lower castes. He rejected

[97]   Ibid.

the notion that traits like color of hair or eyes, color of skin, and stature indicated the race of any particular body of people.

As most foreigners who invaded and settled down in India got completely absorbed in the local population, modern anthropology and ethnology do not support different racial origin of higher and lower castes. The argument that because one is a Brahmin one must be an Aryan or one who belongs to South India must be a Dravidian or one who comes from various tribes must be an Aborigine is simply ridiculous. Max Muller, who is often credited for being the first to call Aryans a distinct racial group, stated that the word 'Arya' would have originally conveyed a 'landholder or a cultivator of land' while 'Vaishyas', from Vis, meant 'householder'. The 'etymological (linguistic) significance' of Arya, he said, seemed to be 'one who ploughs or tills'.

Ambedkar quotes Max Muller, "There is no Aryan race in blood; Aryan, in scientific language is utterly inapplicable to race. It means language and nothing but language; and if we speak of Aryan race at all, we should know that it means no more than Aryan speech" and that he had "declared again and again that if I say Aryas, I mean neither blood nor bones, nor hair nor skull . . . To me, an ethnologist who speaks of Aryan race, Aryan blood, Aryan eyes and hair, is as great a sinner as a linguist who speaks of a dolichocephalic dictionary or a brachiocephalic grammar".[98]

Although Max Muller used the word 'Aryan' in a linguistic sense, the British administrators and some historians and social anthropologists kept dividing India on racial basis into Aryan North and Dravidian South. Ambedkar found no evidence of racial intention in the use of the word Arya 'with a long a' (Aarya) in the Vedic literature. There are a number of versions of the origin of Aryan race, but the commonest theory is that Aryan came from the steppes of Caucasia. Ambedkar quotes Prof. Ripley who criticized the theory for 'the utter absurdity of the misnomer Caucasian', applied to the 'blue-eyed and fair-headed' Aryan race of Western Europe. People of this description, Ripley said, did not occur 'within many hundred miles of Caucasia' and that there was not a single native tribe making use of a purely inflectional or Aryan language along the great Caucasian chain. He concluded, "Nowhere else in the world probably is so heterogeneous a lot of people, languages and religions gathered in one place as along the chain of the Caucasus Mountains."[99]

---

[98]   Ibid.: 69
[99]   Ambedkar, 1990: Vol. 7: 71

Ambedkar supports his statement by quoting verse 22.8 from Rig Veda: "We live in the midst of the Dasyu tribes, who do not perform sacrifices, nor believe in anything. They have their own rites and are not entitled to be called men. Oh! Thou, destroyer of enemies, annihilate them and injure the Dasa." Rig Veda did not describe Dasyu *tribes* as slaves and serfs. It criticized them because they were without the Aryan rites or had different rites. Ambedkar argues that besides many descriptions of wars between the Aryans and the Dasas and Dasyus in Rig Veda there are also instances of compromise between them. The point to note, he concludes, is that 'whatever the degree of conflict, it was not a conflict of race', but was in the nature of 'religion' or 'religious practices' or, perhaps, for political and territorial supremacy. The British time theories of Dravidian slaves, serfs and Aborigines, untouchables and backward and discriminated tribes in the form of Scheduled Castes and Scheduled Tribes, and their continuing progeny persisting in similar condition for centuries has haunted the nation for long. Unless these notions are discarded, we cannot come to the real causes of backwardness in the society. Unfortunately these theories are quoted even now.

Ambedkar then describes two Sanskrit words *Mridhravak* and *Anasa* mentioned in the Rig Veda, but differently interpreted by the Western writers. '*Mridhravak* means one who speaks crude, unpolished language.' The word *Anasa* has two meanings. Max Muller understood *a-nasa* as 'without nose'. Ambedkar says this makes no sense as at no other place Dasuyus are described as 'noseless or flat nosed.' While Risley and other writers adopted Muller's interpretation to differentiate between 'dark snub-nosed' Dravidians and Aborigines from the 'fair sharp featured' Aryans, an ancient commentator Sayanacharya interpreted *Anasa* as *an-asa* meaning 'mouthless or devoid of good speech'. Ambedkar agrees with the latter and states, 'There is no reason to hold that Sayana's reading is wrong.' Mridhravak and Anasa are synonyms and indicate person or persons with crude and uncultured speech and could be both Aryans and non-Aryans and could belong to any group community or race. Ambedkar then quotes a number of verses to prove that Aryans and Dasuyus were the same people and concludes that the theory of Aryan race falls to the ground at every point because it was based on nothing but pleasing assumptions and 'inferences based on such assumptions'. The theory was preconceived and 'facts' were purposely 'selected to prove it'.[100] To prove his point Ambedkar quotes from

---

[100]   Ibid.: 76-77

Bhavishya Purana, another ancient Indian text, which says, "Since members of all the four castes are children of God, they all belong to the same caste. All human beings have the same father, and children of the same father cannot have different castes."[101]

Ambedkar retracted even from the accuracy of anthropometry when he conveyed his findings in a highly significant passage that the nasal index of the Churra (the untouchables) of the Punjab is the same as the nasal index of the Brahmin of the United Provinces; the nasal index of the Chamar (the untouchables of Bihar) is not very much distinct from the Brahmin of Bihar, and so on.[102] He contests historian Kane's view that the word Dasa means a 'serf or a slave' and that 'Dasas and Dasyus conquered by the Aryans were gradually transformed into the Shudra'.[103] Ambedkar also decries the hypothesis that Dasa and Dasyus were slaves or serfs just because the word Shudra is said to be derived from two words *Shuk* (sorrow) and *dru* (overcome), meaning one who is 'overcome by sorrow', and points out that why take a sinister view when the word could as well mean one 'who overcomes sorrow.'

In 1996, N. N. Bhattacharya wrote in *Indian Religious Historiography* that study of races of India made by British officials was 'politically motivated and made arbitrarily'. It was based on 'insufficient data and (with) immature outlook.' He criticized them for describing 'Dravidians' (Shudra) in the 1931 census as 'the black skinned medium-statured dolichocephals of inferior racial status.'[104] Quoting various verses from scriptures, Ambedkar rejects the notion that Shudras were slaves and for that reason they were denied Upanayna. Shudras not only participated in the coronation of kings but they also were ministers. Bhishma advised Yudhishtra to choose three of his ministers from among the Shudras 'who should be humble and of pure conduct and devoted to daily duties'.[105] He admitted that the 'Western theory' was of no help in determining 'who were Shudra and how did they become the fourth Varna'.[106]

---

[101] Ibid.

[102] Ambedkar: Vol. 7: 302-303

[103] Kane

[104] N.N. Bhattacharya, 1996: 11 *Indian Religious Historiography*: Munshiram Manoharlal Publishers Pvt. Ltd. New Delhi

[105] Ibid.

[106] Ambedkar: 111-113

Having demolished the Aryan invasion theory and the role of color or complexion in separating people, Ambedkar embarked upon an uncertain *'technique,'* which he thought 'the Brahmins employed to bring about the degradation of Shudras from the rank of the second to the rank of fourth Varna'. The technique, he believed, was denial of *Upanayana* to the Shudra.[107] As a rite, *Upanayana* was originally a very simple ceremony for a student to beg the teacher to allow him to stay with him for the purpose of study and to be initiated into the study of Vedas.[108] Unless this was accomplished, even a Brahmin or a king remained a Shudra and 'once-born'. The ceremony was individual specific, not caste specific. Individuals were once-born or twice-born, not their Jatis. Yagnopavita or wearing of thread was meant to acquire one's father's *gotra*.[109] Women were permitted to take part in both the ceremonies.[110] So far as Yagnopavita was concerned, even a Shudra wore the thread. Thus, loss of the right to wear the thread could deprive a person of one's *gotra*, but not the right to study the Veda or vice versa. R. S. Sharma (1996) writes in: *The State and Varna Formation in the Mid-Ganga Plain: An Ethno-Archeological View* that Shudras were Vratyas—meaning of low caste, yet like the Brahmins and the Kshatriyas they 'performed the Ashvomed Yagya'. There was no bar on their studying Vedas or acquiring wealth, education, and status. The meaning of 'low caste' is not explained. Ambedkar summarizes his findings as under:

1. Shudras was one of the Aryan communities of the solar race". Shudras ranked among Kshatriya Varna in the Indo-Aryan society.
2. There was a time when the Aryan society recognized only three Varnas, namely, Brahmins, Kshatriyas, and Vaishyas. The Shudras were . . . a part of Kshatriya Varna.
3. Due to a continuous feud between Shudra kings and Brahmins, *Brahmins* were 'subjected to many tyrannies and indignities'.
4. Brahmins 'refused to invest the Shudras with sacred thread' to avenge their tyrannies and oppressions.

---

[107]   Ibid.: 141-151
[108]   Ibid.: 156 (emphasis in original)
[109]   Ambedkar: 157-159
[110]   Ambedkar: 160-161

Loss of the sacred thread caused social degradation of Shudras. They 'fell below the rank of Vaishyas and came to form the fourth Varna.'[111] Ambedkar then quotes a few authorities like Senart to support his thesis that Shudras were Aryan Kshatriyas. Unfortunately, he did not give importance to the prediction that in the *Age of Kali* only people with attributes of Brahmins and Shudras would survive. With so many scams, corruption in every sphere of life, rapes of small children, terrorism, and fall in moral values, can there be difficulty in calling most non-Brahmins, even most Brahmins in India, Shudras in the contemporary derogatory sense?

Shudras in Contemporary Society

Ambedkar rejects the notion that because Shudras formed a large part of population in ancient times, their population in the present time too would be large. He emphasizes that 'such an inference' was without foundation, for the Shudras of the Indo-Aryan society were 'absolutely different from the Shudra of Hindu Society', and continues:

> The Shudras of the Hindu Society are not the racial descendents of the Shudras of the Indo-Aryan Society . . . the meaning of the word 'Shudras' in the Indo-Aryan society is quite different from the meaning it has in the Hindu Society. In the Indo-Aryan Society the word Shudra was proper name of one single people . . . The word Shudra, as used in the Hindu society, is *not* a proper name at all. It is a general cognomen of a miscellaneous and heterogeneous collection of tribes and groups, who have nothing in common except they happen to be on a lower plane of culture. *It is wrong to call them by the name Shudra.* They have very little to do with their namesakes of the Aryan society, who had offended Brahmins.[112] (Emphasis added)

800 or more years of Muslim rule, two centuries of exploitation by colonial rulers, and the appearance of a feudal society after the third century AD were good enough reasons to cause widespread poverty and illiteracy in the Indian population before 1947. The question is who were these

---

[111] Ambedkar: 204
[112] Ibid.: 200-201

heterogeneous collections of 'innocent and backward people' with large population whom it was wrong to call Shudra and what was the cause of their backwardness? But for the Shudra identity judicially imposed upon them in 1992, these backward people, now called Other Backward Classes, could well be backward due to vast socioeconomic inequalities that have been present in society for centuries. The observations of Dr Ambedkar in which he rejects the Shudra identity of those apart from the lowest, the untouchables, tell the true story of backwardness in contemporary India. Many had traditional occupations which produced some of the finest material in ancient and medieval India, but there was no caste occupation nexus or restriction in change of occupation, which are responsible for centuries of backwardness. This has been also discussed in other places.

Court Cases

Ambedkar relates the complexity faced by the Privy Council in 1837 while distinguishing between Kshatriyas and Shudras:

> The question at issue was whether in India at the relevant time there were any Kshatriyas. The contention of one side was that there were. The contention on the other side was that there were none. The later contention was based upon the theory propagated by Brahmins that the Brahmin Parshurama had killed all the Kshatriyas and that if any were left they were all exterminated by the Shudra king Mahapadma Nanda. The Privy Council did not accept this theory which they regarded as false and concocted by Brahmins and held that Kshatriyas still existed in India. The Privy Council, however, did not lay down any test by which a Kshatriya could be distinguished from a Shudra.[113]

That the Privy Council could not distinguish between a Kshatriya and a Shudra tells the true story. In another case of Marathas, the court decided that "there are three classes of Marathas in the Bombay Presidency: (1) the five families; (2) the ninety six families; (3) the rest. Of these, the only first two classes are legally Kshatriyas". The *second* court adopted the use of word 'Das' as surname to determine backward status; the *third* court relied

---

on the 'wearing of sacred thread' and ability to perform 'homa'; the *fourth* court applied the period of 'impurity'; the *fifth* court used the criterion of the competence or incompetence of 'illegitimate' sons to succeed; the *sixth* court adopted "general repute" in the community; *the seventh* court applied the criteria of 'consciousness of the community'; the *eighth* court used the wearing of *Upanayana* or thread and stated that 'all non-Brahmins are Shudra'. Perhaps, that was the only court which was right. The *ninth* court adopted 'consciousness of the caste, its custom and acceptance of that consciousness by other castes'.[114]

In a contemptuous remark, Ambedkar observed, "It is most confusing medley of opinions which settles little and unsettles much." And "no one who knows anything about the subject can say that the criteria adopted by the various courts are the right ones".[115] Post independence courts are no wiser.

Untouchability and Untouchables

Here only Dr. Ambedkar's views are recorded. Ambedkar describes the category of untouchables as 'an entity beyond human intercourse where mere touch is enough to cause pollution'. He blames the Hindu community for 'inculcating . . . false beliefs in the sanity, superiority and sanctity of Hindu Civilization', which he attributes 'entirely to the peculiar social psychology of Hindu scholars'. He expresses his disappointment at the absence of investigation into the origin of untouchables and regrets that barring unproven inferences there is no unanimity either on reason for appearance of untouchability or on the period in which it first appeared. The situation remains the same even today.

Ambedkar differentiates untouchables from 'impure'. 'The impure came into existence at the time of Dharamsutras', but *'the untouchables came into being much later than AD 400'*[116] That was the time when Buddhism was at its decline. He admits that there was no untouchability in ancient India and the terms impurity and impure did not mean untouchability or untouchables. He confesses that in the absence of any historical evidence his theses or any thesis cannot be final, but there was a serious lacuna

---

114   Ibid.: 165
115   Ibid.: 164-165
116   Ibid.: 242

which, Ambedkar admitted, occurred due to insufficient attention he paid to the philosophical, ethical, and spiritual side of the scriptures. When he was criticized for being vague and subjective, he tried to silence his critics by saying, "I am not so vain as to claim any finality for my thesis . . . All I say to them (critics) is to consider whether his hypothesis is workable or not or whether it fits in or gives meaning to all surrounding facts and that he seeks nothing from them but a fair and unbiased appraisal".[117] He was not unreasonable.

He argues that though sense of impurity and pollution in some form or the other was found in many ancient civilizations (he cites a number of such instances), they were mostly concerned with 'occurrence of certain events, contact with certain things and contact with certain persons'. The events were 'birth, puberty, menstruation, marriage, cohabitation and death'. Sometimes events and even persons had to be isolated. He also concedes that there were no people primitive or ancient who did not entertain the notion of pollution and Hindus were '*no* exception'. Differences were about the source of pollution and methods of purification.[118]

Ambedkar then brings up the theory of 'broken men' or those captured after warfare and cites the example of his own community of Mahars to prove his thesis. The fifty-two rights given to the Mahars in lieu of doing the duty of watch and ward on behalf of village "included the right to collect food from the villagers, the right to collect corn from each villager during the harvest season, and the right to appropriate the dead animal belonging to the villagers." It is strange that the fifty-two privileges given to some people for watch and ward duties and entrusting to them the safety of the villages should earn them the title of 'broken men', centuries later of untouchables and in modern times of Dalits. It was not unlikely that they were the hired guards or the able-bodied men who stayed at the periphery of the village because that facilitated their duty of watch and ward. Mahars might have been extremely poor, but it is doubtful they were untouchables, ostracized and impure, or even discriminated castes. Kotani and his colleagues record that Mahars were soldiers and fought in the army of Shivaji. During the British times, there was a Mahar Regiment in the Indian Army which still continues and has won laurels. Mahars might or might not have been the 'broken men' whose previous fifty-two rights were restored by the Muslim king of Bedar, but with so many rights they

---

[117]   Ambedkar: Vol. 7: 245
[118]   Ambedkar: 249: 253

certainly could not have been untouchable.[119] Even Ambedkar admits that Mahars and Marathas had common *gotras*, i.e. they had the same origin or were once brothers or brothers and sisters. Today, they are doing quite well. Their untouchability is only for politics.

Ambedkar acknowledged that the broken men, even when they became Buddhists and attracted the ire of Brahmins, were not treated as untouchables. He wrote, "Can the hatred between Buddhism and Brahmanism be taken to be the sole cause why Broken Men became Untouchable . . . It is obvious that there were some additional circumstance which has played its part in fastening untouchability upon the Broken Men. What that circumstance could have been?"[120] He had answered it earlier by saying 'beef eating' which was more a behavioral problem or problem of conduct which even the Buddhists disapproved. Hatred for Brahmans and Brahmanism was a colonial invention to denigrate an ancient religion. Three to five percent of Brahmins could not be the cause of all the social ills in the Hindu community.

Sadasivan, apparently a neo-Buddhist author, who is highly critical of Brahmins and the Hindu religion, stated, "There was no single caste comprising all Brahmins . . . Many of them belonged to lower castes and tribal population. In Punjab there are ninety subgroups or castes of Brahmins which do not refrain from inter-marrying." Husaini Brahmins claim their existence 'only from Mohammedans'. Among Marathas, there are thirteen main castes of Brahmins. There are said to be eighty Brahmin castes in Gujarat. In Tamil Nadu, there are eleven clans. 'Kanyakubja have more than 100 different steps.' Kshatriya was a later name. Rig Veda called them Rajnaya. They were originally members of various tribes. Later, each tribe had a totem to show their exalted origin from sun, moon, or fire. They disappeared early in history, and 'all subsequent Kshatriyas could be traced to the lower castes and tribes'. Sadasivan further says that 'there was no Vedic sanction either for Varna and caste and it was absurd to equate one with the other'.[121]

Such divisions in a caste are also described by others. Hindu population, according to Prof. A. M. Shah, is divided into caste division of the first order, or the 'main or major divisions. This is followed by further divisions.

---

[119] Ibid.: 279-280
[120] Ambedkar: 311
[121] Sadasivan, 2000: 229

Banias from Gujarat, for example, are "caste of the first order". Shah divides them into "30 or 40 divisions of the second order" and gives their various names. "Each one of these is divided into divisions of the third order called ekdas or gols, meaning *endogamous units or circles*. And some of them are divided into divisions of even a fourth order, called "tads or factions" (emphasis provided). The situation gets complicated due to use of word Jati by people 'for caste divisions of all orders.' Situation further worsens when an endogamous unit spreads in due course over a number of villages, towns or cities and has a 'huge conglomeration of small castes, sub-castes,' each with a population running into thousands, and hundreds of thousands in one caste cluster. Shah gives the example of Jats, Yadavs, Rajputs, Maratha, Kolis, Kurmis and Lingyats and Brahmins to illustrate his point.[122] Karvey gave the example of Gujars and others. Quigley describes Rajput caste as a grouping, which was frequently viewed as homogeneous from the outside, but which was endlessly fragmented into hierarchically ranked sub-groups in the same manner that 'castes' were.[123] There are *exogamous* clans forming a *biradri* and many *biradris* form a caste. Then what is the functional unit of a caste, fit for reservations?

In an unpublished article titled '*Revolution and Counter-Revolution in Ancient India Part 11*', which appeared on the Internet a few years ago, Dr Ambedkar discusses the decline and fall of Buddhism, as given in Chapter 5. The editors clarify, "Dr B. R. Ambedkar had written 'The Decline and fall of Buddhism', as a part of the treatise, Revolution and Counter-Revolution in Ancient India. We have found only 5 pages in our papers which were not even corrected. Copy of this essay has been received from Shri S. S. Rege, which shows some corrections in Dr Ambedkar's handwriting. This essay is of eighteen typed pages which is included here—Editors."

Ambedkar draws a distinction between the fall of Buddhism and decline of Buddhism in this essay and states, "There can be no doubt that the fall of Buddhism in India was due to the invasions of the Musalmans. Islam came out as the enemy of the '*But*'. The word 'But' as everybody knows is an Arabic word and means an idol. Not many people however know what the derivation of the word 'But' is. "But is the Arabic corruption of *Buddha*. Thus the origin of the word indicates that in the Moslem mind idol worship had come to be identified with the religion of the Buddha." For the decline of Buddhism, Ambedkar blamed the Hindu priests. It is,

---

[122]   Shah A,M. 1996: 180-183
[123]   Quigley 1993: 88

however, recognized in the literature that the decline could have also set in due to internal degradation and disenchantment of the people in general. Ambedkar concludes by saying, "Period of Buddhism in India, which was also one of the richest in India and in world history, came to an end with the collapse of Buddhism in India and the rebuilding of Hinduism." Another author of a recent work also quotes Ambedkar, "The reason for the collapse (of Buddhism) was the Mohammedan invasions and the killing of Buddhist monks by the Mohammedans."[124] Ambedkar summed up his views on untouchability:

1. There is no racial difference between the Hindus and the Untouchables. The distinction between the Hindus and Untouchables . . . is distinction between Tribesmen and Broken Men.
2. Just as Untouchability has no racial basis so also it has no occupational basis.
3. Untouchability has sprung (from) contempt and hatred for the Broken Men as of of Buddhists . . . (due to beef eating).".
4. . . . . care must be taken to distinguish Untouchables from Impure . . . Untouchables are distinct from the Impure." Impurity was transitory and 'removed with removal of cause.' Impure as a class came into existence at the time of Dharamsutras the Untouchables came into being much later than AD 400.[125]

In the English language, there is no separate word like untouchableness. Untouchability and untouchableness, impurity and pollution, essentially, represented the same phenomenon with difference probably in degree and duration. Their separation was descriptive. If Ambedkar would have been alive today, his opinion on the events of his times might have been different. He was genuinely hurt by the indifference of some people, but at the same time he was too learned to be rigid and too temperate to be sectarian. He fought well for the cause dear to his heart.

---

[124] *Demoralization and Hope*: Asian Human Rights Commission: www.humanrights. asia › Resources › Books
[125] Ambedkar: 242

Summary

According to Ambedkar, there was no evidence to say that the present-day Shudras were the progeny of the Shudras who lived 4,000 years ago. He rejected the name Shudra for the large population of poor and illiterate, who went under the name of Other Backward Classes. Untouchability was not seen in ancient India and appeared much after fourth century AD. His argument that caste system would not end by violence and a political movement such as communism, was almost prophetic. He predicted that caste system would only end "when individuals change from within, when all individuals are free to choose, are equal under law and have the liberty to create and accumulate material and spiritual wealth."[126] Till the end of the nineteenth century, Hindu society, he said, was strictly an exogamous society, because marriage within blood relations and class relations was culturally forbidden. Caste, according to him, "should be defined as any social group that develops to impose endogamy in a population that is otherwise exogamous".[127] He advocated annihilations of caste. What is actually happening is exactly the opposite of what he had hoped.

---

[126] K. Jamanadas. 'Ambedkar and Communism', http://en.wikipedia.org/wiki/Caste#cite_note
[127] Ibid.

CHAPTER 3

SOCIAL STRATIFICATION—CASTE

Society from Vedic Age to Colonial Period

Before the Europeans came to India, there was little documented evidence on the nature of caste. Cohen wrote that the Portuguese observer Duarte Barossa reported at the beginning of the sixteenth century that the major cultural features of caste system were 'high position of Brahmans; relationship of pollution to untouchability; commensality among hereditary groups; and sanctions to maintain caste customs and political organization, but without referring to Hindu theory of Varna'. For the next 250 years, the 'European accounts did not progress much beyond that', and the official view persisted with the same.[128] Even people's intelligence and conservatism were related to their caste, and India was said to be a sum of its parts and the parts were castes. The change in perceptions occurred when anthropologists began to admit that politics had a role among castes; exogamy in the form of *gotra* was more central than endogamy and its violation attracted greater penalty; endogamy was not exercised at the level of the entire caste; even an 'inferior' caste could refuse food from a 'superior' caste, and there was no fixed occupation for all members of any caste.[129]

In *Hindu Social Organization* published in 1936 with a foreword by the former President of India Dr S. Radhakrishnan, Prof. Pandharinath Prabhu, a distinguished professor of social anthropology, stated that in ancient times a person's place in society depended upon *Desa* or place where one functioned, *Kala* or period in which the activity took place, *Srama* or effort that one put into development of one's own nature, and

---

[128] Cohen, 1996: 5: The Study of Indian Society and Culture
[129] L.M. Khanna, 2002: 48-56—quoting various authors

gunas or traits or 'psycho-biological' attributes which one was born with or which one acquired subsequently. Gunas or traits depended partially upon one's genetic makeup and largely upon effort. Birth was a factor, but the personal effort and social environment were more important. Prabhu blames 'some modern protagonists of Indian culture' who lay too much stress on 'everlasting and unchanging norms and values', while the 'ancient Indian thinkers themselves held changing view of their society and values'.[130]

Historian Subodh Kapoor, a professor of History, further elaborates upon the above by saying that the ancient Hindu social structure was marked *first*, by complex 'educational organization by which the highest results were accessible to the humblest members of the social organism'. *Second*, 'evolutions of forms of polity' and 'political institutions' were dictated 'without sacrificing local needs or curbing the native instincts of various groups and communities.' *Third*, creation of immortal forms of art, architecture, sculpture, painting, and iconography was open to all. *Fourth*, there were efforts to inculcate 'industrial arts and metallurgy, the scientific background of sociology, and the foundation of philosophical systems and schools of thought'. Their *last* endeavor was to 'build up systems of dogma, metaphysics, spiritual culture and religious realization'.[131]

Ancient Indian texts suggest that caste system was not rigid. Even a lower caste person like Valmiki composed Ramayana, which was widely adopted and became a major Hindu scripture. There are numerous such examples cited in ancient texts to show that the individuals could move from one status to another during their lifetimes.[132] In 300 BC, Megasthenes recorded seven categories of people that formed the society on the basis of function. They included Sophists or saints; tax-paying tillers of the soil, herdsmen, handicraft men, and retail dealers; the military men; the advisers, councilors, and those engaged in spying and collecting information.[133] Arian, his translator, stated that Magasthenes also 'tells us further this remarkable fact about India that all Indians are free and not one of them is a slave'.[134] There is no mention of four castes.

---

[130]   Prabhu, 1936
[131]   Subodh Kapur, 2002: Introduction. In *Ancient Hindu Society*, 6 volumes, published by Cosmos
[132]   James Silverberg. 'Social Mobility in the Caste System in India: An Interdisciplinary Symposium'. *The American Journal of Sociology*, Vol. 75, Iss. 3 (1969), 443-444
[133]   Quoted by Klass, 1993: 22-24
[134]   Ibid.: 29-31

A Buddhist pilgrim from China, Fa Hein visited India during the reign of Chandragupta Vikramaditya around AD 400. He reported that throughout the country the people did not kill living creatures or drank intoxicating liquor. Only Chandal were considered unenviable because of their degrading work of disposers of the dead. No other section of the population was notably disadvantaged.[135] Hsuan Tsang, the Chinese scholar, was not aware of Jati system in the seventh century. Basham relates the emergence of the modern Jati system to historical events in the Indian polity, which occurred with the invasions of the Turks.[136] Jatis were not Varnas.

In a Japanese study quoted in this book, Yamazaki said that the distinction between Shudras and Vaishyas disappeared in early times and Buddhist Jatakas made no distinction between Vaishyas and Shudras.[137] 'In ancient times, low caste men, washer men and others frequently became kings.' They were quite 'honorable people'.[138] "Even Kshatriyas, Brahmans, and Vaishyas would rise early and go to bed later to please their sudra master who has amassed wealth, grain, silver and gold and work at any occupation ordered by their sudra master."[139]

A well-known medieval historian Raghuvanshi also found that people from three Varnas other than Brahmins were associated with political power, wealth, and mundane matters. Though more prosperous Vaishyas were confined to trade, commerce, and banking, Shudras were as powerful as others.[140] Therefore, the idea of continuing discrimination of 75 percent of the total population of India for generation after generation and century after century on caste basis becomes a suspect both in the ancient and medieval India, particularly when the definition of caste is disputed and no one is prepared in present times to define Shudra. A small number of people did stay away or were *Achhyuts*, but due to objectionable traits or behaviors or, perhaps, occupations like scavenging which involved lifting of human night soil and dealing with dead bodies.

According to Spellman, the *Age of Kali* stems from the concept of cyclical, rather than lineal, time and is the last of the four Ages described in

---

[135]   John Keay, 2000: *India: A History*. London: HarperCollins Publishers Ltd., 145, 189
[136]   Basham, 1967: *The Wonder That Was India*: 145
[137]   H. Kotani, 1997: 45
[138]   G. Yamazaki, 1997: 119-120
[139]   Ibid.: 25
[140]   Raghuvanshi: as quoted by S.V. Desika Char: 22-25

the scriptures. It was force of greed and possession that marked the difference between various *Yugas*. 'As greed increased, so did anger and violence and government (the need of), theft and increased focus on satisfying desires.'[141] The Age of Kali started after the Bharata war, and its various descriptions are found in third, eighth, and tenth centuries AD. When R. S. Sharma quotes the prediction in Puranas that in the Age of Kali only Shudras and Brahmin would survive and that the Shudras would be the oppressors of Brahmins, all that it meant was that Tamsic qualities would prevail over the Sattavic qualities. Legends have it that Kshatriyas lost their qualities and were killed first by the sage Parusharam and those who were left were killed by the Shudra king Mahapadma Nanda. Similarly, the Vaishyas, who were the multitude, degenerated in moral values and became indistinguishable from Shudras. Whatever be the reality, it was obvious that society lost its previous sanctity, and the term Shudra became a symbol of people who no longer studied and followed the scriptures and became insensitive and immoral. The Age of Kali assumes importance in social sciences and law also because to determine the social identity of some people it was cited in the courts and also in the Privy Council during the colonial period. Shudra were not caste, but a description of people with certain traits. Most of the following account comes from the writings of three of the most prominent Indian historians: R. S. Sharma, Romila Thapar, and B. D. Chattopadhyay.

By the third century AD, the condition of Vaishyas, who were traditionally agriculturists, cattle keepers, and those engaged in commerce, had worsened and they were reduced to the rank of Shudras. On the other hand, the condition of the Shudras improved with the assimilation of numerous 'Aboriginal tribes and foreign elements'. These *'new tax-paying Shudra''* of historians now comprised old Shudra, shudarised Vaishyas, foreign elements, Aboriginal tribes, and a new category of 'landed intermediaries' and receivers of land grants.[142] The 'new' Shudras now formed the major part of society and not only pursued their own occupations but also learnt new methods of agriculture which turned them into tax-paying peasants.[143] They had hardly any disability other than that they could not read Vedas and Sanskrit. Warriors came from able-bodied men of all sections of society (Romila Thapar). Chattopadhyay describes some of the more affected as 'subject peasantry'. The disappearance of Kshatriyas and Vaishyas and the

---

[141] Spellman, 1982: 214
[142] B.D. Chattopadhyay, 1996: 147. Also quoted by Khanna, 2002
[143] Ibid.

emergence of 'new' Shudras comprising most of the Hindu population appear to be an eventful period in the social history of India.

According to Sharma, it had been predicted that *Kaliyug* would be a period of severe 'social crisis' in which 'heretical sects and foreign non-Brahminical rulers would predominate' and 'in the struggle between the Brahmins and the Shudras the latter would be the oppressors and have an upper hand'. Brahmans would be treated with disrespect and Shudras greeted respectfully and addressed as 'Aryas'. The traders, too, would indulge in fraudulent practices and possession of wealth would become the only symbol of high family status. Sharma describes *family* as a measure of one's status and not Jati.[144] Romila Thapar records families of non-Kshatriya origin like Nandas and Mauryas who, though said to be of Shudra origin, were actually rulers. She describes them as lesser dynasties of 'vratya dvija, sudra and mleccha', which rose due to 'inevitable degeneration in the Kaliyug of all norms'. 'Vratya' means 'of low origin'.[145] Vratya Kshatriyas were Indo-Greeks, Sakas, Parthians, and kusanas, which were collectively called Yavanas. Denial of Varna status did not reduce their power and dynastic status was 'not confined to any particular varna'. From the mid-first millennium AD onward, kingship often observed the formality of claiming 'kshatriya status'[146] and whosoever rose because of the acquisition of power 'often articulated in the taking of royal titles such as maharajadhiraj'.[147] With the high degree of mobility and frequent change in the fortunes, no sections of society could remain the ruling classes for long as no section could have remained backward and out of power for generations and centuries.

Sharma suggests that 'strong corrective measures' in some scriptures might have been recommended to meet the situation which arose when the society became insecure and lawless and the lower classes began to adopt the customs and practices of the previous higher classes. He uses the word 'classes' and not 'castes.' He reiterates that this should not be dismissed as 'speculation and figment of imagination'. This created an 'intermediate class' of 'new' Shudras and the Varna model was replaced by a 'modified model of feudal type'[148] bringing with it all its ills. The same (new) Shudras,

---

[144] Sharma, 1982: 186-200
[145] Romila Thapar, 1986: 366-367
[146] Ibid.: 372
[147] Thapar, 1996: 14
[148] Sharma, 1982: 186-200. Also Khanna, 2002: 33-36

which included the ruling classes and most of the population, must have gone through many upheavals during the Muslim and colonial rule, for otherwise the 1901 census would not have shown almost 96 percent of Indian population illiterate and almost whole of it poor by the British standards (1901 census report).

In South India, K. K. Pillay did not find any reference to Kshatriyas in the Sangam literature. Next to Brahmins were Chettis (merchants), Vir Panchals (artisans), and Kaikolas (weavers and barbers); all were from the low castes. In the eighteenth century, Rajputs, who were not considered Kshatriyas, ranked lower than Wanias in caste hierarchy. Shivaji, the Maratha king, was grudgingly recognized as Kshatriya, but his progeny was downgraded to Shudras after his death. In Bengal, people were also divided into Brahmins and Shudras (Buchanan). In 1980, the Mandal Commission projected the population of Brahmins in South India to be 3 percent of the total population. The rest were Shudras. 97 percent of South Indians could not have been backward castes, which the term Shudra implied.[149] Seeing this, a dissenting judge lamented in the Mandal case that the obsession of caste has made the commissions and courts to view backward classes only as backward Hindu Castes,[150] and worse, Shudras, as slaves and serfs.

While there was plenty of mobility among castes, most sociologists now claim that the rigidity was added during the British regime. Sociologists such as Srinivas and Damley found considerable flexibility and mobility in their independent studies and asserted that it was not correct to say that the position of each component of any caste was fixed for all times.[151] Even Herbert Risley noted in 1915 that there were many misconceptions about India's caste system. He disagreed with Sir Henry Yule that Indian people were so superstitious that no one of a higher caste could eat or drink with those of a lower caste. In his experience, social customs among the people of India about eating and drinking with other sections and castes, rather than being rigid as claimed by Yule, were 'fluid and transitory'.[152]

---

[149]   Desika Char, 1993: 173
[150]   *A.I.R.* Supreme Court 1993: Justice R.M. Sahay in his dissenting judgment in Mandal Case: 735: (5): 641
[151]   Silverberg, 1969: 'Social Mobility in the Caste System in India'. *The American Journal of Sociology*: 443-444; M.N. Srinivas, 1952: *Religion and Society among the Coorgs of South India*, p. 32 (Oxford); and *Caste in Modern India and Other Essays*: p. 48. (Media Promoters & Publishers Pvt. Ltd., Bombay; first published: 1962, 11th reprint: 1994)
[152]   Risley, 1915: *The People of India*: 67-110

Jati, which is the nearest equivalent of caste, in biology means "a subset of individuals within a colony of social animals (e.g. ants) that is specialized in the function it performs and distinguished by anatomical or morphological differences from other subsets". However, among human beings, "it is essential to distinguish between large-scale and small-scale views of caste society, which may respectively be said to represent theory and practice, or ideology and the existing social reality".[153] While it is true that Varnas represented the theory and the ideology of social stratification and Jatis portrayed 'practice' and existing 'reality' more political and less social, both were two different ways to classify society and there was nothing like a caste system.

In Varna, attributes or traits of individuals were important. In the case of a Jati or a caste with its many sub-castes, there is still controversy about its functional unit. Commenting upon Dumont's theory that the principle of purity—impurity keeps the segments (castes) separate from one another and reinforces hierarchy, Quigley states that "practitioners of [recent anthropology] cling on to the flotsam of a theory, which their own evidence devastatingly undermines. Unable to visualize a general structure of caste which would displace Dumont's theory they hang on to it unremittingly even though their own evidence shows again and again that this theory simply does not explain what is known about India . . ." The ingrained idea that Brahmans are the highest caste hinders the 'alternative formulation of how caste systems work'.[154]

Jatis are found among all living beings including flora and fauna, even gods. According to Marriot and Inden, 'Among human beings a jati can designate a distinct sex, a race, a caste or a tribe, a population, the followers of an occupation, or a religion or nation.'[155] There is no hierarchy among Jatis. Endogamy is not practiced at the level of caste cluster or caste, but at a sub-unit level which is not easy to define. This was also discussed in the chapter on Dr. Ambedkar. Today the important question is the definition of the functional unit of social stratification. If sixty-six years after independence, the courts cannot say whether caste is a synonym of class or antonym, or both, or whether it is 'open' or 'closed' or whether it represents a race, a nation, a region, a cluster of social units, or only a small localized

---

[153]   British Encyclopedia 2009
[154]   http://en.wikipedia.org/wiki/Varna_(Hinduism) quoted by Declan Quigley, 1993. *The Interpretation of Caste.* Oxford: Clarendon Press
[155]   Marriot and Inden: quoted by Galanter, 1984: 134

unit or it is biologically akin to a colony of ants or, perhaps, none of them, then it is a reality, not sarcasm. According to historian Romila Thapar:

> *Jati* comes from the root meaning 'birth' and is a status acquired through birth. *Jati* had a different origin and function from varna and was not just a subdivision of the latter. The creation of varnas appears to be associated with ritual status, a status denied to the *shudra* who was debarred from participating in all rituals. Whereas the three higher *varnas* were said *to* be strict about marrying within regulated circles, the *shudra* varna described in the normative texts was characterized as originating in an indiscriminate marriage between castes, creating mixed castes—a category abhorrent to those insisting on the *theoretical* purity of descent. This sets them apart and they were often labeled as *jatis*.[156] (Emphasis in original)

Thus, the lower status of Shudras was due to their inability to take part in rituals, and the Jatis came up due to mixed marriages. Mahabharata says, "If one is factually situated in the occupation of a brahmana, he must be considered a brahmana, even if born of a ksatriya or vaisya family." Similarly, a Shudra is one who is actually engaged in a particular occupation. "Therefore, neither the source of one's birth, nor his reformation, nor his education is the basis of a brahmana. The vrtta, or occupation, is the real standard by which one is known as a brahmana."[157] A warrior is one who by occupation is warrior, not because he was born to a warrior. The rigidity attached to Varna classification was a construct.

When the Europeans stated that the roots of caste system lay in the fusion of two systems in which Jati system was considered an all India phenomenon of a 'pre-Aryan culture' and the Varna scheme an 'institution of Aryan culture' they messed up the whole social structure. To simplify perceptions, they called Varnas primary castes and Jatis sub-castes. That was not true. If Jatis existed before the Varnas, they could not be the sub-castes of Varnas. Finally, when in 1837 the British enacted a legal fiction in the form of *Hindu Law* in which they called Varnas primary castes and Jatis

---

[156]   Thapar R., 2002. *Early India: From the Origins to AD 1300*. Berkeley, CA: University of California Press

[157]   Mahabharata Anusasana Parva, ch. 163: Quoted in Wikipedia Caste system among Hindus

their sub-castes, they destroyed the original meaning of both and created a monster that still haunts the nation.[158] The Mandal Commission's statement in Chapter IV of its Report that ranking of the Hindu society into four Varnas was 'the bed-rock' on which the caste structure was erected cannot be accepted. In fact, it was the cause of all troubles. Varnas applied to people or individuals. Abe Dubois was a prominent Christian priest in the early nineteenth century. He admitted the multiplicity of castes, but could not 'resolve' them into four main castes 'known as varnas'.[159] He did not mention any fifth Varna by the name of Panchama or a separate category of untouchables. Known for his frequently expressed antipathy, he would have castigated the Hindu community if 14 percent of its population were untouchables.

Risley quoted in 1915 from Dr Fick's work based on Buddhist Jatakas: "Then (in ancient times as *now*, the traditional hierarchy of four castes had no distinct and determinate existence; *still less* the so called mixed castes supposed to be derived from them; while of Shudras *in particular* no trace at all was to be found." Indian society, he said, had been a '*medley of heterogeneous groups*' for centuries with the only difference that they were apparently 'not so strictly endogamous as the castes of today' (emphasis added).[160]

Sir Denzel Ibbetson was another noted British anthropologist administrator. In 1881, he questioned the theory of fourfold classification of *Hindus* into four main castes of Brahmins, Kshatriyas, Vaishya, and Shudras and wrote that there were 'Brahmans' who were looked upon 'as outcasts' by those who under the fourfold classification would be classed as 'Shudras', that Vaishyas no longer existed, that there was no 'such a thing as Kshatriya', and that 'Shudra' had '*no* present significance save as a convenient term of abuse to apply to somebody else whom you consider inferior'. He found 'nothing more variable and more difficult to define than a caste' and stated that "the fact that a given generation is descended from ancestors of any caste creates a *presumption*, and nothing more, and that generation is of same caste, a presumption liable to be defeated by an infinite variety of circumstances"[161] (emphasis added).

[158]   Yamazaki, 1997: Caste System, Untouchability and the Depressed; in certain States, Ed. Kotani
[159]   Dubois as quoted by Morton Klass in *Caste*: 1993
[160]   Quoted by Risley, 1915; Reprint 1969: 261
[161]   Ibbetson quoted by Risley, 1915; Reprint 1969: 411-412

The above two observations put an end to the supposition that the present generations could be traced to any particular people who lived thousands of years ago and their subsequent generations were discriminated against for centuries. The theory of atonement for past misdeeds and compensatory reservations had no relevance in the past, not to speak of contemporary India. Thus, Varnas and Jatis are unconnected units of social division, and the social identity of the term Shudra is hazy. Therefore, any notion based on the concept of rigidity of Varnas without defining the manner in which the term Shudra has been used officially or judicially would be highly controversial, if not totally unacceptable. To say that one is backward and discriminated, just because one's ancestors once carried the name of barbers, tailors, carpenters, cannot be accepted. On the contrary, *real* discrimination started when reservations were given to people of subjectively chosen castes or occupations. The courts do not answer in clear terms whether the Constitution aimed to remove socioeconomic inequality and illiteracy from *all* sections of society or those who had only selected castes, religions or occupations. Even in the case of depressed classes, the census commissioner of the 1931 census admitted 'insuperable difficulties in framing a list of depressed classes which will be applicable to India as a whole' and explained that 'it is not intended that the term should have any reference to occupation as such' and is applicable only to those who were denied access to temples or had to use separate wells or were not allowed to sit inside a school.[162] Also, "No specific definition of depressed castes was framed.'[163] The Other Backward Classes were never denied temple entry and if occupations were not necessary to refer to in the identification of depressed classes in 1931 census; they could not be relevant in identification of Other Backward Classes after the independence, and now in 2014.

The conversion of Harold Gould's perception that 'occupation and individual was one' in pre-industrial Europe into 'caste and occupation was one' had so much impact that in 1992 even the Supreme Court said,

> "Lowlier the occupation, lowlier the social standing of the class in graded hierarchy. In rural India, occupation—caste *nexus* is true even today. A few members may have gone to the cities or even abroad but when they return—they do, barring a few exceptions, go into the same fold again. It doesn't matter if he

---

[162]   1931 Census: 471 Appendix2
[163]   Ibid

has earned money. He may not follow that particular occupation. Still the label remains . . . For the purposes of marriage, death and for all other functions, it is his social class—the caste—that is relevant."[164]

With the highest respect, in marriages, deaths, and other religious functions, it is the *gotra that* is asked, not caste, Jati, or Varna. Nicholas Dirks in his excellent work *Caste of Minds* writes that during the colonial period, the British census commissioners found so much confusion and difficulty in securing correct information on caste that they hoped no attempt would be made in the future to obtain information on castes and tribes of the population. Brahmins were easily identifiable, but even they did not all belong to one caste. In only one city of 'Benares' the enumerators found '107 distinct castes of Brahmins'. Kshatriya 'caste' was 'regionally and socially' restricted. Of these too, only 'Rajpoots' were said to be 'proper' Kshatriyas. The Vaishyas were 'occupied in agriculture and trade' and 'overwhelmingly' defined by occupation. Finally, "the great majority of the Hindoo population was *indiscriminately* thrown together into the fourth, namely, the *Soodra*, or servile classes"[165] (emphasis added).

W. R. Cornish, the Madras Commissioner, found in 1871 that caste was a subject upon which "no two divisions, or sub-divisions of the people themselves are agreed, and upon which European authorities who have paid any attention to it differ hopelessly" and that it was frustrating "to describe every sub-caste, or to trace the offshoots in all cases to the parent stems" and that it "would be extraneous to the purpose of this report, and I shall not attempt it".[166] Cornish was the census commissioner in 1881, when he wrote this. He found that the 'order' in which the castes were entered and on which the 'native authorities generally agreed upon' was only the order of their 'relative importance' and there could not be any 'unanimity on such a question', when every man thought his own caste was superior to that of others and that 'the lower the caste, the more it now claimed pre-eminence for itself'. Therefore, he advised against the use of *occupational* criteria for subsequent enumerations, especially for the vast majority of the population grouped under the 'dubious rubric of Sudra'.[167] It became the opposite in

---

[164] *A.I.R.* Supreme Court 1993: 553: 82
[165] Waterfield: as quoted by Dirk: 202-203
[166] Ibid.
[167] Cornish: quoted by Dirks: 224

the twentieth century when politics intervened and the lure of reservations made the higher castes to seek lower or still lower status. Then, how was the 2011caste censor conducted after the last one in 1931, and Varna status determined by untrained college students and other equally ignorant or hurriedly tutored enumerators, especially, in the case of other backward classes?

When no objectionable traces of caste were discovered in the Vedas after the 1856 'rebellion', Max Muller advised the Government not to consider 'caste as part of religious system of the Hindus' and inflict penalties for observation of the rules of caste as this would not violate the Queen's earlier promise that the State would not interfere with the religion of natives.[168] However, the emphasis shifted in the late nineteenth century, and the spread of racial ideology, projection of Indians as an inferior race, and extension of the empire took precedence over the 'message of Christ'. When the attempts to compartmentalize people in the Varna scheme failed, the British government gave up recording Varnas in census operations and stuck to Jatis. Therefore, no grading in Varna's terms could be done before or in the 1931 census. The scramble for the backward status only started when reservations came into vogue in 1936. Thus, barring Brahmin and a few others, all backward and forward classes had come from *within* those whom the British had indiscriminately given the name of Shudra. Manufactured Kshatriyas and sanskritized Shudras, too, were Shudras and so were the new 'tax-paying' Shudras.[169] These assorted people have played a considerable part in the caste politics of post-independence India.

East India Company did not come to rule India. It was sucked in by vast economic possibilities, newly developed gun powder that gave it immense power; pressures from its clergy, and the ability of a divided India to further divide. When the then rulers and their clergy saw the possibilities of a demographic change in a demoralized civilization through propaganda and conversions and realized that no complete military victory was possible, they began to 'sponsor the study of ancient scriptures in order to meet both practical and ideological needs of the Imperial rule'.[170] The opportunity came when they became conscious of a small but sizeable section of society that had been the victim of purity and pollution and which could provide a nidus from where they could pursue their goal of 'God, Glory and Gold'

---

[168]   Dirks, 2001: 132
[169]   Chattopadhyay, 1996: 147
[170]   D. Lorenzen, 1982: 84

to ensure economic, political, and cultural dominance of India. The British knew that cultural dominance would be more lasting than economic or political dominance. It meant convincing the young and educated Indians of the superiority not only of the European culture and religion but also, more importantly, of the 'inferiority of their own'.[171]

According to Lorenzen, the French historian, the British constructed a 'mature Imperialist ideology', which consisted of two approaches. 'Evangelicals' proposed 'education and conversion' and the Utilitarian 'education and constitutional reforms'. Both courses were followed. The economic struggle of classes in history was converted into conflict between forward and backward castes and the natural fight of races into a divide between the Aryan North and the Dravidian South.[172] Their success is visible even sixty-six years after the independence.

Many British social anthropologists in the early twentieth century had started to view social stratification of Hindu society in terms of multiple *castes* or even smaller units. Abu'l Fazal Alami had already stated in *A'in-Akbari* that "the operational level of Hindu social system was not at the level of the four varna, but at the level of kin based social categories such as we are familiar with in the twentieth century literature".[173] Kin-based social categories are defined as related to family, relations, relatives, kith and kin, or kinfolk. *Notes and Queries on Anthropology*, first published in 1920 by the Royal Anthropological Institute of Great Britain and Ireland, defines caste system as 'an institution most highly developed in India where Hindu society is divided into large number of separate groups, mostly functional or tribal in origin'. It did not elaborate upon the groups, but the 'large' numbers certainly could not be four Varnas, perhaps, not even Jatis. Mendalbaum believed that caste, as a combination of Varnas and Jatis, was 'a graft via English language' a suspect on account of its 'ambiguity', but still got identified with many social entities like 'endogamous groups, a category of such groups, and as a 'system of social organization.' 'Its multiple usages' became apparent not only to the observer, but also to the user who could 'sift' social entities as the occasion arose. Finally, castes were ranked into 'hereditary kinship groups associated with division of labour' with the hope that they would now give the impression of 'a unified and organized whole'. Marc Galanter pointed out that despite this effort, Varnas and Jatis could

---

171   Ibid.: 84 onwards
172   Ibid.
173   Cohen, 1996: 5: The Study of Indian Society and Culture

not be combined, for Mendalbaum and Marriot had already interpreted the functional unit of Hindu society in terms of kindred notions, which were different from caste, but akin to those which were noted during the Mughal period.[174]

Castes were 'held by ties of kinship' and inter-dependence in a village through *Jajmani system*, which was an economic system based roughly on barter. Oscar Lewis defined Jajmani as a system under which each caste group within a village gave certain standardized services to the families of other castes. It was, in fact, a relationship between families and not between whole castes—'a form of relationship in which one family was hereditarily entitled to supply goods and render services to the other in exchange of some others'.[175] In all important dealings in a village, family was the central point of exchange in the system and not caste as a whole. Family was also the unit of social and spatial mobility. It was neglected not only during the colonial period but also after the independence.

Fox describes a 'bewildering and irregular set of regional and sub-regional groupings of castes' with 'a common name and function', which are composed of several 'endogamous groups' that gives a false impression of 'commensality, hypergamy and differential status between their constituent jati groups'.[176] *These Jati groups or caste clusters* form caste associations and may be relevant in politics, but are not suitable for reservations. Jawaharlal Nehru wrote in *Discovery of India*, "The conflict is between the two approaches to the problem of social organisation which are diametrically opposite to each other: the old Hindu conception of group being the basic unit of organisation and the excessive individualism of the west, emphasizing the individual above the group." Nehru did not clarify whether the groups, he implied, were Varnas, Jatis as castes, sub-castes, their kin-based families or nuclear families. When the courts ignore these subdivisions in the pursuit of reservation for caste clusters or castes as a whole they also ignore the considerable differences between their sub-divisions and thousands of families and millions of individuals that go into their making. The politicians fail to visualize the absurdity of the situation when they project 23 percent Scheduled Castes and Scheduled Tribes, 52 percent Other Backward Classes, roughly 50 percent of the total population of women, and around 20 percent of minorities, in addition to the agitating backward classes from

---

[174] Galanter, 1984: 7-8
[175] Ibid.
[176] Fox, 1969: 32: quoted by Galanter, 1984: 11

the upper castes as potential candidates for reservations. Visualizing this, the Government of India aptly commented in G.O. 1956, "If the entire community, barring a few exceptions, has thus to be regarded as backward, the really needy would be swamped by the multitude and hardly receive any special attention and adequate assistance, nor would such dispensation fulfill the conditions laid down in Article 340 of the Constitution."

The nineteenth-century Orientalists viewed castes as a scheme of Varnas, without clear cut hierarchy. The official view also held that the effective unit of social division was an exogamous unit (gotra) in which no marriage could take place among people of the same gotra. It was only when an endogamous unit replaced the exogamous unit in the beginning of the twentieth century that the 'Indians increasingly began to identify themselves with the caste names like Brahman, Kyasthas, Nadar etc.'[177] When challenged, not only Risley justified his 'new concept' by calling the change as 'social precedence as recognized by native public opinion,' but also the official version acknowledged that the nineteenth-century perception (gotra) was altered to accommodate the other 'cultural' category called 'jats or jatis.' The change from an exogamous to an endogamous unit was not an easy task, but in making it successful, "the census, the constant need for government application to identify oneself by caste, the application of varying laws to different castes, all played a crucial part."[178] Few understood what had happened.

In a villager's life, there were three societal formations: Jat, Biradri, and Kula. In vernacular Kula meant Kumbha or a family group. Jat (Jati) roughly had the *same* position in the caste hierarchy of a region as the others. There was no hierarchy among Jatis. Cohen clarified in 1996 that for the last fifty years it was 'jat' that was meant when someone used the word 'caste'. In contrast, a *biradri* was a social group made up of males who belonged to the same *gotra* and believed to have the same ancestors. They did not marry among each other and there was exogamy among the members of the same *biradri*. Therefore, "when one talks of caste ranking, inter-caste relations in a village, vote banks in a caste, in fact, face-to-face actions in the rural system in terms of caste it is the brotherhood that is being talked about". When Vedas, Dharamshastras, and Orientalists talked of Varnas, they talked of

---

[177] Cohen, 1996: 17
[178] Cohen, 1996; Risley, 1915: 11, quoted by Cohen: 17 and 18

ideological division of society, but when the British administrators and their assistants carried out a survey they could only find 'jats' and 'biradris'.[179]

Biradri is still important in rural areas, but it has lost most of its sheen in urban areas. Recently, focus has again shifted to family, which has been the unit of social, spatial, economic, and educational mobility since ancient times. While Jati dictates much of the social as well as political action in a villager's life, most economic activities continue to operate within the family groups. Increased mobility and education have broken down even these barriers.[180] All families in a caste are also not equally situated. According to Burton Stein, the modern phenomenon of competition between castes was not appropriate in medieval India. The units of social mobility still remained '*individual families*', because the 'open agrarian system' favored spatial mobility, which, in turn, 'facilitated social mobility' at the level of families.[181] Historian Prativa Verma argues that the family had been a unit of social mobility since the days of Mahabharata, and the mobility still continues to occur in terms of families. Therefore, a caste with thousands, hundreds of thousands, or even millions of families cannot be backward or forward as a whole. The *lack* of hierarchy among castes further facilitated mobility.[182]

Therefore, a biradri, a kula, or a clan as a group may be relevant occasionally, but *family* remains the most suitable and easily recognizable functional social unit for the purposes of social benefits, including reservations, in present times. This criterion can be applied also to backward classes of other communities. Reservations for entire castes have worsened inequalities even in the same castes, occupational groups, and religious communities. An ever-increasing creamy layer concept is irrational. On the political level, too, there is competition among the 'grades of the same castes'. Wide economic and cultural gaps also exist between the leaders and well-placed sections of backward classes and the other members of the same castes.[183]

Mendalbaum played a major role in matters of social relations by bringing the family to the forefront, but was eclipsed in the 1970s and the 1980s by the simultaneous appearance of Dumont. Things have changed

---

[179]   Ibid.: 24
[180]   Mandelbaum, 1996: 34
[181]   Burton Stien as quoted by Srinivas in Singer and Cohen, 1996: 196
[182]   Varma Prativa. 1980: 198
[183]   Srinivas in Singer and Cohn, 1996: 197

since then. He argues that a person's family is not only a 'module' or a 'model for jati relations' but also the basic unit of community and the source for interaction with other families within the same Jati, and the families in the other Jatis, even in the 'production' and the 'economic activities'.[184] As there are considerable differences in wealth and power and in goals and ideas, even in the social company, among the families within a Jati, Jatis are not the homogeneous units that have been presumed by the courts.

Leela Dubey relates inequalities in the caste system to 'unequal distribution of resources and exploitive relations of production', particularly when the 'resources, property and entitlements' get unevenly allotted on the basis of '*kinship*'. A Jati or caste group then functions through its constituent family units or large-scale kinship units, *not* Jati as a whole, but through 'the lineage of *familial units which hold material resources*'[185] (emphasis added). This leads to concentrations of material resources into the hands of the select few even among the families. In such a case, social status at familial and kinship levels depends upon their economic, educational, and occupational status. Therefore, unless intra-caste disparities are corrected at the familial or *kula* levels, social benefits derived from increased mobility and fading of the joint family system would not reach the rest of the caste population. A religious community is even more diverse. The corrections must be made at intra-community level and at the level of families. The rest is politics.

Another sociologist discards the view that caste and class are 'closely interrelated, almost inseparable, basic processes of social life'. In real life, he says, it is quite different. Castes are 'highly differentiated internally' and permit immense built-in social inequality. Inter-caste marriages, external forces of change, and internal contradictions have ruled out caste to be homo hierarchicus, or have any alleged 'absolutist, unchanging and holistic nature'. Quality of the agricultural land, infrastructure for cultivation, trade and commerce, invasions and migrations, and in recent times education, occupation, power, style of life, ownership, control and use of land, inter-caste feuds and bargaining for higher wages have further added to the mobility and social status of individual families. The symbols of high status have shifted from high castes to the possession of political power, education, and a share in the new economic opportunities. Therefore, the idea that caste, if it is backward as a whole, turns into a backward class is erroneous.

---

184 Mandelbaum in Singer and Cohn, 1996: 34-35
185 Leela Dubey, 1996: 2

As its parts and families are not situated similarly, it must cease to be the unit of social benefits.

The genetic endowments cannot be improved at present, but it is possible to provide a similar environment and equal opportunity to strive for one's goal in life. Family or a small group of familial units, irrespective of which Jati, religion, region, or sex it belongs to, is a more potent and easily identifiable functional or effective unit of social division for the administration of social justice than getting lost in the crevices of unsustainable and politicized collectivities like castes and religious communities. Therefore, to bring about conditions where "the whole of the rising generation, irrespective of income or social position, grows up in an environment equally conducive to health, enjoys equal opportunities of developing its powers by education, has equal access to ability, to all careers, and is equally secure against being crushed by the contingencies of life",[186] social justice in modern times should be logically provided at the family or suitably defined extended family or, in some cases, even at individual level. A properly defined backward class or classes of similarly affected people from all sections of society could be the determinative factor at group level for all social benefits, including reservations, but even here the status of individual families that should finally matter.

Officially and judicially there was nothing lower than 'once-born' Shudra during the British regime. Once-born or twice-born status was always individual centric, not group centric. The Indian Constitution and Dr Ambedkar did not give Shudra label to the Other Backward Classes. In the absence of any rule, clear definition, fixed parameters, or an accepted convention or agreement among the judiciary, even the Indian courts tended to avoid assigning a Varna status to a particular individual. Yet there was so much misinformation and pressure on the judiciary that in one of their judgments Chief Justice Gajendragadkar denounced *Varna* as a blot in 1951 and in another judgment Justice Krishna Iyer suggested that untouchables were those who were outside the four-fold Hindu division. No evidence was cited from the scriptures or history for such supposition. Marriott and Inden were aware of the ambivalence of courts when they commented in 1959 that courts were 'goaded' into grading Hindu society to avoid its 'immense variation' and 'extensive investigation in each case', but the values that graded the society were less ritual and more *moral,* ethical, and eternal at the individual level. In a rare, but dissenting judgment in 1959, when Justice

---

[186] Tawny, 1952: 13-14

J. L. Kapur of the Apex Court stated that 'caste varies as a consequence of the *gunas*, (attributes) *karma*, (past actions) and *subhavana* (inclinations) and is dependent on actions', he was talking of Varnas, but found no support from the majority.[187] Galenter's comment that the apprehension of courts that change of caste by individual's traits, deeds, or inclinations could expose them to a torrent of litigation might have been genuine, but succumbing to the incorrect and divisive versions of colonial period has "heavily contributed to the present unacceptable situation".[188]

The interpretation of Indian social structure in its true perspective, therefore, becomes mandatory. Even the lowest castes are not confined to any single occupation. Society is a composite of thousands of Jatis, not four watertight compartments. Writing the preface of a book based on the *Conference on Social Structure and Social Change in India* held in Chicago in 1965, Stinger quotes Hazlehurst who stated that caste is 'a composite of tenuously articulated parts whose principle function has been political more than social for centuries'.[189] Such vague political units could not be the social units for giving or denying social benefits and reservations in modern time.

In recent years, the colonial regime has been severely criticized for misrepresentation of Hindu society. Meenakshi Jain, a reputed professor of history in Delhi University, criticized the Mandal Commission's Report for creating a stereotype image of the caste system and the Hindu society, which our colonial masters popularized with devastating effect in the nineteenth century. She emphasized that the India of rigid social stratification and hierarchical ranking was largely a British creation, and in order to understand and control the Indian social order, the British transformed the 'older system in a fundamental way'.[190] Quoting from an eminent historian, C. A. Balyay from Cambridge University, Jain points out that even in the eighteenth century 'the hierarchical ordering of Hindu society was not an established fact'. The Brahmins had no influence over the large bands of nomads, such as Gujars, Bhattis, and Rangar Rajputs, with their huge herds of cattle, which 'plundered the North Indian countryside.' They settled down into

---

[187] Galanter, 1984: 303
[188] Ibid.
[189] Stinger in Preface in Structure and Change in Indian Society 1996: x
[190] Jain: Pre-British India: The Myth of Caste Tyranny: *The Indian Express*, 26 September 1990: Posted on Internet on 8 April 2008—8.37 p.m. by India Forum Discussions. http://www.india-forum.com/forums/

an 'agrarian society' when the British destroyed their hideouts in the dense forests. In a devastating final comment, Jain wrote in 1990:

> The striking feature of the caste system in the *pre-British period* then, was its *local character*. There was no all-India horizontal organisation of castes . . . there was hardly any question of all-India tyranny of any caste group, especially so of the Brahmins who usually also lacked the political and armed strength . . . Based as the Mandal Commission's Report is on a totally distorted view of the past, it deserves to be rejected in toto[191] (emphasis added).

In a recent article on the Internet, Farida Majid brings out how the British changed the structure of caste in India. By enacting a series of 'land ownership, revenue collection and other agricultural and commerce laws' after the end of the eighteenth century, they dispossessed and disenfranchised the peasantry and the ordinary laborers and then codified the lower castes in such a way that they smothered whatever upward mobility they earlier had. By the time the British left India, she says, they had already turned the caste system of modern India into an instrument of 'extreme cruelty and social injustice' and converted caste into as it is seen in 'today's India'.[192]

Srinivas's 'theoretical model of 'Sanskritization' in which the lower castes not only accepted and absorbed the customs, rituals, belief, ideology, and style of life of upper castes but also exhibited the 'tremendously flexible' dimensions of caste, was a widespread social and cultural process found even among the Adivasis.[193] How the Varnas, which were not even Jatis, got reflected in the 1992 judgment as a tremendously rigid watertight structure is difficult to say. Historians have gone further even than Sanskritization. They call the modeling of dominant castes on the pattern of the 'king the Kshatriya' as 'Rajputization'. The process was further 'refined' by Herman Kulke to call it 'Kshatriazation'. The landholders, the agriculturists, the pastoralists, the once cattle keepers, and the sellers of milk products, perhaps lower in the cultural or behavioral sense, dissociate themselves from the main community or tribe through 'a narrow linage of single families' to

---

[191]   Ibid.
[192]   http://groups.yahoo.com/group/akandabaratam/message/52854: 14 February 2011
[193]   Ishita Banerjee-Dube, 2008: xi, xii

'claim Rajput origin'[194] and acquire the 'symbols and practices' expected of the true Kshatriyas. Despite their manufactured genealogy tables which connect them to the solar and lunar dynasties of kings, most Rajputs and Thakurs are the progeny of the 'Kshatriazed' lower caste chiefs.'[195]

Till the early 1980s, sociological literature continued to struggle with 'caste approach' and 'social distance' to make sense of 'social stratification' and 'analysis of 'social mobility.' Only in the late 1980s the researches shifted their focus to the link between caste, politics, and religion. Ritual dominance as determinant of caste relations was soon discarded and social scientists began to lay stress on the 'post-Dumontian approaches' to put caste and hierarchy in their 'proper place'.[196] Post-1980 studies have challenged not only the "primacy given to caste but also its relevance as 'a religious institution' and a 'closed system'. It is now generally agreed that caste has always been 'in a state of flux' and as a 'system' was never as 'systematic' as it had been taken for". Even Dumont's view of 'ritual dominance of Brahmins' and Brahmanism has been discredited by the recent assertions of Dalits and backward classes.[197] The present attitudes and postures of the alleged lower castes are for political reasons and the continuation of reservations.

Therefore, which was once contemplated an instrument of social justice, has become an instrument of caste hatred. Scholars argue that the acceptance of the 'logic of caste' by the courts has not only produced a 'legal muddle', but has also created a dichotomy between the constitutional assurances of equality and equal opportunity and the social order defined by stratification.[198] Caste has compromised the easy affiliations of national unity and civilization history by influencing the body politics of post-colonial India and "segmented the society into class, gender and religion".[199] When Conlon saw the contradictory ways in which the Hindu social structure had been presented in the last two centuries, he argued in a recent essay that "we should move on from dwelling upon the powerful role of the colonial project" and give "greater agency and autonomy to Indians to interpret their own history".[200]

---

[194]   Ibid.: xxii-xxiii
[195]   Ibid.
[196]   Quoting Neeilson: Banerjee-Dube: xxvi
[197]   As quoted by Banerje-Dube: xxvi
[198]   Ibid.: xxvii
[199]   Dirks, 2001: 17
[200]   Banerjee-Dube, 2008: xiv

Till 1950, the views of colonial administrators and social scientists on the development of caste consciousnesses and validations of claims to a higher or lower status were mainly shaped on the data and conceptions which grew out of census operations. Even today, much of the scholarly activity on caste and related subjects is taken as part of census operations.[201] That only messed up perceptions. Calling castes with more than one lakh (hundred thousand) population 'communities' in the early twentieth century and creation of thousands of communities among the Hindus, six among the Christians, and only one among the Muslims was not so innocuous, as it looked.[202] Bayly refers to Fox and, what she calls, 'large literature on the construction of colonial knowledge', which, she says, was used in a 'systematic scientific sense' to fragment a complex and dynamic society and to 'atomize' it into martial races, criminal tribes, Brahmans, non-Brahmans, and the like and to bring in a 'new arena of representative constitutional politics'.[203] She rejects the nineteenth and twentieth-centuries' ethnographic literature and writes that 'no one wishing to write credibly about caste today' would accept the colonial ethnographic literature that divided people into different races and then applied the same to castes on the pretext of 'scientific observation and fact'.[204]

Politicization and misrepresentation of caste during the colonial period prevented not only the emergence of an Indian nation-state but also enabled the colonial rulers to crush those in search of an all-India identity. Anthropometry became 'the wedge' to separate 'Orient from Occident', and though the cephalic and nasal indices became obsolete within a few decades of their origin, those of the 'supposed Indo-European descent were categorized differently from the alleged Dravidians and Aborigines'.[205] Different languages further lent credibility to different racial origins of populations.

Susan Bayly quotes Ronald Inden who, in a 'bracingly acid account of the crimes of past and current collection of European romanticists, empiricists and miscellaneous essentialisers', blasted a one-sided exercise of 'hegemonic power' by which it 'created an imagined India in which caste

---

[201]   Ibid Cohen, 2008: 31
[202]   *A.I.R.* Supreme Court 1993: 549: 75
[203]   Banerjee-Dube: 166
[204]   Susan Bayly, 1995: 166. Caste and Race. In *The Concept of Race in South Asia*. Ed. Peter Rob
[205]   Ibid.

was a mere fabrication, designed to demean and subjugate the supposedly demeaning, politically impotent Indian 'Other'.[206] Ashish Nandy and other Indian historians, too, debunked the 'orientalist' scholarship as a 'farrago of destructive, white male fantasies', and Dirks criticized the Victorian age data collection of a domineering foreign power, which it used to exercise an ominous influence over a weak and susceptible people.[207]

In an interesting episode on the origin of Shudra in Bengal, Cohen quotes from the Bengal census of 1891, "Shudra, found in Eastern Bengal, descended from maid servants by their masters of good taste; also called Golam or Golam Kayastha." Prof. M. N. Srinivas's remark, that the Shudra spanned such a wide cultural and structural arc that there are at one extreme the dominant and land owning peasant castes which wield power and authority over local Vaishyas and Brahmins and on the other extreme are poor Untouchable groups just above the pollution line, is worth repeating.[208]

In the face of such a situation, if the Constitution makers avoided the term Shudra, which had been described earlier as of having no existence on the one hand to including all non-Brahmins on the other, it was for good reason. The dominant and landowning peasant castes still wield power and authority over local Vaishyas and Brahmins, despite being labeled as backward and discriminated Shudras by the Mandal Commission. The country has still to emerge from the after-effects of the adoption of divisive hypotheses of colonial rule by the post-independence Indian State with the courts watching, as if, helplessly.

Summary

Modern historians and historiographers have severely criticized the British for constructing a distorted version of Hindu social structure. The whole idea of Varnas being four primary castes and Jatis their sub-castes was misconceived. The theory of caste—occupation nexus did not find support even in the colonial period. For ages, there had been nothing lower than once-born Shudra. Even Shudras had different versions. There were both upward and downward mobility among castes, and the lowest castes often

---

[206] Ronald Inden quoted by Bayly, 1996: 165: Caste and Race. In *The Concept of Race in South Asia*

[207] Ibid.: quoting Asish Nandy and Dirks: 165

[208] Srinivas. As quoted by Khanna, 2002: 96

rose to occupy reins of power. No people remained backward and forward for centuries. Economic and educational differences between the haves and have-nots are, therefore, increasing. Jati was always a political more than a social unit of the community, while a family, which has the characteristics of both a small group and an individual unit, has been an effective unit of social mobility and economic exchange since the ancient times. Its relevance in administration of social justice has been ignored for too long.

CHAPTER 4

RACE AND CLASS

Stratification on the Basis of Races

Comte de Gobineau was a French diplomat, writer, ethnologist, and social thinker. His theories of racial determination were largely responsible for the subsequent development of racial theories in Europe. In the nineteenth century, he and his English disciple Houston Stewart Chamberlain propagated a notion that a superior 'Aryan race of the 'Germanic people', who now represented 'the summit of civilization' and spoke the 'Indo-European languages', was not only morally superior to the 'Semites', the 'yellows', and the 'blacks' but was also responsible for all the progress made by the mankind.[209] In the mid-nineteenth century, the British imported the Aryan theory and divided Indians into three racial categories of Aryans, Dravidians, and Aborigines. Later, Risley used nasal and cephalic indices to determine non-Aryan Tribes of Negrito, Australoid and of Proto-Dravidian antecedents. Despite repudiation by other anthropologists and the editor of Risley's second edition of *People of India* admitting in 1969 that the present population of India was a mixed population and if Risley was alive he would have made amends, this racial hypothesis has continued to plague the Indian nation.

The ancient term Mlecchas caused further confusion. The Western writers construed Mlecchas sometimes as 'foreigners' and at other times as races. As Mlecchas were not mentioned in the Vedas, foreign writers interpreted them as 'non-Vedic barbarians' who did not conform to the moral and religious norms of the Vedic society, ate 'meat', indulged in 'self-contradictory statements', and were devoid of 'righteousness and purity of conduct'. Mlecchas referred to the Scythians, Persians, Sakas, Hunas,

---

[209] British Encyclopedia

Yavanas, Kambojas, Pahlavas, and Bahlikas. Christopher Jefferlot quotes Romila Thapar who described them as those who did not observe 'varna vyavastha and vedic rituals' and did not study Sanskrit. They differed from the 'Aryas' in the nature of 'ritual purity' and not 'ethnicity'. Inter-caste marriages between Aryans and Mlecchas were 'open'.[210] Their progeny formed a 'new caste' of Shudra and 'if they accepted the local laws' and adopted the local religion and its practices, they were not excluded. Greek, Sakas and Huns, after adopting local religion, were recognized as Kshatriyas. This not only showed the ability of Hindus to 'assimilate' others but also to give status according to their traits or 'ritual' purity'.[211] Jafferlot quotes from Mimasa, 'Sudra are as capable as twice born are; in matters of world, aryas and mlecchas have equal capabilities.'[212] Therefore, around the ninth century AD, 'references to large number of indigenous people as mlecchas began to decrease'.[213] During the colonial regime, attempts were made to identify the same Mlecchas as belonging to lower races like Aborigines and Dravidians in the South. Later, the same Mlechas were interpreted as part of Panchama or a fifth Varna in Encyclopedia of Hinduism by Walker quoted in this book, and as outcastes and out of pail by others.[214]

Sir Herbert Risley took advantage of the Aryan invasion theory and constructed 'the outline of the process' which, he said, took place when the second wave of Indo-Aryans made their way into India through Gilgit and Chitral, subdued the local inferior race, and established themselves as 'conquerors'. They 'captured women according to their needs' and closed 'their ranks to further mixture of blood' and behaved toward the Dravidians as did the planters in America toward the African slaves.[215] This left an indelible impression on the Indian psyche that even now, whenever anyone talks of uplifting backward classes, he or she psychologically compares them with American Negroes. This closing the ranks was later interpreted as 'closed class' or caste, and the courts approved reservation for backward classes on the basis of closed classes or castes. The theories of different races based on morphological differences, such as color of skin, texture of hair, stature, and nasal and cephalic indices, too, were discarded within a couple

---

[210]   Jafferlot Christopher, 2008: 327-328: Caste and Race. In *The Concept of Race in South Asia*
[211]   Ibid: 327-328
[212]   Ibid.
[213]   Ibid.
[214]   Walker B. 1995: 172 Also Khanna L.M. 2002: 86-87
[215]   Risley, 1915: Reprint 1969: 264-265

of decades, though continue to be cited by some even now. The classification of castes on racial basis has attracted considerable criticism in recent years. In the early twenty-first century, India was dragged even to United Nations forums by Indian protagonists of racial discrimination, but when they failed to impress, they stated that caste was even worse than race.

Racial theory was born in an article written in 1664 by French doctor Francois Bernier, but it was Max Muller who brought it to India from 1850 onward. Despite Max Muller's repeated assertions that by race he only meant language, the old impression of race continued. Race was differently viewed in different parts of the world. The English varied their concept of race from 'ethnicity, tribe, clan, caste, nationality to religion and so on', while to the Germans race meant physical, mental, and intellectual differences. When the linkage of race with language was discovered in the form of Indo-Aryan family of languages, 'race theoreticians had to tie themselves into intellectual knots to preserve white supremacy'. Rajanyagam quotes Ronald Inden who demonstrated that the English and German scholars 'looked less to what India was' as to what 'they thought it was'. He criticized them for inventing a superior Aryan race which conquered the inferior race of Dravidians, and when they could not deny the evidence of 'great empires in the South', they discovered a new twist: 'A settled agricultural civilization' suddenly became 'stagnant', and the pastoral, nomadic, hunting culture of early Aryans became 'dynamic and progressive'.[216]

Race influenced even 'Hindu revivalist thinkers', especially those who were Western schools educated. Inden mentions Swami Dayanand Saraswati, who described the Vedic Aryas in his book *Satyarth Prakash* or *Light of Truth* as 'primordial and elect people to whom the Vedas has been revealed by God'. In his view, all Hindus in certain areas were Aryans.[217] The Western writers often cite this as acceptance by Indians of different racial origins of their ancient society.[218] The fact may be that the Indians never heard of division of humanity into different races before the nineteenth century and the word Arya or Aarya meant to them nothing more than a gentleman.

Ultimately, the racial theory reached South India when the German word 'Wesen', which meant 'essence' or 'one defining characteristic of a people' or race, was equated with the Tamil word *inam* and Tamilians were converted into a separate race of Dravidians. One important community

---

[216]   Degmar Hellmann-Rajanyagam, 2008: 109-111: *The Concept of Race in South Asia*

[217]   Ibid.: 328-329

[218]   Christopher Jefferlot, 2008: The Concept of Race in South Asia: 127-128

which Rajanyagam discusses is Vellalars, who were Shudras. In addition to kings, there were seven, 'probably mythical', famous patrons and chiefs who possessed land and certain amount of wealth. These chiefs (velirs) were landowners and farmers who later became Vellalars. Although 'in the Manudharma', Vellalars were considered 'Sudras' and the British, too, included them among them, the Cancum literature showed them as more powerful than the kings. Vellalars gave up their right to rule in lieu of the 'right to crown the king' only because they wanted to be occupied with farming. As they were very rich, Brahmins elevated these landowners and farmers to the highest status after the Brahmins and downgraded the warriors as mercenaries and 'criminal tribes'.[219] Vellalars were not restricted to any caste group or race and their 'inam' was not immutable. Anybody could become a Vellalar, or 'an exemplary Tamil', provided one followed 'Vellalar Saiva creed'.[220] Today, these land holding classes and farmers form a large chunk of 69 percent Other Backward Classes in Tamil Nadu and are called Shudras, implied as serfs and slaves for centuries.

Attempts to reduce Tamils or Dravidians to a biological 'race' were in the last resort unsuccessful and a Dravidian South could not be established. Tamil Nadu emerged, but after independence. By that time, the racial division of India in terms of Aryan North and Dravidian South had been so much enmeshed in the Indian psyche that the terms Aryans and Dravidians are still used to distinguish the North Indians from the South Indians. On the question of Aryan invasion of India, Romila Thapar, an eminent Indian historian, who has been often blamed for bringing Aryan invasion theory in the school textbooks, explained in 2006:

> For the last thirty years I, together with other historians, have been refuting the concept of an Aryan race or a Dravidian race . . . Aryan is a linguistic label and not a racial category. And . . . since I am frequently misquoted on this by some people, I argued further that although I did not accept the notion of an Aryan invasion, I did support the idea of a graduated migration of Aryan-speaking peoples from the Indo-Iranian borderlands into north-western India. This resulted in an interface of various cultures and this interface needs to be explored.[221]

---

[219] Ibid.: 123-125
[220] Ibid.: 127
[221] http://varnam.org/blog/2004/03/romila_thapar_no_aryan_invasion

It is not the intention to get involved with the genetics of racial theory, but few observations would be in order. American Anthropological Association in a statement on "Race" dated 17 May 1998, clarified:

> "In the United States both scholars and the general public have been conditioned to viewing human races as natural and separate divisions within the human species based on visible physical differences" but now 'it has become clear that human populations are not unambiguous, clearly demarcated, biologically distinct groups'. Analysis of genetics (e.g., DNA) indicates that 'most physical variation, about 94 percent, lies within so-called racial groups'.[222]

If you walk from London to Beijing, there would always be a gradual change, a 'gradient'. You will never find distinct races or clear-cut change anywhere. These gradations are given the name of *clines*. Geneticist Richard Lewontin observed that when 85 percent of human variation occurs within populations, and not between populations, both 'race' or 'subspecies' could not be the 'appropriate' or useful ways to describe populations. In the face of these controversies, some evolutionary scientists have simply abandoned the concept of race in favor of 'populations' and some others in favor of 'clines.'

The lack of concurrence on the meaning and identification of races continued into the twenty-first century, and contemporary scientists are no closer to agreement than their forebears. Thus, race has never in the history of its use had a precise meaning. What is race? Are Negroid, Mongoloid, Australoid races? Not so, according to science. Relethford is quoted from Wikipedia, 'Race is a concept of human minds, not of nature. Unfortunately, this view hasn't completely caught on outside of scientific circles. Still, there are signs times have changed.'[223] Andre Beteille, too, stated "I am now convinced that identifying the races in the population of India will be an exercise in futility . . . It is sad but true that many forms of invidious discrimination do prevail in the contemporary world. But to assimilate or even relate them all to 'racial discrimination' will be an act of 'political and moral irresponsibility.'[224] He also stated, "The Scheduled Castes of India

---

[222]   Ibid.
[223]   Wikipedia—Free encyclopedia 2010
[224]   Beteille Andre, 2001: 'The Hindu: Discrimination that Must Be Cast Away' at Hinduonnet.com, June 3, 2001—quoted from Internet

taken together are no more a race than are the Brahmins taken together. Every social group cannot be regarded as a race simply because we want to protect it against prejudice and discrimination." And also "treating caste as a form of race is politically mischievous; what is worse, it is scientifically nonsensical".[225]

In view of this rejection of race, many social scientists have replaced the word race with the word "ethnicity" to refer to self-identifying groups based on beliefs in shared religion, nationality, or race, but it must also be understood that 'religion, nationality, and race itself are social constructs and have no objective basis in the supernatural or natural realm'.[226]

2009 Research Study[227]

It was stated that this pioneering research study, conducted jointly by Centre for Cellular and Molecular Biology (CCMB), Hyderabad, Harvard Medical School, Harvard School of Public Health, and the Broad Institute of Harvard and MIT, USA, 'will rewrite the Indian anthropological and genetic history'. The study sets aside the theory that the present North Indian and South Indian people are genetically different. According to it, nearly all Indians carry genomic contributions from two distinct ancestral populations and both the groups are a genetic mixture of the Ancestral South Indian population and the Ancestral North Indian population, which arrived in India 60,000 years ago. Unlike the South Indian ancestral group which is distinctly unique, the North Indian ancestral group is closely related to European populations. Ancestral South Indian (ASI) population and Ancestral North Indian (ANI) population had married among each other groups long enough to give birth to the present mixed Indian population, which is distinct from both. K. Thangaraj, a senior scientist, stated that the Indian population was a mixed population, which was neither Dravidian nor Aryan. This 'genetic mixture of ASI and ANI is quite distinct from the original ancestral groups'. The 'great Indian divide along north-south lines

---

[225]   Ibid.: Also http://en.wikipedia.org/wiki/Andre_Beteille

[226]   Wikipedia Oxford Dictionary Oxford University Press: Retrieved 28 December 2013.

[227]   www.hsph.harvard.edu ›. . .› Press Releases › 2009 Releases and Aryan-Dravidian divide a Myth: Study, *TNN*, 25 September 2009, 1.16 a.m. IST; first published in Nature 461, 489-494 (24 September 2009)

now stands blurred' and the hitherto believed 'fact' of separate ancestries of North and South Indians have proved to be a 'myth'.

ASI in their purity is very small in number and is only found in Andaman. Thangaraj states that the study analyzed '500,000 genetic markers across the genomes of 132 individuals from 25 diverse groups from 13 states'. All the individuals were from 'six-language families' and traditionally 'upper' and 'lower' castes and tribal groups. The study found that the genetics proved that 'castes grew directly out of tribe-like organizations during the formation of the Indian society' and 'that it was impossible to distinguish between castes and tribes since their genetics were not 'systematically different.'[228] Because the Allele frequency differences between groups in India were found to be larger than in Europe, it was concluded that they 'reflected strong founder effects whose signatures have been maintained for thousands of years owing to endogamy'. These findings also suggest that Indians must have gone to the West and spread their culture rather than the Aryans came and conquered India. It rejected the Aryan invasion theory.

Wikipedia in 2010 sums up in the situation from 1930-2010"

> There have been several historians and scientists who have proved that there are no separate races of so called Aryans or Dravidians as they belong to the same race. This has picked up strong footing, as on one hand, there are no evidences till date in support of Aryan invasion theory, and increased number of historical and scientific evidences that prove that there is only one race, on the other. Evidences include a ground-breaking research in 2009 that has been conducted jointly by Centre for Cellular and Molecular Biology (CCMB) Hyderabad along with Harvard Medical School, Harvard School of Public health, Broad Institute of Harvard and MIT of USA. The research team has made this claim after observing that North and South Indians are genetically similar.

A 2010 review, however, claims that there are at least four population groups in diverse India. Other than Ancestral North Indians and Ancestral South Indians, the population consists of Tibeto-Burman, Austro-Asiatic, and Andamanese genetic pools suggesting human beings migrated into India from Africa, Eurasia, Tibet, and Southeast Asia. The caste system

---

[228] *The Times of India*, 25 September 2009

in India is possibly a complex intra-group and inter-group admixes of interactions between various population groups. This alludes to the mixed origin of castes. The review paper admits the study is so far incomplete.[229]

A report in *Times of India of 7 December 2012*, on genetics study undertaken on gypsies of Europe and published in the scientific journal *Cell Biology* confirms that the gypsies, known as the Romani people that live in many countries of Europe, are of Indian origin. The study tested the DNA of gypsies drawn from various countries and compared it with the DNA of people from Europe, India, and Central Asian countries, using the genome-wide sequencing technique. It was found that 11 million Romani can be traced back to a single group that left India about 1,500 years ago from its north-western region, suggesting that Indians for whatever reasons migrated even to far-flung countries. The non-genetic imprints were found earlier in many eastern countries.

In an interesting follow-up study, the same Howard Group, quoted above, published more of its findings on 8 August 2013, in the *American Journal of Human Genetics*. "Only a few thousand years ago, the Indian population structure was vastly different from today," said co-senior author David Reich, professor of genetics at Harvard Medical School. Researchers found that people from different genetic populations in India began mixing about 4,200 years ago, but the mingling stopped around 1,900 years ago. This is related to the diseases carried through the genes.

Stratification on the Basis of Classes

One of the worst effects of British rule in India was not that they ruled India, but that they made Indians caste maniac. Even courts were affected and equated castes with classes on one excuse or the other. Dictionaries are quoted one after the other to equate caste with class. One example of actual difference between the two is cited. According to Webster's Encyclopedic Unabridged Dictionary of the English Language, meaning of the words 'class' and 'caste' is as follows:

> Class: a number of persons or things regarded as forming a group
> by reason of common attributes, characteristics, qualities, or

---

[229]   Majumdar (February 23, 2010). 'The Human Genetic History of South Asia: A Review'. *Current Biology*, Vol. 20 (2010), R184-R187

traits, kind, sort; any division of persons or things according to rank or grade.; a social stratum sharing basic, economic, political or cultural characteristics and having the same social position; the system of dividing society; caste.

Caste: (1) Social, *an endogamous and hereditary social group* limited to persons of the same rank, occupation, economic position etc. and having mores distinguishing it from other such groups; *any rigid system of social distinctions. Hinduism, any of the four social divisions, the Brahman, Kshatriya, Vaisya and Sudra, into which Hindu society is rigidly divided*, each caste having its own privileges and limitations, transferred by inheritance from one generation to the next; any class or group of society sharing *common cultural features.*; *a caste society; a caste system; a caste structure* (Emphasis added).

The differences between caste and class are marked in italics and need not be elucidated further. To give one example, castes are hereditary groups, classes are not. A caste may have people with different status from different classes, but a class can have people with only the same or similar position or status. Similarities between the two are vague, if not hardly any. Among Hindus, four social divisions or Varnas qualified persons, not castes, which were in thousands. The courts cite three reasons for equating caste with class. *First*, practically in all the dictionaries and encyclopedias caste and class are exchangeable expressions, but this is a generalization, for all encyclopedias when they go onto the specifics distinguish the two. One example is cited above. Only castes are taken as hereditary 'status groups'. In the absence of any definite notion of caste in 1880s, the British converted depressed castes into depressed *classes*, but corrected their factual error in 1936, when they renamed depressed *classes* as Scheduled *Castes*. Little could they imagine that castes would be equated with classes in post-1947 court decisions?

Second, because Ambedkar described caste as closed *class*. From a 1916 quote of Dr Ambedkar, the majority judgment brings out that . . . "society is always composed of classes . . . early Hindu society could not have been an exception . . . as a matter of fact, we know it was not." This division, Ambedkar stresses upon, was a *"class* system in which *individuals*, when qualified, could change their class and therefore classes did change their personnel"[230] (emphasis added). Castes, by definition, cannot change their personnel.

---

[230] Ibid.: 549-550

In fact, Ambedkar distinguishes class from caste in this definition and admits individuals could change their class, or a Brahmin could become a Shudra and a Shudra, if qualified, a Brahmin. His later expression, 'closed class' or caste, prohibited such change. Open and closed are antonyms, not synonyms. Ambedkar described 'Brahmins as priestly *class*; Kshatriyas as the military *class*; Vaishyas as the merchant *class*; and the Shudra as the artisan and menial *class*', accepting that each of them could change to any other class. He did not call any one of them caste. When he advocated annihilation of castes, he meant annihilation of Jatis. It could not be otherwise. *Third* reason was given by Justice Jeevan Reddy; when writing for the majority, he observed in the majority judgment:

> The above material makes it amply clear that caste is nothing but a social class—a socially homogeneous class. It is also an occupational grouping, with the difference that its membership is hereditary. If one ceases to follow that occupation, still he remains and continues to remain a member of that group. To repeat it is a socially and occupationally homogeneous class. Endogamy is its characteristic. Its social status depends upon the nature of occupation followed by it. Lowlier the occupation, the lowlier is the social standing of the class in the graded hierarchy. In rural India, occupation—caste nexus is true even today.[231]

In Para 83A, the judgment clarifies, 'Once a caste satisfies the criteria of backwardness, it becomes a backward class for the purpose of Article 16(4).' In addition, caste must be 'inadequately represented in services under the State.' With respect, the presumption that all members of a caste with a population of hundreds of thousands, even millions, are homogeneous and identically situated in terms of income, education, occupations, and social position in society, or they are backward or forward as a whole, is not a fact. Mobility and change have been occurring for centuries in terms of families and individuals. Those who are left behind are also not homogeneous. Occupation in all members of a caste is not fixed and caste occupation nexus was denied even by the British administrators.

In fact, it is the economic condition that puts an individual in a particular class, whether one is from rural area or urban setting. An occupational class will have people from the same occupation and people

---

[231] *A.I.R.* Supreme Court 1993: 553: 82

with the same economic earnings will have the same socioeconomic class. Such people could be from any caste and community On the contrary, a caste or community may have people from many occupations, educational qualifications and may be of different socioeconomic status. Caste is heterogeneous, but class is homogeneous.

In one of the submissions before the Court, a counsel argued in the Mandal Case that under clause (4) of Article 16, reservations are given on the basis of backward class of citizens, and not in favor of citizens. Therefore, he argued, what is to be identified is backward class of citizens, not backward citizens.[232] There is a definition of class in Reader's Digest Family Word Finder (1975) that states that the status of a class can be determined either in terms of a group as a whole or separately in terms of its individual members. The dictionary states:

> Usage note: Class can be followed either by a singular or a plural verb, depending upon whether you consider the class as one unit or as composed of individual members. Thus you may correctly say the class *is* graduating in June (which implies that you consider the class a unit, acting together) or the class *are*, in general, very bright (implying that you consider the class as composed of a number of very bright individuals). And if you had used is or are in either of these examples that would be all right, too, because it is how you feel about the class, if it is a unit or they are individuals. Thus whatever you use is correct.

In another example, the British Encyclopedia and Ultimate Reference Suite DVD 2005 describes 'Social Class, also called class' as a *group* of people within a society who possess the same socioeconomic status and 'as collection of *individuals*' which have similar 'economic circumstances'. This, it says, 'has been widely used in censuses and studies of social mobility'. Thus, if one views class as group of certain economic, educational, occupational, or social status, those who are from a higher or a lower status, to whichever caste or community they belong to, would not be eligible to be members of the same class, but will continue to remain members of their original caste or community. Similarly, if one takes class in the above examples as separate individuals, each individual would have to be of the same economic, educational, occupational, or social status, to be put in the

---

[232]   Ibid.: 544: 66

respective class.[233] Their caste and community would not change. A class can, therefore, identify both, a homogeneous group or a number of similarly placed individual citizens, but a caste or a religious community cannot. A *social* class or class is a recent term which had no equivalent in the ancient societies.

Social classes are primarily based upon economic interests while the status groups are constituted by evaluations of 'honour or prestige of an occupation, cultural position, or family descent'. Caste in that sense is a status group. In the early nineteenth century, due to industrial and political revolutions of the late eighteenth century and decline in rank and feudal distinctions in the Western European societies, class replaced 'the major hierarchical groupings in society'. The present social groups of 'commercial and industrial capitalists' and the 'urban working class in new factories' are now defined in economic terms, either by the 'ownership of capital' or, conversely, by the 'dependence on wages'. Their social class changes with the change in economic position.[234]

Caste, on the other hand, is a generic term in which all types of people or classes exist. Names like Lingyats, Gujars, Jats, Ahirs neither indicate socioeconomic nor educational status of their members, nor even their ritual or social standing. Caste does not change with change in socioeconomic status. If a caste has to be labeled as Shudra, then the word Shudra has to be defined in specific terms, because a Shudra and a Brahmin can both be the members of the same social class. When the Supreme Court talks of birth, fixed occupation, purity and pollution, hereditary occupations, and endogamy, it talks of status acquired by virtue of birth in particular families, but when it talks of classes, these parameters should have no relevance. It is now 'established' that even within the hierarchical groupings (like, for example, castes) many 'social classes' exist.[235]

For Carl Marx, one type of society differed from another by its mode of production, which comprised of technology and division of labor. Each mode of production brings about a distinctive class system in which "one class (dominant class) controls and directs the process of production while another class is, or other classes are, the direct producers and providers of services to the dominant classes". In the present class system, too, status is not dissociated from political and economic controllers. In the earlier

---

233   British Encyclopedia 2005
234   Ibid
235   Ibid.

times, though status was expected to be separate from political power, but in practice, the king remained superior to the priest. The Brahman that was venerated was different.

On the other hand, Weber derived his concept of study of social stratification from his studies in Germany. He formulated a three-component theory of stratification, which saw political power as an interplay between 'class', 'status', and 'group power'. He believed that class position was determined by a person's skills and education rather than by relationship to the means of production. While Marx was convinced that stratification would only disappear along with capitalism and private property, Weber believed that the solution lay in providing equal opportunity within a competitive, capitalist system.

The British Encyclopedia continues, "There has always been a conflict between the controllers and directors of production and direct producers and providers of services over the appropriation of what is produced." This particularly happens when the mode of production itself changes with 'developments in technology' and change in 'utilization of labour'. When conflicts become extreme, a new class is said to appear to confront the existing rulers of society. Maoist movement in India, which arose due to the failure to plug the ideological gap left open by the fragmentation of communists, is finding roots and sympathizers in almost every caste and class in India. If the Maoists can eschew violence, they have a potential to fill the existing space. Caste is marginal in this struggle.

In Marxism, there are three classes: upper, working (or lower), and the middle. 'The upper class in modern capitalist societies is often distinguished by 'the possession of largely inherited wealth, property and the income derived from them.' They confer many advantages upon the children of upper class. In India, a new upper class is emerging which is based on inherited political power which, in general, brings with it the associated economic power. Within the working class, distinction exists between 'skilled, semiskilled, and unskilled workers' that broadly correspond with 'high, middle and low income levels'. The middle class in the West include "the middle and upper levels of clerical workers, those engaged in technical and professional occupations, supervisors and managers, and such self-employed workers as small-scale shopkeepers, businessmen, and farmers". At the top level in the Western countries, the middle class merges into the upper class, while at the bottom, the poorly paid in jobs, in sales, distribution, and transport merge into the working class.

On the contrary, the unskilled workers in India lack economic and educational resources. Their wages are low and they have no property and no social security. Unemployment is another factor. Shift in the economy from manufacturing to service industries has further reduced the employability of manual workers. Ninety percent of unskilled workers in India come from Adi Shudras and most backward classes in which abject poverty is more critical than caste. Benefits of reservations rarely reach them. They are exploited by the upper, middle, and better off lower castes, which do not pay them even minimum wages. Middle class might be gradually expanding in India, but the gap between the incomes of middle and lower classes is so high that a recent paper published in India denied the existence of an economic middle class. The purchasing power has decreased despite increase in pays. Medical facilities are out of reach of most. Even the definition of below the poverty line is controversial and more political than realistic.

A general diminution of class differences from higher standards of living, greater social mobility and a better redistribution of wealth and income seen in the West have not been reflected in India. Differences, in fact, have increased due to lopsided development, increasing gap between the highest and the lowest income groups, insistence on illogical reservations on the basis of an undefined caste, non-determination of functional unit of social division, and rampant corruption. In the Western countries, these changes generally reflected a decline of class ideologies and class conflict, but in India, the growth of caste politics and restriction of social benefits to only a few even among the castes has increased inequalities. It is, therefore, imperative for the purposes of social benefits, to revert from castes to families, where the actual differences start.

There is another class of people who are dismally neglected. They are the poor and the illiterate who live in ghettoes and slums of urban areas, which have sprouted in all large- and middle-sized cities. *United Nations Environmental Programme* and *United Nation's Control of Human Settlement* reported in 1999 that India was no longer an overwhelming rural society: 'About half of India's population would be urban at the dawn of new millennium."[236] Sociologists find it difficult even to separate rural from urban areas. This rapidly growing and restive proletariat has received little attention. Owing to growing interest of Maoists in the urban population, it is difficult to say how long this proletariat would remain quiet.

---

[236] *Hindustan Times*, 17 January 1999

Finally, if the Constitution had meant Other Backward Classes or backward class of citizens other than Scheduled Castes and Scheduled Tribes to be *castes*, there was no earthly reason for its makers to call them economically or economically, educationally, and socially backward *classes* comprising of similarly situated families and in some cases even similarly placed individuals. A religious community is neither a class of citizens nor a caste. In fact, each community is a combination of differently placed classes, groups and, where applicable, castes. The Supreme Court recognized this in 1992 when it ruled that besides Scheduled Castes, Scheduled Tribes, and Shudras there were "similar backward social groups among Muslims and Christians (which) had no entry into the administrative apparatus. It was this balance which was sought to be addressed by providing reservations in favor of such backward classes"[237] (emphasis added). However, it compromised when, instead of identifying 'similar social groups', of all religious communities it did not object to reservations already given to a whole religious community in certain states.[238] Majorities and minorities can be due to factors other than the religion and can be found also within the same castes and communities. The only common sub-groups are families, where caste, religion, region, and sex become immaterial. Even among the Scheduled Castes and the Scheduled Tribes the constitution provides social benefits for the affected backward parts and groups which, logically, should be families. Then, why not among the Other Backward Classes?

Summary

Castes cannot be divided on the basis of different races. Genetically India's population is a mixed population. Castes and classes are two different ways of dividing society; classes are homogeneous while castes and communities are heterogeneous. Barring in SC and ST, the constitution provides social benefits for classes. By definition, class means both a group and its similarly affected families or individuals. Therefore, reservations should be possible on both accounts. Family remains the most suitable group for social benefits even under the constitution, for it does not compromise individual rights.

---

[237] *A.I.R.* Supreme Court 1993: 554, 555: 83
[238] Ibid.

The constitution lays stress on individual rights. If group rights had been implemented at family or individual level, there would have been no problem also in discontinuing after certain parameters were met. The omnipotent expression, "nothing in this article will prevent…" in Article 15(4) and 16(4), the way it was implemented to bring in caste and religion, did away with the individual rights and with it the original intention of the constitution.

Caste based reservations have benefitted relatively few. Instead of removing, they have enhanced the intra-caste inequalities even among the backward classes. There is no basis for a forced caste and occupation nexus.

CHAPTER 5

HINDU LAW AND LAW OF CASTE

Dumont's timeless essences of *essentialism* described in the Introduction refer to the belief that people and/or phenomenon have an underlying and unchanging 'essence', where an essence is the attribute or set of attributes that make a thing what it fundamentally is and without which it loses its identity. *Constructivism* is the way people create the meaning of the world or society through a series of individual constructs. Varnas and Jatis were 'essence' of the Hindu social structure, but Varnas represented as primary castes and Jatis as their sub-castes were constructs, malevolent or innocent depending upon one's perception. The British interpretations of the essences of the social structure of the Hindu society changed the very shape of the established law and the meanings of customs and practices. In the process either they produced hybrids or altogether new constructs. These distortions of social structure were also carried into their version of the *Hindu Law*. If mixing up of Jatis (castes) with Varnas destroyed the original character of both, the creation of a fifth Varna of Panchama, produced an entirely new construct, a total plant, to misrepresent thousands of years old social structure. Therefore, there is a call for reflection and more refined explanations in order to understand how the scriptures originally visualized the society and how the British invented a new *caste system* to damn the Indian nation. Some colonial constructions were uncovered earlier and some will be in the following paragraphs.

Gupte describes three phases of Hindu Law: Classical Hindu Law, Anglo-Hindu Law, and Modern Hindu Law. There is little information on the practice of law in India prior to the eighteenth century. During the classical period, law was based upon the teachings of the Dharamshastras, the known sources of dharma as instructed by the learned in Vedas. According to Hindu conception, law in the modern sense was only a branch of dharma, which included religious, moral, social, and legal duties. The author says if Hindu Law was law of status, it was also law by acceptance.

It was highly elastic with enough scope for growth and was not obligatory. The subsequent rulers and regimes often changed it and imposed their own laws.[239] By linking castes to their own class system, the British administrators in India viewed the old laws as indicators of occupation, social standing, and intellectual ability. They overlooked that many dynasties of obscure origin, which had captured political power and acquired Kshatriya status, had actually come up from the previous lower strata due to social mobility.[240] Their genealogy tables were manufactured later to connect them with a traditional lineage.[241]

The British, at least notionally, considered three sources before they made up their own version of Hindu Law. The *first* source was Srutis, the Vedas, and the Upanishads, which were described as the 'principle source'— 'the source rather of ultimate authority or sanction of the rules of law themselves'. In the case of differences with the Smritis and other documents, the Srutis 'would prevail'.[242] The *second* was the 'Smritis' or Puranas and Dharamshastras based on written or unwritten recollections composed by Hindu rulers. They were described as 'real source', and because of 'scantiness of law in the Vedas', the British made them, at least theoretically, the sole exponent of the Vedic authority. Even out of them, only Manusmriti was given pre-eminence. The *third* source was the 'commentaries and digests', described as the 'laws of actual usage', by which the British ultimately superseded even the Smritis.[243] Thus, in practice, the Srutis were reduced to a nominal source, and out of Smritis, the Manusmriti was chosen for intense propaganda, but finally, the British took to foreign translations of commentaries and digests to construct their own version of Hindu Law. They also engaged some Brahmin priests in doing this.

The colonial version of *Law of Caste* in the Hindu Law, which was adopted unchanged after the independence, even today ignores the original insight or intuitive understanding of an ideal society foreseen in the Srutis. Varnas and Jatis came up at different times and were two different ways of classifying society, but the colonial rulers, to make sense of their version, applied caste to both the terms and distorted the original open-ended fourfold classification into watertight compartments. Gandhi objected to

---

[239]   S.V. Gupte, 1981: *Hindu Law*: 1-3
[240]   http://en.wikipedia.org/wiki/Caste_system_in_India
[241]   Gupte, 1981: 55 Also Burton Stein
[242]   Ibid., 1981: *Hindu Law*: Chapter 3: 33
[243]   Gupte, 1981: *Hindu Law*: Chapter 3: 33

the colonial version of Varnas, but ultimately gave up before an unrelenting propaganda.[244] Gupte comments, 'In the course of interpretation of Hindu Law, some of the decisions have deviated completely from the original rule or created innovations and laid down rules alien to the spirit of Hindu Law.'[245] After independence, the compilers of the Indian Constitution and later the Parliament, despite doing extensive amendments of the *Hindu Law* after 1947, left the British time 'Law of Caste' in the form of Article 11 unchanged and accepted the colonial distortions without a second look.

The original structure of the ancient society as conceived in the Srutis, however, cannot be dismissed as academic. In the earlier times, Jati did not convey a rigid description of an occupation or the social status of a group. The caste as a 'system' became more rigid, when the British started to enumerate castes in ten-year censuses and codified the caste system they shaped under their rule.[246] They ignored the Srutis, which viewed the social organization from the point of whole humanity, and stuck to their own contrived version. The ancient Indian thinkers held a changing view of their society and perceived it in three different ways.

First, the Vedas classified humanity in the cosmogony of Purusha Sukta into four types of people or four Varnas. The stress was on *differentiation*, which is a characteristic of nature in both animate and inanimate world. John Karkala was a distinguished professor of philosophy and visitor to many foreign universities. He wrote, when "Purusha, the all pervading Universal Spirit, cosmic energy, the life giving principle in animated things", represented allegorically as 'Person', 'submitted Himself to sacrifice', meaning activity or manifestation, the society was 'classified' on the basis of 'function and occupation' 'into four *types* of people'. They were 'like speech that came from mouth, reflecting the thought of the mind'; like arm that 'protects and defends the society'; like the thigh that 'sustains the society'; and like feet that 'provides locomotion and moves the society'.[247] Four Varnas represented the thinkers, the protectors, the sustainers, and the movers of society in which sustainers and movers of society were as important as the thinkers and the protectors. People's individual disposition and qualities put them in a particular Varna, not family or birth, but since it has been taught from the colonial times that Varnas are primary castes

---

[244]   Galanter, 1984
[245]   Gupte, 1981: 30: Para 13
[246]   http://en.wikipedia.org/wiki/Caste_system_in_India, 2011
[247]   John Karkala, 1980: 36

and Jatis their sub-castes, unless the country starts from the school books, it will not be easy to reverse old perceptions.

To view the society in its true essence, one has to discard the notion that a Brahmin by birth was superior just because he was said to have come out of the mouth of the Creator and a Shudra by birth was inferior because he came out of the feet. Words like Brahmans, Kshatriyas, Vaishyas, and Shudras qualified people for their qualities. Every thinker was not a Brahmin and every scavenger a Shudra. or every Shudra a scavenger or every Brahmin a thinker. Risley found only 8 percent Brahmins working as priests in Bihar in the 1901 census. The others were in all sorts of occupations. In the past even the rich Shudras had servants, who would be ordinarily considered Brahmins, Kshatriyas, and Vaishyas. All depended upon one's socioeconomic position. Saints and thinkers like Vyas and Valmiki came from poor families, but by qualities they were Brahmans. When asked, "Who is a Brahmana?" Yudhishtra replied, "He in who are noticeable truthfulness, charity, forgiveness, good character, mercy, ascetic tendencies and compassion is regarded by authorities as Bramana." When told that such qualities could be present in a Shudra too, he said, "The Shudra in whom these traits (*lakshna*) are found is no Shudra (but a Brahmana) and a Brahmana in whom they are lacking is no Brahmana (but a Shudra)."[248] The term Brahmana of the Vedas is accepted even by the Buddhists as a term for a saint, 'one who has attained final sanctification.'[249] Warriors and rulers were not confined to particular Jatis. Many prominent rulers Nandas, Mauryas, Guptas, etc. were all from non-Kshatriya castes, if there were any such castes.

The *second* way in which the ancients divided the humanity, even the universe, was by *gunas* or attributes. The German Indologist Herman Oldenburg observed in 1916 that the three *gunas* called *sattav, rajas, and tamas* were considered as 'interwoven in a covering . . . wherein the soul dwells'.[250] He then quotes a verse from Svetasvatara Upanishad which describes *Prakrati,* the Fundamental Principle of Material World, as *a red, white, and black she-goat,* which litters many young ones.[251] Prakriti, the Creation in its infinite variety, was a mixture of all *gunas* or attributes and

---

[248] Pandharinath Prabhu: Reprint 1993: 303: *Hindu Social Organisation*
[249] S. Radhakrishnan, 2004: The Dhammapada (Chapter XXVI: Brahmanavaggo). In The Buddhism Omnibus.New Delhi: Oxford University Press
[250] Oldenberg, 1963: 138
[251] Ibid.: 13

so was its litter. Sattava meant balance, order, or purity. Rajas meant change, movement, or dynamism. Tamas denoted "inertia" and was associated with dullness and ignorance and with those who fell in moral values and had objectionable behavior. Everything in nature was a blend of three *gunas*. Black was as much a part of nature as white or red. Among human beings, the identity of an individual depended upon a more predominant *Guna*. Except for Justice B. L. Kapur of the Supreme Court, quoted earlier, the Supreme Court barely looked at Varnas in their right perspective. Luckily, in recent times there has been more recognition in social sciences.

The *third* way was when everyone, king, saint, or commoner, was regarded at birth as 'once-born' Shudra. 'Twice-born' status came with education and the study of Vedas. The terms applied to individuals and not groups or Jatis. There was nothing lower than the 'once-born'. These were the *essences* of Hindu thought. To turn them into once-born and twice-born *castes* and to try to create a third category lower than the two were *constructs*. People can be twice-born or once-born or educated and uneducated, not their Jatis or castes.

Thus, *the society was made up of four broad categories of people in which everyone was born as 'once-born' Shudra and acquired three types of traits in different proportions during one's lifetime. Twice-born status came with education and the study of Vedas,* which in modern times could be the study of humanities, arts, sciences and religions in their different forms. Only the illiterate remained once-born. These were the *essences* of social stratification in terms of scriptures. The rest were aberrations or constructions. Impurity and pollution disappeared with removal of cause. Physical untouchability was scourge, but applied to individuals. Risley invented a class of untouchables in 1901 despite opposition for ten years from his staff, and the 1931 census overstated their number for political reasons.

In a recent publication of newspaper *Hindu*, Balasubramanium points out that the origin of caste system in India has been a contentious subject. A strong group of scholars think that it was brought in by people from West Asia, who migrated and settled here around 3,000-4,000 years ago. On the other hand, there are other scholars who suggest it to be the result of "cultural diffusion" among the original inhabitants themselves. They feel that social hierarchy or stratification was not an imported imposition but an indigenous invention. This alternate model suggests that caste system has been present for the last 30,000-10,000 years. What is meant by caste *system* is not told.

G. Arun Kumar and others published a combination of genetic and anthropological analysis in the journal *PLoS ONE* dated 28 November 2012, to address this question. After studying the socio-cultural habits of South Indian males and analysis of the specific part of Y chromosome that does not get diluted by recombination and tells the genetic history or parentage, they concluded that whereas 'all mating and marriage' is mixing of 'genes' and more diverse the mixing, the greater is the variety and enrichment of traits, the genetics also tells us 'that the whole world is but one family'. They quote Maha Upanishad which states: 'ayam bandhurayam neti ganana laghuchetasam udaracharitanam tu vasudhaiva kutumbakam.' ("Only small men discriminate saying: One is a relative; the other is a stranger. For those who live magnanimously the entire world constitutes but a family. Caste or any such social pigeonholing restricts this width of choice from an ocean into a gene pool or even a pond!")[252] The prediction that in the Age of Kali people with only sattvic and tamsic qualities would survive was more of a lament than an essence. It was a reflection on the fall in the moral fabric of the society. It did not mean administrators, warriors, merchants, agriculturists, artisans, sweepers, priests, or hosts of other similar classes would vanish. Even today one can be a teacher, a soldier, a businessman, and a barber in the same family and the same Jati, but belong to different Varnas. Emergence of 'new' tax-paying Shudras and the replacement of the Varna model by a feudal type were the indicators of fall in morality. Privy Council's refusal to accept the notion of two Varnas in the Kaliyug in the case quoted by Ambedkar was extraordinary. It could decide on the caste of an individual, which too would be difficult, but it could not decide on what was only a notion.

The origin of Jatis, the nearest equivalent of castes, is still uncertain. The foreign views hold that Jatis were based on occupations, but in one ancient view, Jatis appeared due to mixing of people with different traits, statuses, and occupations. Terms like anulomas and pratilomas indicate the same. Considering India's mixed population and genetic pooling, this is not unlikely. Description of Marriot and Inden that 'among human beings a *Jati* can designate a distinct sex, a race, a caste or a tribe, a population, the followers of an occupation, or a religion or a nation' tells us the extent of its use.[253] A Jati may also mean 'genesis', origin or birth, and is applied to all living things including flora, fauna, human beings, and even gods. One

---

[252]   *The Hindu*, 10 January 2013: Caste system: an indigenous invention in South India?
[253]   Marriot and Inden: as quoted by Galanter, 1984: 7

meaning is species. How the Europeans reduced Jatis to mere hereditary endogamous units during the last few centuries is difficult to know. Their number increased with the migration of their members or families to other places, where they mixed with others and either retained the same Jati name or acquired another. Most sociologists and historiographers now agree that Jatis were not sub-castes of Varnas, no caste considered itself inferior to the other, no cultural hierarchy could be determined among them, and finally, there was no caste—occupation nexus. Throughout the ages, their role has been more political than social. In religious functions, *gotra* was important, not Jati. Notion of purity and pollution had many reasons and was temporary. Achhyut or untouchable existed for different reasons but as individuals. The depiction of Varnas as four watertight compartments; acceptance of a fifth Varna, and addition of a third category below the once-born *castes* in 1992 were the *constructs* of the colonial period, not 'timeless essences' of the ancient social structure.

The 'Law of Caste' in Article 11 of the *Hindu Law* is another construct of the colonial times. Article 11 states that a Hindu is governed by rules of law applicable to his *caste*. It divides the society into four primary castes, which were previously Varnas, and numerous sub-castes, which were earlier Jatis. "Primary castes are (i) the Brahmins, or priestly caste, (ii) the Kshatriyas, or warrior class, (iii) the Vaishyas or agricultural or trading caste and (iv) the Shudras." The Article says that the members of the first three castes belong to twice-born or regenerate class and every Hindu belongs to one of the two classes, but in the case of dispute, the question must be determined on evidence. It is surprising how the Indian states and the courts accepted the terminologies like 'regenerate classes' and 'two classes'? If caste is fixed by birth, how can it regenerate? Second, twice-born and once-born were constituted by four and not two classes. Brahmins, Kshatriyas and Vaishyas were not identical and could not be lumped under one class. Moreover, all the four types were people, as individuals, not as Jatis. Finally, the Hindu Law concedes on the identification of Shudra, "*The question whether a given person is a Shudra or not is not easy to answer, for there seems to be no authoritative principle, test or text which would help to decide the question*"[254] (emphasis added). In the Japanese study quoted in this book, Yamasaki stated in 1997 that as *no* fifth Varna was mentioned in the Smritis and in the Hindu Law first enacted in 1837, "the classical distinction between upper three varnas and Sudras was retained and all castes that could not be called

---

[254] Yamazaki, 1997: 17

twice born were considered to belong to Shudra varna."[255] Consequently, depressed castes, also called outcastes and Scheduled Castes, 'did not have any special status distinguishable from sudra castes under the Hindu Law.'[256] The British courts did the same. The whole separation of Shudras was illogical and biased. Therefore, the question remains: Who are Shudras and how are the present socially and educationally backward classes Shudra?

According to the *Hindu Law*, the law of Dharamshastras was applicable only to descendents of the Aryans and not to descendents of non-Aryan Dravidians, but perhaps, as a concession, the British and their successors permitted Dravidians of South India to be governed by the Hindu Law, unless the law 'modified their custom' or the community did not adopt it.[257] This was despite the fact that Max Muller clarified in mid-nineteenth century itself that there was no Aryan race in blood; Aryan, in scientific language, was utterly inapplicable to race and Aryan meant language and nothing but language, and Ambedkar had already rejected the racial theory. South Indians were not Dravidian serfs and slaves. Indians have been a mixed population for thousands of years, and any derivations derived from the racial theory were false. The Hindu Law needs to be amended in line with the scriptures and the present knowledge.

The origin of Indian population from Ancient South Indians and Ancient North Indians was described earlier. The same Hyderabad group published a study which has appeared in *American Journal of Genetics* on 9 December 2011. It destroyed the myth that Indians were descendents of Aryans who migrated to India 3,500 years ago. It says, "There is no genetic evidence that Indo-Aryans invaded or migrated to India or even something such as Aryans even existed." And it also says, "The genetic component which spread beyond India is significantly higher in India than in any other part of the world. This implies that this genetic component originated in India and then spread to West Asia and Caucasus"[258] This supports Pargitar, who had stated much earlier that the Indian tradition knew nothing of any Aila or Aryan invasion of India from Afghanistan. In fact, there was Aila outflow of the Druyhus through the North-west into countries beyond which they formed various kingdoms and introduced Indian religion in other nations. 'Druyhus did not come, but went to North-West to establish

---

[255]   Ibid. Also Hindu Law 1981: 56
[256]   Ibid.
[257]   Gupte, 1981: *Hindu Law*: 15-16
[258]   *Mail Today*, 10 December 2011

their kingdoms.'[259] In such an event, the present Hindu Law based on racial division of Hindu society into Aryans, Dravidians, and Aborigine becomes obsolete. Another shift in the colonial stand occurred, when the Hindu Law was made to state that it 'governs the descendents of Aboriginal tribes provided they are sufficiently hinduised though they may retain their old customs'. The criteria for 'sufficient' and 'insufficient' Hinduisation were never told.[260] Nor, as we now know, there were any Aborigines tribes. As if this was not enough, the British brought in the terms like 'Tribal Religions', 'Animism', and 'Animists' to separate the alleged descendents of the non-existent 'Aborigines' of India living in the forests and the mountains in isolation and poverty, so that they could be separated from the mainstream Hindus and become ready material for conversions.

The term animism was first developed as animismus by German scientist Georg Ernst Stahl in 1720. It referred to the 'doctrine that animal life is produced by an immaterial soul'. Sir Edward Tylor in his 1871 book *Primitive Culture* defined animism as 'the general doctrine of souls and other spiritual beings in general', which often includes 'an idea of pervading life and will in nature', i.e. a belief that natural objects other than humans, too, have souls. As a self-described 'confirmed scientific rationalist', Tylor believed that this view was 'childish' and typical of 'cognitive underdevelopment' and that it was therefore common in 'primitive' peoples such as those living in 'hunter gatherer societies'. Wikipedia, on the other hand, contends that animism is widely found in Hinduism, Buddhism, Pantheism, Christianity, and Neopaganis.[261]

This only shows a belief in the oneness of Creation. If souls in some form did not exist in the lower formations, how did they suddenly appear among the human beings? Evolution is a chain of events and implies progression and continuation. If one could evolve to higher formations, there is no reason why under contrary circumstances one could not devolve to the lower. A separate religion of Animists was not created with pious intentions.

Commenting on it, G. S. Ghurye, doyen of sociology in his own time, observed in 1963 that "the only sound conclusion is that the creeds of the so called Animists and the Hindus of some sections of Hindu society have so much material which is either similar or common or both, that

---

[259] J.N. Yadav, 1992: 47-64 Yadavs Through The Ages Vol.1 Sharda Publishing House Delhi

[260] Gupte, 1981: *Hindu Law*: 15-16

[261] http://en.wikipedia.org/wiki/Animism

the demarcation between the two, being almost impossible, is thoroughly artificial" and "the only proper description of these people is that they are the imperfectly integrated classes of Hindu society. They are in reality Backward Hindus".[262] Prof. M. N. Srinivas agreed with him in 1992 and stated, 'I find that the British classified the tribal as animists in contrast to Hindus and I find this very unfair anthropologically.'[263] K. S. Singh, former Director General of Anthropological Survey of India, found in 1992 that almost 98 percent of Scheduled Castes and '86.7 percent Scheduled Tribes describe themselves as Hindus'.[264] In fact, it can now be said that the Adivasis were the progenitors of those who lived in plains and not any Aboriginals. Racial theory divided people and also the country into Aryan North and Dravidian South.

Jaipal Singh, a member of Constituent Assembly, requested President Rajendra Prasad in 1950 to issue instructions to call Scheduled Tribes as 'Adivasis' (meaning original inhabitants). In September 2004, national assembly of indigenous people took exception to the word 'primitive' in the draft of National Policy on Tribals and demanded 'recognition of rights to ancestor lands, territories and natural resources'. Recently, Adivasis even questioned the term Scheduled Tribe that implies 'primitive traits, distinctive culture, shyness with the public at large, geographic isolation, and social and economic backwardness'. Other tribal organizations, too, resented epithets like primitive, people with intellectual limitations, and criminal tribes.[265] Genetic evidence shows no difference between those from hilly areas and the plains. Jatis appeared with the appearance of an agrarian society. The Scheduled Tribes were poor because of isolation in difficult terrains and the practice of *jhooming*, described as subsistence agriculture, in which they stayed at a place till all the trees were cut and consumed, leaving the area denuded and unfit for cultivation. Post-independence reforestation and other measures have brought back a radical change. That the British played havoc with the Indian people was understandable, but leaving a vital portion of Hindu Law without critical analysis after independence was due to an indefensible neglect or politics or both on the part of the national leaders. This resulted in debatable interpretations of the constitutional provisions by the courts.

---

[262]   Ghurye, 1963: Reprint 1965: 7, 19
[263]   Srinivas. Quoted in *People of India*, Vol. 1. Ed. K.S. Singh
[264]   *People of India*, Vol. II: 12
[265]   *Frontline*, 5 November 2004

The *First Challenge*, therefore, is to remove the colonial constructs, modify *Hindu Law* in the Sruti terms, amend Article 11 of the Hindu Law in line with ancient perception of Varna and Jati, remove the illegitimate racial division of Hindu society and the country in line with the latest scientific findings, and finally *review* the perceptions of Hindu society in the 1992 judgment.

The *Second Challenge* would be to interpret the relevant constitutional provisions in line with the corrected perceptions. While commenting upon the '*Ancient Varna system and the origin of Caste*' in his book *Classifying the Universe* (1994), Brian K. Smith aptly remarked, 'To paraphrase Santayana's maxim those who cannot remember the past are doomed to repeat other people's version of it.' It is time to discard other people's versions which have unfairly influenced many generations and re-interpret the composite Indian social structure in its true perspective and apply the law accordingly.

CHAPTER 6

MANDAL CASE—PERCEPTIONS

In a scathing attack on the Hindu social structure in the *Indra Sawhney vs. Union of India case*, the Supreme Court blasted the Hindu community in Para 2 of its majority judgment:

> The Constituent Assembly was composed of men of vision . . . They understood their society perfectly. They were aware of *historic* injustices and inequalities . . . They were conscious . . . that the Hindu religion . . . *as it was practiced*—was not known for its egalitarian ethos . . . it divided its adherents into four *watertight* compartments. Those outside this four-tier (*chatarvarnya*) were the *outcastes* (*Panchama*), the lowliest. They did not even belong to caste system ugly as its face was. The fourth, the *Shudra, were no better,* though certainly better than Panchamas. The lowliness attached to them (*Shudra and Panchama*) by virtue of their birth in these castes, unconnected with their deeds. There was no deliverance for them . . . except perhaps death. They were condemned to be inferior. All lowly, menial and unsavory occupations were assigned to them . . . In the rural life, they had *no alternative* but to follow these occupations, generation after generation, century after century. It was their *karma* they were told, the penalty for their sins they allegedly committed in their previous birth . . . *Poverty, low status in Hindu caste system and the lowly occupation constituted and do still constitute a vicious circle* . . .[266] (Emphasis added)

This was a devastating comment on the Hindu religion and its society. It is not that there were no Varnas or Jatis or traditional occupations or no

---

[266] *A.I.R.* Supreme Court 1993: 502: Para 2

notion of purity and pollution and Shudra in the Hindu social structure, only Varnas were not four watertight compartments; there was nothing lower than the 'fourth caste Shudra'; fifth Varna of Panchama had no reference in the original classification; 'outcastes' were another added entity contested even by census commissioner of 1931 census; caste was not a socially homogeneous class or a single occupational grouping; and the theory of caste—occupation nexus was not supported by many sources. These issues were discussed earlier and will be further taken up in this chapter.

On the Karma theory, which is a part of every religion that came up in India, Buddhist Rev. Mahasi Sayadaw says that Karma is the law of moral causation. "The theory of Karma was prevalent in India before the advent of the Buddha. Nevertheless, it was the Buddha who explained and formulated this doctrine in the complete form in which we have it today."[267] The Hinduism of the past believed that Karma was important, but effort was more important than birth. India became a country of slaves when Indians gave up effort and took to unqualified belief in Karma.

The Court might have based its above observations on two sources. *First*, Prof. Wadia's comment quoted in the Mandal Commission's Report that "the high metaphysics of Upanishads and ethics of Gita have been reduced to mere words by the tyranny of caste. Emphasizing the unity of the whole world, animate and inanimate, India has yet fostered a social system which divided her children into watertight compartments, divided them from one another, generation after generation, for endless centuries". He further qualified that 'this process of divisions, groups called castes have been permanently assigned high or low rank on the basis of birth'.[268] Prof. Wadia did not explain the meaning of caste and how castes were allotted a permanent position, when even the colonial rulers recorded that no caste or Jati ever considered itself inferior to the other. Even the National Backward Classes Commission records, "Till information regarding the position of each caste in the Government of India's services becomes readily available, it may be *presumed* that this factor is fulfilled by a caste/community/sub-caste/synonym/sub-entry on the basis of their own observations and other relevant materials that may be available to it"[269] (emphasis added).

In a seminar on Casteism and untouchability held in Delhi by the Union Government in 1955, the Government of India defined 'untouchables' as

---

[267] http://www.buddhanet.net/e-learning/karma.htm: extracted on 5 August 2011
[268] Report of 2nd Backward Classes Commission: Chapter IV: Para 4.1
[269] Appendix 1

"those who were not allowed entry into Hindu temples and to draw water from common wells and tanks, as their touch polluted caste Hindus".[270] Speaking on the occasion, where Prof. A. R Wadia was also present, the eminent sociologist Irawati Karve called the untouchables Shudras. Neither the Government nor Prof. Wadia nor anyone else objected.

The second source was Encyclopedia Britannica, which the Court cited to support its theory of four watertight compartments and the fifth of Panchama:

> More abundant than slavery was serfdom. Within the *rigid* classification of social classes in ancient India the *Sudra caste* was obliged to serve the Kshatriyas or warrior caste, the Brahmins or priests; and the Vaishyas or farmers, cattle raisers and merchants. There is an *'unbreakable barrier'*, however, separating these castes from the inferior Sudra *caste*, 'the descendents of the primitive indigenous people who lived in serfdom'. Shudras were little better than Untouchables[271] (emphasis added).

To call Varnas as castes was conceptually unacceptable. The little difference between Shudras and untouchables could not change their basic Shudra identity. Such differences are seen even among untouchables. Finally, the encyclopedia insists that the Hindu society was divided into *four* castes, and the lowliest caste was the *'inferior sudra caste'*, 'the descendents of the primitive indigenous people who lived in serfdom', and there was an *'unbreakable barrier'* between the upper three 'castes' and the 'sudra caste'. Anomaly occurred when the 'unbreakable barrier' was *shifted* from between the three upper castes and Shudra caste *to* between three upper castes *plus* Shudra caste, the 'descendents of the primitive indigenous people', and a hypothetical *fifth 'caste'* called outcastes and Panchama. Panchama had a furtive origin which will be discussed later. Here it is enough to say that if there was any fifth Varna in the Hindu religion, there was nothing to prevent the encyclopedia from saying so. The farmers, the cattle raisers, small merchants, and many artisans that formed the bulk of the society and now form the Other Backward Classes, are described as Vaishyas in the encyclopedia, quoted by the judgment itself. Then how did they suddenly become Shudras? What was meant by Shudra?

---

270 Report on Casteism and Untouchability, 1955: 5: 56
271 *A.I.R.* Supreme Court 1993: Page 550

Conversion of four Varnas into four watertight compartments was not only misleading, but also converted the previous 'caste orders' in which Varna were 'four kinds of people' and Jati, the "endogamous unit taken to be primary reference to caste", into a new 'twentieth century *caste system*' which depicted Varnas as castes and Jatis their sub-castes. Marriot and Inden criticized this conversion and commented that 'serious students of Indian history regard it (caste) as a suspect on ground of both its foreignness and its ambiguity'.[272] Finally, when the British rulers could not group castes into broad categories of four Varnas and one category of outcastes (Aborigines) in 1871—2 census due to intrinsic difficulties, absence of uniform classification, and the wrong assumption that 'an all India system of classification of caste could be developed',[273] they discontinued recording of Varnas in subsequent census operations and included only those castes which were either prominent or had a population of more than 100,000. In 1993, the British sociologist Quigley showed two mistakes in the colonial understanding. There was 'no such thing as the caste system'. There were 'only so many political units divided into different castes'. The second mistake was the assumption that 'there is one unambiguous interpretation of Varna system'.[274] Roche commented in 2008, 'Very few scholars have explored the possibility of the British having strengthened such traditional elements as caste on the pretext of centuries old customs.' In an astonishing report on hierarchical position of castes, he pointed out that when the British could not determine the actual position of castes in social hierarchy, from the 1881 census onward 'standard names were ranked alphabetically' and not according to any precedence.[275] This observation would have astounded the courts, which imported the 1906 lists and accepted them as a proof of hierarchy among castes. A couple of examples are quoted in Chapter 8

The shifting of Vaishyas, with the bulk of their population formed by the farmers, cattle keepers and artisans, to the new category of 'new taxpaying' Shudras, could be the main reason for the Mandal Commission to show the population of Vaisyas, banias etc in 1980 as less than 2 percent of the total population and Kaysthas of a little over 1 percent. Vaishyas were, thus, restricted to only better placed merchants. Over a time, the same new Shudras lost their kingdoms and independence due to the onslaught

---

[272]   As quoted by Galanter, 1984: 7

[273]   Cohen, 1996: 32: *Caste in History*

[274]   Quigley, 1993: 20

[275]   Patrick A. Roche, 2008: 4: *Caste in History*. Ed. Banerjee-Dube

by foreign rulers and become poor and illiterate. This was reflected in 1901 census figures, which showed nearly 96% of Indian population illiterate and almost whole of it poor by the British standards. Another reason of their being called Shudra could be the Puranic saying, which stated that with the decline in moral values in the Age of Kali, only people with the qualities of Brahmin and Shudra would survive. Whatever are the reasons, their original identity and diversity among them could not be obliterated, because the British created a new community of "Other Hindu" and included them under the Shudra. (Infra) The 'new tax-paying Shudras' described earlier had nothing to do with the Shudras, who were called dasas and menials or who were labeled as Accyuts and untouchable. In the early 20th century, the same 'new' Shudras called themselves Backward Hindus and later became Other Backward Classes.

As the word 'depressed' carried a connotation of untouchability, many backward classes were reluctant to call themselves depressed. The United Provinces Hindu Backward Classes League was founded in 1929. It proposed before the Franchise Commission, of which Ambedkar was a member, that depressed classes might be called 'Hindu Backward', to differentiate them from the existing Backward Hindus or Other Backward Classes. The League submitted a list of 115 castes which included 'all candidates from the untouchable category as well as *a stratum above*. All of the listed communities', it said, "belonged to non-Dwijas or degenerate or *Sudra* classes of Hindus." It meant that even in 1929 the untouchable and the stratum above were regarded as Shudras. Panchama were not even mentioned. However, the nineteenth and twentieth-century notion of Varnas as primary castes and Jatis as sub-castes, continued to persist. Marc Galanter admitted in 1996 that he had to use the word caste for both the Varnas and the 'existing endogamous groups or Jatis', because the 'judicial treatment of the relation between Varna and caste was plagued by confusion'.[276] He recounts several criteria used by the courts to determine place of Jatis in Varna 'hierarchy', but found every criterion as subjective and contradictory as the other. The inability to differentiate between Varnas and Jatis was one of the fundamental flaws, which created uncertainty and resulted in miscarriage of justice.

Varna differentiation was neither absolute nor hierarchical nor hereditary nor unchangeable nor endogamous nor involved commensality, which

---

[276]   Galanter, 1996: 102: Changing Legal Conception of Caste in Structure and Change in Indian Society. Eds. Singer and Cohen, Rawat Publications, Jaipur

become the hallmarks of Jati during the colonial period. In fact, every Jati had people with characteristics of each Varna in different proportions. Varnas were individual based and pertained to an un-stratified society, while Jatis represented stratified society. Answering his own question, 'whether Caste was only an 'Orientalist Construct', Quigley replied that representation of "Indians as prisoners of the outrageous institution of caste addicted to hierarchy, ritual, concepts of purity and pollution, and other absurd theories of society and cosmos only contributed to the political subjugation of the East while simultaneously reinforcing the rationality and moral righteousness of Western Institutions".[277]

Therefore, it is necessary to get rid of the colonial psychology which has corrupted our understanding and be prepared to start from the beginning. Suppositions, presumptions, divisive politics and relentless propaganda, which started under the colonial rule, have no role in the administration of social justice. 2014 is not 1807, when the term Panchama came into existence, or 1901, when the British made up an all-India category of untouchables, or 1947, when the colonial baggage spilled over to plague the nation with unabated politicization of caste.

That Varnas were primary castes and Jatis their sub-castes was false. Even before 1901, the anthropologists' 'fieldwork' had established that caste meant *jaati* and 'not *varna*'. *Varna*s were four kinds of people and *Jati* an endogamous unit taken as the primary reference of caste. Occupation, language, and place of origin were relevant to only endogamous groups, but even they were of 'different kinds' and practiced endogamy at 'different levels'.[278] While the British census takers were not puzzled in 1901 over difference between Varna and Jati, the knowledgeable in India are perplexed even now.

Charsley comments that determination of castes in census operations in 1901 was not an easy task, because the 'ignorant masses' gave anything like occupation, sub-caste, clan, or some title by which they were known to their fellow villagers as their caste and the 'localized bases' of the endogamous groups varied from place to place. Only after they were trained to cite Ahirs, Gujars, etc. as their castes that the castes came into limelight[279] and became the basis of reservations in due course of time.

---

[277] Quigley, 1993: 14
[278] S. Charsley, 1996: 3
[279] Ibid.

Community

The way the expression 'community' was used during the colonial times created another red herring. A community was defined as one whose population was approximately 2 percent of State's population or more than 100,000. Brahmins with only 1.8 percent population was an exception. The British divided Hindus into eight communities consisting of Brahmins, other *caste Hindus*, five others of Nayar, Kummula, Nudar, Ezlmva, Chermar (Pulaya), apparently all from South India, plus *one* of undefined "*Other Hindu*" in singular as one community. Christians were divided into six communities, but Muslims were retained as one community.[280] Why there were only six communities among the Christians and only one among the Muslim was not explained. Why five communities from the South India were mentioned separately from other Hindus was also not clear. Obviously, their population would be small. "Other Hindu" was later called Shudra and now contained bulk of the Hindu population. The expression 'other caste Hindus,' included Kshatriyas and Vaishyas.

'Other Hindu,' whom the British administrators had called Shudra was, probably, the same category which, according to Dirks, the British created by throwing bulk of the Hindu population indiscriminately among the Shudras. It now included the future Scheduled Caste, which were extracted from it in 1936; Backward Tribes converted into Scheduled Tribes after the independence; and finally, 52% population of Hindus of socially and educationally backward classes which the Mandal Commission culled out from 1931 census and called Shudra. They could also be the same, which the historians had called 'new tax paying Shudras' and Ambedkar as "a general cognomen of a miscellaneous and heterogeneous collection of tribes and groups, who have nothing in common except they happen to be on a lower plane of culture and it is wrong to call them by the name Shudra." Some of them were later described as upper Shudras and others lower Shudras. Puranas describe all non-Brahmins as Shudra. The Sanscritised, rajputised and kshatrized lower castes are also Shudas. The issue is who, in fact, are the Shudra and how can they be identified? If social justice has to be delivered with justice, it is incumbent that the State clarifies these contentious issues and courts adjudicate.

When the Mandal Commission tells us that except for the twice born castes, it had included all others among the socially and educationally

---

[280] *A.I.R.* Supreme Court 1993: 549: 75

backward classes, it does not tell us how it determined the twice-born Kshatriyas and Vaishyas and their population on *Varna* basis or the basis of four watertight compartments. The British had discontinued recording Varnas in census reports after insurmountable difficulties in 1871-2 census. 1931 census only contained alphabetically collected castes. If we take the figures of Mandal Commission and reduce 5.52 Brahmins from the total of 17.58 of forward castes culled out of 1931 census, other caste Hindus—a perverted name for Kshatriyas and Vaishya - would be a little over 12 percent of total population. Once constituting the major portion of Hindu society, these warriors, ruling classes, administrators, huge number of farmers and agriculturists, cattle keepers, merchants and those in business and most artisans were now reduced to a little over 12 percent of Hindu population; and the rest 82 percent were those who were classically dasa, slaves and serfs and those engaged in other lower and menial occupations like sweepers etc.[281] This was incredible, if not preposterous. With this composition, how did the community survive for thousands of years? That more than 90 percent population was poor and illiterate in 1901 was different matter. Even now almost 30 percent people live below the poverty line and many more not too far above it.

The whole story of backward classes begins in the colonial times when 'twice born *castes*' were arbitrarily constructed by combining Brahmins, Kshatriyas and Vaishyas into one category and giving them an Aryan origin. Similarly, rest of the population was given the racial cover of Dravidians and Aborigines and called once born Shudras. The former were branded as discriminators and the latter backward and discriminated. The same perception continued after the independence and adopted in educational system without a whimper, because the British and the British trained Indians had attributed 96 percent illiteracy and poverty of almost the whole of Indian population to British formulated 'caste *system*.' In 1980 when the Mandal Commission presented its report it was the same situation and so also was in 1992, when the Supreme Court gave its verdict in the Mandal case. In the process, the nation ignored and still ignores the effect of foreign rule of more than thousand years before 1947, in which India was robbed and crippled. The racial theory has been rejected convincingly, but the perception of racial discrimination of backward castes by forward castes continues.

---

[281]   Ibid: 513

The political nature, the scheming and the absurdity of the above classification of British rulers was evident. In 1980, when the Mandal Commission culled out 52% of total population of India from 1931 census as socially and educationally backward classes and found only 3 percent Brahmins in South India as forward castes and the rest Shudra, one could hardly believe. In the North it was more liberal and, as stated earlier, found more than 17 percent as forward castes. It was not without reason that the petitioners in the Mandal case argued before the Constitution Bench, which first heard the Mandal case, that the whole identification was a farce. The criteria devised by the commission, if applied, could determine poverty, illiteracy and social backwardness, but not different racial origin or Shudra identity of the affected. Now there is genetic evidence to show that Indians were a mixed population and there were no racial basis for determining forwardness or backwardness. Therefore, it is time to either re-determine backward classes and forward classes, or better, go to socio-economic factors, for which there is evidence and also provision in the constitution.

To show that Dr. Ambedkar used class and caste inter-changeably in 1916, the court quotes him in Para 76 of its majority judgment, "… society is always composed of classes. It may be an exaggeration to assert the theory of class conflict, but the existence of definite classes in a society is a fact. Their bases may differ. They may be economic, intellectual or social, but an individual is always a member of a class. This is universal fact and Hindu society could not have been an exception to this rule." Ambedkar unambiguously showed that the Hindu society was divided into classes, by which he meant Varnas. Only when he stated that 'a Caste is an Enclosed Class'[282] that the caste lobbies thought it was a chance to equate caste with class, but they were mistaken. Ambedkar had said classes were *open* and changeable, not castes. He described caste as enclosed or closed class and, therefore, not changeable. Open and closed were antonyms, not synonyms. The fact is, Other Backward Classes are classes, economically backward because of poverty; intellectually backward because of illiteracy; and socially backward because of the other two. Their composition and status change with the removal of poverty and by imparting education.[283] It is the equitation of caste on class that created the problem.

Charsley quotes a famous passage from *Laws of Manu x. 4* by Buhler (1886). It reads, "The Brahmana, the Kshatriya and the Vaisya castes are

---

[282]   Ibid:249-250: 76
[283]   Ibid

the twice born, but the fourth, the Sudra, has only one birth; there is no fifth caste.".[284] Varnas were called castes in translation.

Cohen recorded in 1987 that attempts were made in 1971-72 census to place castes in four Varnas and categories of Outcastes and Aborigines by assuming that an all India system of classification could be developed. [285] However, they failed, for after 1881 census recording of Varnas was discontinued in census operations. There were no Aborigines and no outcastes. There were only four Varnas, as shown by Manu.

Fifth Category—Genesis of Panchama

Whether to meet their administrative requirements, or for religious expansionism, or to make sense of the lowest classes, the colonial rulers invented a number of terms in the nineteenth century, which had no relation to the ancient social structure. Two such terms were 'outcastes' and 'Panchama'. Panchama was coined in 1807 probably from the 'ancient' word Panchum which meant the fifth. Panchum had been used at some time in the history to show Puranas as a fifth Veda. Panchama is also the name of a small village in the South. It is also the name of a single caste among the Scheduled Castes in South India. The British had not included a fifth Varna or a fifth primary caste in the Law of Caste in the Hindu Law. Some respondents in the Mandal case resurrected Outcastes and Panchama in 1991 to influence one of the most crucial Supreme Court judgments in the history of free India and argued that "backward castes in Article 16(4) meant and only meant the members of Shudra *caste* which is located between the upper castes and the outcastes (Panchama) referred to as Scheduled Castes".[286] Its adoption by the Court in 1992 created an artificial threefold division of Hindu society, converted Shudra Varna into middle caste or, what respondent's called, Shudra *caste*, and added a new lowest *caste*—a fifth 'caste' or outcaste called Panchama. The respondents gave no reasons for adoption of these terms. Their relevance was explained in Archives on the Internet:

---

[284] Charsley Simon: 1996:3
[285] Cohen: 1987 Quoted by Quigley: 15-16
[286] A.I.R. 1993 Supreme Court.: 543: 63

The Panchama are, in the Madras Census Report, 1871, summed up as being "that great division of the people, spoken of by themselves as the fifth caste, and described by Buchanan and other writers as the Pancham Bandam". According to Buchanan, the Pancham Bandum "consists of four tribes, the Parriar, the Baluan, the Shekliar, and the Toti". Buchanan further makes mention of Panchama Banijigaru and Panchama Cumbharu (potters). The Panchamas were, in the Department of Public Instruction, called "Paraiyas and kindred classes" till 1893. This classification was replaced, for convenience of reference, by Panchama, which included Chacchadis, Godaris, Pulayas, Holeyas, Madigas, Malas, Pallans, Paraiyans, Totis, and Valluvans. "It is," the Director of Public Instruction wrote in 1902, "for Government to consider whether the various classes concerned should, for the sake of brevity, be described by one simple name. The terms Paraiya, low caste, outcaste, carry with them a derogatory meaning, and are *unsuitable*. The expression Pancham Banda, or more briefly Panchama, seems more appropriate." The Government ruled that there is no objection to the proposal that Paraiyas and kindred classes should be designated Panchama Bandham or Panchama in future, but it would be simpler to style them the fifth class.[287] (Emphasis in original)

Description of "Paraiya, low caste, outcaste, carry with them a derogatory meaning, and are *unsuitable*" tells the true story of their imposition on Hindu social structure. Yet, the terms outcaste and Panchama were used in the Mandal case judgment, just because it was brought in vociferously by some well known lawyers of some respondents. It created a false fifth class and messed up the Hindu social structure. The country is still suffering from its after effects.

Charsley also quotes Cornish on the highly controversial origin of Panchama, and stated that Panchama was created in 1807 in Madras by Buchanan by a combination of 'slaves of the inferior caste sudra' and four tribes of 'Panchum Bandam', called it 'pariah', which was a single caste, and later equated it with Panchum Bandam or Panchama.[288]

---

[287] http://archive.org/stream/castestribesofso06thuriala/castestribesofso06thuriala_djvu.txt
[288] Cornish, 1874: 16-17, 168 quoted by Charsley, 1996: 5

The inclusion of 'Sudra' was sufficient to show its actual identity. A dozen other castes constituting Panchama could not create a fifth caste or fifth Varna, or produce the 'great division of people' with a population of tens of millions spread over the whole of India. It was nothing short of chicanery. Cohen records that attempts were made to include castes among four Varnas and Outcastes and Aborigines in the census report of 1871-2 under the assumption that an all-India system of classification could be developed,[289] but when they failed, recording of Varnas in census operations was discontinued after 1881.

Though the British were reluctant in 1902 to use the title of low caste, outcastes and Paraiya for the above castes because they were 'derogatory and unsuitable', they agreed to call them Panchum Bandhum or Panchama or simply fifth class, not visualizing its future implications. As a single caste in South Indian states, Panchama continues to be recorded among the Scheduled Castes. The Anthropological Survey of India carried out a macro-level study of Indian population in the 1980s and published its findings in 1990s in various volumes of *People of India*. It found that the population of Panchama *caste* in the 1981 census in Andhra Pradesh was 9,265, in Karnataka 785, in Maharashtra 17,595, in Kerala 134; in Orissa 269, and in Tamil Nadu only 76. Thus, the total population of Panchama *caste* in the 1981 census was just over 28,000, while the population of Panchama, as Scheduled Castes, was 15 percent of the total population. Then, who were the others? K. S. Singh, the Director General of Anthropological Survey of India and one of the main authors of the study commented that in spite of a 'large number of groups covered under Panchama their population is small'. He described Panchama as 'a non-existent fifth Varna'.[290] Considering that Panchama or 'fifth class" was constructed from 10 or 11 castes, its population of 28,000 calculated by Anthropological Survey, quoted above, seems reasonable.

However, some incorrigibles still persisted. Benjamin Walker reports in *Encyclopedia of Hinduism* that to rationalize Panchama in the early 1920s some people arbitrarily included five categories of people among them. *First*, there were Mlecchas or foreigners including non-Aryan barbarians, Scythians, Persians, Huns, and in recent times Muslims and Europeans; *second*, non-Aryan Tribes with Negrito, Australoid, and those of proto-Dravidian antecedents; *third*, Panchama Tribes; *fourth*, the group called

---

[289] Cohen 1987: quoted by Quiglet 1993: 15-16
[290] K.S. Singh: *People of India*, Vol. 2; 1046

Antyaja; and the *fifth* were the Pratiloma or those whose fathers were from a lower caste than their mother's.[291]

Mlecchas were described earlier. They became Kshatriyas after they adopted Hindu religion. Otherwise, too, they had their own kingdoms and priests in ancient times and were not 'lower' than Shudra.[292] The Muslims and the Europeans ruled India for more than 1,000 years and could not be called lower than the lowest. The racial categories of Negrito, Australoid, and those with proto Dravidian antecedents are nowhere visible in the mixed population of India. The new evidence presented in the chapter on 'Race and Class' rejects even the theory of different races. The word *Antyaja,* according to Ambedkar, meant 'end of a village' and not the end of the caste system. In any case, the word 'ant' means end, not outside. The lowest castes might be at the *end*, but they were not outside the community. Mixed marriages among the Indian population, especially Anuloma marriages, where the female was from a lower caste, were accepted. Pratiloma, where male was from a lower caste, were certainly looked down upon, but were relatively few. Risley ridiculed the various combinations and permutations that went into their creation by saying, "No one could examine the long lists without being struck by much that is absurd and inconsistent."[293] Therefore, the terms like outcastes, Panchama, and middle castes have no role in describing the social structure of Hindu society. The respondents could dupe the nation and the court in 1992, but the times have changed.

Outcastes, Outcasts, out of Pail and Exterior Castes

The other highly controversial term accepted by the Court was 'outcastes', which, as shown above, was rejected in 1902 in favor of Panchama as it was 'derogatory' and 'unsuitable'. Sir J. J. Hunt, the census commissioner of the 1931 census, was also not satisfied with the nineteenth century term 'outcastes' and replaced it with '*Exterior Castes*'. According to him, the controversial word 'outcastes' (with e) showed that some people did not belong to caste system and therefore were outside the Hindu society. Dissatisfied with the word 'outcastes with e', he replaced the term with exterior castes to 'avoid a taint which was unjustly attached to it. Exterior

---

[291]   Walker, 1995: in Vol. II of An Encyclopedic Survey of Hinduism
[292]   Yamazaki, 1997: 4
[293]   Risley, 1969

castes, he said, '*may* connote exclusion, but not extrusion'.[294] His anxiety was to dispel the notion that depressed classes were extruded or forced out from the Hindu community. Actually exterior meant peripheral or outer aspect of something, like an outside wall, but an integral and important part of the main house or society. The word exclusion meant exclusion from rituals not exclusion from society, as was known in the case of Shudras. Out of pail was another term to show some people outside the Hindu community. Pail means a bucket or a container. The Hindu community was neither a bucket nor a container in which you could put anything you liked and took it out whenever you liked. It is pity that such contrived terms, which affect hundreds of millions of lives, are still used to construct the edifice of social justice. They have no equivalent in religion, even local languages.

Avarna—Not the Fifth

When Panchama did not work, some people brought in *Avarna* to convert it into a fifth category outside the society. 'A' meant 'without' and Avarna meant without a Varna. Avarna in Sanskrit applied to *people* who did not believe in Varna classification or were atheists like charvakyas or followed faiths such as Jainism. Avarna is a negative phrase which indicated the absence of Varna and not a positive assertion of a fifth. On the other hand, the foreign writers interpreted that 'Avarna denoted those sections of people in Hindu fold who did not belong to the four major castes'.[295] They may or may not have belonged to four 'castes', but having rejected fourfold Varna classification it would be amazing height of imagination to say that they would invent a fifth Varna or its foreign version 'fifth caste' for themselves. This was a diabolical colonial construct, which was not as innocent as it looked.

The incorrigibles, however, persisted. They tried to convert an outright denial of a fifth category in the Manusmriti into the presence of a fifth by asking, "Why the Laws of Manu should have excluded the possibility" of a fifth category "unless it was already a matter of contention at the time it was written"?[296] If I say I have two rupees, could it mean that because I thought it necessary to clarify I must have actually three? The very manner

---

[294] 1931 Census Report: Page 471—Appendix 2
[295] http://en.wikipedia.org/wiki/Avarna: extracted on 5 August 20011
[296] Charsley, 1996: 4-5

of constructing a fifth caste was enough to reject it outright. Proverbially, this was the last straw to add a fifth into the fourfold division of humanity. It failed in the face of a positive statement by Manu. Finally, when all experiments failed, Risley took refuge in the racial theory and embarked upon a fifth category in 1901 census. He called this category *untouchable*, but this time he overtly extracted a fifth from the existing four of the Shudras. He was aware that even the lowest sections were parts of Shudras. Therefore, to differentiate between them, he gave them a racial cover.

Shudra, Untouchable, Dalit

The 1901 census was a watershed in the history of India. New terms were coined and old ones deliberately misinterpreted. Charsley describes four kinds of Shudras in 1901. First, there were "*Satsudras* who were a special high status sect"; second, those from whom Brahmins took water; third, those from whom Brahmins would not take water; and lastly, the prototype of the untouchables, which Ethovan had described as *Aspriscya Shudras*, one whose touch was so 'impure as to pollute the Ganga water'.[297] Ganges water was held to be the most pure and sacred, and therefore, there was nothing more polluting than what could desecrate even Ganges water. A similar classification of Shudras based on degree of 'intake of water and food' was used by the census commissioner of the 1931 census to identify depressed classes.[298] The first three categories, like in the previous classification, were not untouchable. They were the same or similar to Ghurye's classification of Shudras quoted by M.N. Srinivas.[299] In the latter, the three categories were as follows: *first*, castes at whose hands the twice-born could take pacca food; *second*, castes at whose hands twice-born could not accept any food but could take water; *third*, castes at whose hands even water could not be taken; *last*, whose touch defiled not only twice-born but any orthodox Hindu— the untouchables. The similarity between the three was obvious, but the application was different. While Charsley, Hutton and Ghurye applied the classification to identify Shudras that were depressed classes, the Mandal

---

[297] Charsley: 3
[298] Galanter, 1984: Chapter on Scheduled Castes. Also quoted by M.N. Srinivas
[299] Mandal Commission's Report: 19: 4.9 quoting M.N. Srinivas. 1954:*caste in Modern India* Asia Publishing House, Bombay

Commission applied it to socially and educationally backward classes or backward class of citizens, which were different from Scheduled Castes.

The term "Dalit" was coined in 1940s to describe the Scheduled Castes. Kanshi Ram used it to carve out a political category of Bahujan Samaj in the 1980s. Now Muslims and Christians have started using the term without explaining its applicability to their communities and their religion. Who can say politics is not irreligious! In Chapter 10 of '*Demoralization and Hope*' the author explains the genesis of three terms: *Shudras-Untouchables-Dalits*: "These three terms are usually used interchangeably. Basically they refer to a common phenomenon . . . Historically they refer to three phases in the history of those who have been classified as the lowest castes of India. While the Shudras period was marked by the imposition of Veda's doctrine and at least considering Shudras as lower in the ladder of Hindu caste structure, the untouchability resulted in creating the total outcasts . . . All forms of contact were forbidden by the use of rules of untouchability."[300] Dalits, the author says, is the recent name for the same. As there was no fifth category in the 'Law of Caste' in the *Hindu Law*, the courts continued to regard the lowest castes as Shudra during the British regime.[301] The important thing was that Shudras, untouchables, and Dalits were three names of the same people at different times and not of different people at any time. Somebody explained on the Internet, "Shudra is a Hindu term. Untouchable is a term coined by the British. While all untouchables are Shudras all Shudras are not untouchables."[302]

Origin of Untouchability and Untouchable (Hindi Achhyut)

Ambedkar had differentiated impurity, by coining a word 'untouchableness', from untouchability. The former was present in many parts of the world, including India. This disappeared with the removal of causes like menstrual periods, child births, or dealing with or touching dead bodies. When Risley invented untouchability, he called the category untouchables. He gave this category a separate racial identity, but finding it impossible to apply, the British courts continued to treat all those

---

[300] 25 March 2004: http://www.ahrchk.net/pub/mainfile.php/demo_and_hope/100/. Article from '*Demoralization and Hope*' by W.P.J. Basil Fernando, a real human rights activist from Sri Lanka; downloaded March 2012

[301] Gupte, 1981: *Hindu Law*: 55-56

[302] http://wiki.answers.com/Q/Are_shudras_untouchables

who could not be called 'twice-born' as Shudra and that included the depressed classes.[303] In 1996 in his article titled *'Untouchable—What is in a Name'* Simon Charsley, Senior Sociologist from the University of Glasgow, discusses the way in which the concept of untouchability was conceived in the twentieth century and created a 'new category of people, the Untouchables'. Till 1909, the term untouchability had not come into use. After that, the Maharaja of Baroda used the term untouchableness as an adjective. In 2010, it was converted into untouchability. Ambedkar differentiated between the two terms much later.

Sir Herbert Risley suggested the words 'untouchable' and 'untouchability' for the first time, when he was the census commissioner of Bengal in 1891, but there were no takers among his staff. In 1901, when he became the census commissioner of India for the 1901 census he tried to revive his pet project, but, again, faced stiff resistance from his census superintendents. The *Achhyut* or the untouchables in the form of fourth division of Shudras, especially, the *Asprishya Shudra* whose even touch was defiling and who could pollute the holiest, the Ganga water, were already present, but as individuals.

Therefore, when Risley found that no uniform classification on the 'status of castes' was possible, and most of his staff had already declined his suggestion of creating a fifth category of Shudra, he shifted towards applying a racial theory to distinguish 'tracts' with different racial configuration. He declared North West of India comprising Punjab, Kashmir and Rajasthan as Indo Aryan tract, but could find no other tract. In Rajasthan, at that time, there were two census superintendents by the name of Bramley and Bannerman, who decided to put the 'English term untouchable' for the first time in the print. However, even they differed in detail. Out of the twelve groups which Bramley branded, he named the eleventh group as 'untouchable castes'. These comprised 'Dhobis, Khanks, Mochis, Dholis and others'. His Group XII, which was still lower, included 'Balais, Chamars, Regars, Kolis and others'. They were the lowest because they ate 'beef and vermin' and were 'filthy'. It was their behavior and habits which made them impure and polluted or untouchable. On the other hand, Bannerman created seven groups of which the last corresponded to the twelfth category of Bramley. He applied the label 'untouchable' only to this last group.[304] Despite no conformity between the two groups, no support from Punjab

---

[303]   Gupte, 1981: *Hindu Law*: 57
[304]   Charsley, 1996: 2

and Kashmir and admitting that no such categorization was possible in rest of the country, Risley officially adopted the term untouchable and applied it to the whole country. That a crucial term like untouchable could get away unchallenged for more than 100 years and got embedded in the psyche of people enough to change the course of social history of India was amazing.

Charsley wrote, "From this unpropitious start representing as it did more of a rebuff than a successful initiative a key term in modern India was launched." [305] Free India recognized untouchability after 1947 in abolishing it. To which race the Asprishya Shudra belonged and to which Bremley's ten extra groups and Bennerman's rest of the six groups was never revealed. It is also not clear whether they ultimately found a place among the depressed classes or not. Risley never viewed depressed classes in terms of abject poverty and total lack of education. He used permutations and combinations, including beef eating, to create eleven caste groups in Madras, which had no relevance to other parts of the country, not even to most parts of South India. Francis (1902) found arbitrariness and lack of any rule in creating another classification, but Risley still labeled the first four of eight categories not twice-born as 'Shudra'. The next three had no label but were taken as an excluded fifth, depending upon whether they ate beef and whether they polluted even without touching. A final category consisted of those who were refused service by Brahmins, because they denied the 'sacerdotal authority of Brahmins and did not want their service'.[306] The whole exercise was mendacious. Charsley sarcastically wrote that howsoever variable was the relevance of the 1901 classification across the different regions of India 'it was *finally sponsored by the official census takers*' (emphasis added). In the end, when the British could not reach agreement on whether to use the Varna scheme 'in four or four plus-one-form' they gave up the effort to place castes under the four Varnas.[307] There was no four plus one form of Varnas in the Hindu social structure.

The fifth category of Francis was 'Lingyat's tradition', an anti-Brahmin reform movement in present Karnataka, earlier a part of Madras Presidency. About Lingyats, Risley wrote in *People of India* in 1915, "In a petition presented to Government of India the members of Lingyat community protested against most offensive and mischievous order that all should be

---

[305] Ibid.: 2, 3
[306] Francis, 1902: *Census of India 1902*: 15, Madras Govt. Press: also quoted by Charsley, 1996: 4-5
[307] Ibid.

entered in the census papers as belonging to one caste, and added that they be recorded as 'virshaiv Brahmins, Kshatriyas, Vaishyas or Shudras as case may be'."[308] According to *Hindu Law* in 1981, "the Lingyats claim to be free from caste distinction" but "in a Madras case the Lingyats of Madras were apparently not regarded as Shudras". And "the Bombay High Court has held that the Lingyats of Bombay Presidency are Shudras and not Vaishyas".[309] After the independence, Lingyats were included among Other Backward Classes. In 1980, the Mandal Commission included Lingyats among OBCs, whom it called Shudras. In 1992, the Supreme Court approved this and the Lingyats accepted. In the 2001 census, Lingyats claimed separate status as now they alleged they were Avarna. Sociologists believe that although Lingyats were relatively less educated, they were powerful landholders with considerable political clout, but kept a low profile to claim reservations.

Lingyats were not alone in this stratagem. There are hundreds of similar landlord groups like Yadavs, Jats, Gujjars, and others among the OBCs, who have ample political clout and yet claim to be backward and discriminated in the specific sense of Shudra. The diversity between and within the lowest castes is seen not only in terms of earnings but also in education and occupations. The obligatory nature of traditional occupations and backwardness of Jatis 'as a whole' are myths or political gimmicks. Identification of socially and educationally backward classes on the basis of comparison of social, educational, and economic parameters with State averages, even if they were determined by the Mandal Commission, of which there is considerable doubt, could not identify Shudras whose every moment 'was negatively influenced by his low caste status'.[310]

In a recent article: *Is There Still Untouchability in India?* Robert Deliège states that in a 'famous study' Moffat pointed out that a new generation of scholars led by Westerners, who were psychologically sympathetic to untouchables, were anxious to show that their study had contributed something new to emphasize the distance between the latter and the rest of society. They tried even to set up what Moffat called 'models of separation', showing the existence of great distance between the untouchables and the rest of society and the persistence of discrimination. These studies were dominated by 'structuralist considerations' (method of sociological analysis based on notions of human society), but did not always match the

---

[308]   Risley, 1915: Reprint 1969: 78-79
[309]   Gupte, 1981: *Hindu Law*: 57
[310]   Mandal Commission's Report: Chapter IV

modern anthropological research on social change in India and the way
untouchability was disappearing. Finally, Deliege concludes that social
realities were no longer what they were. Indian untouchables have come
a long way and have made remarkable progress since independence. In a
significant remark, he dismisses the usual perceptions:

> The vast majority of them (untouchable) may still be poor; but
> poverty is an economic, not a caste, condition. The problem of
> poverty in India cannot be reduced to caste and one finds poor
> people basically in all caste groups; according to the various
> estimates, between 30 and 60 percent of the Indian population
> live under the so-called "poverty line," whereas Untouchables are
> only 15 percent . . . Finally they form less than ever a homogeneous
> social category owing to the state's protective measures, but also
> to their own dynamism and courage, many among them have
> climbed the social ladder . . .[311]

Deliege further points out that in contemporary India, relative purity
no longer lies at the basis of caste struggles. Castes now fight to compete
for 'limited economic and political resources'.[312] His prediction that the
'untouchable' would become a major force is already true not only in States'
politics but also as king makers at an all-India level. Other Backward Classes
are even more vocal and influential. Untouchables were never a single
category and there was always an inherent diversity in untouchability and
the untouchables. Other Backward Classes are even more diverse externally
and internally, and yet thousands of castes struggle to be treated as one
category.

When Dumont recognized incongruity in his theory of *Homo
Hierarchicus* he abruptly ended his review on diversity and complexity of
inter-caste ranking and admitted that 'pollution and separation were variable
features'. He wrote, "We have taken it (i.e. untouchability) absolutely, while
it was commonplace to observe its looseness even between the Brahmin at
the top and the Untouchable at the bottom."[313] Dumont admitted in a way

---

[311]   Robert Deliège, *Is There Still Untouchability in India?,* http://archiv.ub.uni-heidelberg.
         de/volltextserver/4010/, 14 January 2013

[312]   Ibid.

[313]   Dumont, 1980: Homo Hierarchicus: the caste system and its implications. Chicago,
         University of Chicago Press

that not only the unsegregated castes like Other Backward Classes but even the majority of Scheduled Castes might not be excluded or polluted castes. He might even have veered round to the presence of untouchableness, which Ambedkar coined to show pollution as a temporary feature. Whether Risley imparted permanence to untouchability or someone else, is difficult to say, but he did transform purity and pollution into untouchability, which was more deceptive than real. Untouchables were not a single uniform category, and untouchability did not have one particular level or extent. It varied not only in different areas but also in its severity. O'Malley, another census commissioner, had recorded in 1932 that untouchability was a name of recent origin; the word 'outcaste' was a misnomer, and even an untouchable could be 'out casted' for accepting food from some others.[314]

While enacting Articles 341 and 342, Ambedkar and members of the Constituent Assembly recognized the variations not only between Scheduled Castes and Scheduled Tribes, but also within each of them, when they recommended reservations for castes and tribes, but could be limited also to their groups and parts thereof. The same was for exclusion. Strangely, the affected parts and groups were never defined and isolated among 150 million Scheduled Castes and those not affected or improved later removed. The same happened for 75 million Scheduled Tribes. Diversity was visible even in 1931 census, when relatively few *depressed classes* could pass the tests of 'purity and pollution' and the State shifted to restriction in the use of wells, segregation in schools, and curbs on temple entry as alternate criteria. When these did not succeed to get a sizeable number, subjective tests were devised to determine whether a person with similar qualifications would be treated equally or not and whether he/she suffered from 'odium' of higher castes. When even this did not work enough, other criteria like residence, etc. were used, and when nothing was left, according to Lelah Duskin, the criterion of 'nearness to the government' adopted.[315] Untouchability was given an illusion of permanence in the twentieth century, though in most instances it might have been as transitory as the composition of the people it was imposed upon. Even the Supreme Court differentiated between scavengers and other Scheduled Castes who were only depressed. The result of all this was that the really affected could rarely get a chance to improve. Despite the fig leaf of creamy layer, the problem among the Other Backward Classes is even more acute.

---

[314]   O'Malley, Reprint 1932: 137-140
[315]   Lelah Dushkin: quoted by Galanter, 1984: 128-130

In a highly critical note, Farida Majid, a writer of independent views, says that except for 'the word shudra' all the words used to describe the lower castes are 'new-fangled, colonial and Gandhian'. Whoever heard of Scheduled Castes or Dalits in the nineteenth century? A Gandhian innovation, Harijan might have made the lowly people proud at being God's own creatures, but did that improve their condition? She quotes Bankimchandra Chattopadhyaya, who, although blamed Varnas for the ills of the Hindu society, had also stated that "the word acchyut or untouchable was an adjective, not a common noun designating a class of human beings".[316] *Achhyut*, however reprehensible the word may be, characterized an individual, not a caste or class. It was Risley who changed an adjective into a common noun in an effort to create more or less a separate class at all India level. Social justice is an abstract idea which must modify with the passage of time. Society has not remained stationary for centuries, not even since independence.

Arguments in the Mandal Case

The majority judgment recorded two opposing sets of arguments in 1992. The petitioners argued that the basic features of the Constitution were a secular unified and casteless society; caste was a prohibited ground of distinction; economic criterion was important and should be applied in identification; as castes did not exist in other communities, they could not be applied to them; and 'caste would perpetuate and accentuate caste difference and generate antagonism and antipathy between different castes'.[317]

In the second set of opinion, the respondents countered: Poverty was *not* a necessary criterion of backwardness—it was in fact irrelevant; reservation was a 'programme of *historical compensation*;' it was neither a measure of economic reform nor poverty alleviation programme; a review of the Government position was possible only if it is a fraud on the Constitution. Another counsel reasoned that in Article 16(4) the class of intended beneficiaries was different from that in Article 15(4); social and educational backwardness in Article 15(4) was only partly true in the case of backward class of citizens; another stated, Article 16(4) was enacted

---

[316] Farida Majid, 2005: Bankim and Gandhi on Caste, http://groups.yahoo.com/group/akandabaratam/message/52854
[317] *A.I.R.* Supreme Court 1993: 542-543: 61, 62

for empowerment of those groups and classes which had been kept out of administration and because Scheduled Castes and Scheduled Tribes were the *intended beneficiaries* under Article 16(4) there was no reason why caste could not be the exclusive criterion for determining beneficiaries; (*comment*: this was highly contestable); another respondent stated that the Constitution gives reservations to backward classes, not backward citizens. He further added, 'The homogeneous groups based on religion, race, caste, place of birth etc. can form a class of citizens and if that class is backward there can be reservation in favor of that class of citizens;'[318] another respondent advocated national consensus. One respondent blamed untouchability and inapproachability, and still another stated that determination of backwardness and representation in services was in the domain of the State. To some counsels, Article 16(4) was conceived only for those 'middle castes' which were categorized as Shudras in the caste system and none else.[319] The majority views of the Court, in general, agreed with the respondents.

Middle/Intermediate Classes—Perceptual Aspect:

When a fifth category of Panchama became controversial, some people took refuge in the term Middle or Intermediate Classes to create a threefold division of Hindu society and ignored the fact that the British courts had treated everyone who could not be called twice-born as Shudra, and there was nothing below than that. In the mid-nineteenth century with the arrival of European theory of different races in India, the Aryans were restricted to Brahmins, Kshatriyas, and Vaishyas upper castes, the Dravidians to the middle classes or middle castes; and the Aborigines, the alleged primitive original Indians, to the lowest castes and given bizarre names like Panchama, outcastes, untouchables, and others. This was the first indications of a threefold division of Indians on racial basis in which Shudras were upgraded to middle classes. It had nothing to do with the classical division of Hindu society into four Varnas and numerous Jatis. Judicially this position was accepted only in 1992. As the racial division of Indian society has been refuted on genetic grounds, this racial division becomes unsustainable.

A three class model in the early 1960s was also the brainchild of the historian B. B. Misra. It caused considerable confusion when he provided a

---

[318] Ibid.: 543-554: 63-66
[319] Ibid.: 543: 63

'comprehensive list of categories (castes or occupations)' which he thought constituted middle classes and included among them whom he called 'peasant proprietors.' When asked to define them, he stated, "The term middle class is much used and since most of us, without the aid of specialist, understand what we mean when we use it in our every day conversation I am not attempting a meticulous definition." These middle classes had nothing to do with the Marx's classification.

Quoting the above from Misra's book, *The Indian Middle Classes*, published in 1961, Prof. Kenneth Balhatchet of the London University commented:

> "This exhaustive, not to say exhausting, book was published under the highest political, if not intellectual, auspices—those of the Royal Institute of International Affairs. Only a few decades after 1947 it was reassuring to British politicians that independent India was not so independent as to reject the three-class model of England. But could one identify three classes in a society with thousands of castes?" He then gave a devastating reply, 'Misra was not the only historian to be confused.'[320]

Dumont, too, created a threefold division of Hindu society in which it called the middle classes as interstitial classes and described them as all those between the highest, the pure, and the lowest, the impure or untouchable. Interstices mean empty spaces or gaps in the tissues or matter. Interstitial means something 'situated within those spaces or interstices of matter or organs, but not restricted to any characteristic of the organ or having any definite character of its own.' It is difficult to know the context in which Dumont used the word interstitial, but to rationalize in moral terms, if the pure and the wise, the highest, are put at the one end and the impure or the vile, understood as ignorant and evil, on the other, the huge space between them, the interstitial space, would be filled by people with innumerable combinations of good and evil, the nondescript interstitial classes or individuals, which are neither absolutely good nor absolutely bad. In fact, Dumont admitted later that there was not much of a gap even between the pure and the impure, represented by the Brahman and the Shudra, which people took it for. In an indirect way, he admitted that a

---

[320]   Kenneth Ballhatchet, 1996: The Language of Historians and the Morphology of History. In *The Concept of Race in South India*: 86-87. Ed. Peter Robb

Brahmin by birth could be Shudra by attributes and a Shudra by birth could be a Brahmin by attributes. Ambedkar, too, quotes a famous verse from Satyakama Jabali to prove that the 'Varna of a man was determined by his *guna* (mental and moral qualities)' and not birth.[321] He quotes sage Prasara:

> "That Brahmana, who for the sake of dakshina (gift of money or fee) offers oblation (religious offering) into fire on behalf of a Shudra, would become a Shudra, while the Shudra (for whom he offers oblation) would become a Brahman" because the merit of the rite "goes to the Shudra and the Brahmin incurs sin" because his motive is 'material gain'.[322]

It was the motive behind the oblation that made one a Brahman or Shudra, not his birth or caste. A few years ago an official paper published by the Library of the Congress of the United States (quoted earlier in respect of untouchables) recorded that "the Orthodox Hindus regarded the hilly tribes of India as untouchables, not because they were primitive or pagan but because they were eaters of beef, village pigs, and chickens. They do not seem to realize that their status was decided purely on behavioral basis or their traits." Actually, hilly tribes were hardly, if ever, called untouchable.

Similarly, *Apastambha Sutras* records that a low-class man by leading a virtuous life could rise to the level of a higher class man and should be ranked as such. In a like manner, a high-class man could sink down to the levels of a class lower by leading a sinful life and should be considered as such. The class or Varna of an individual depended upon one's qualifications, character, and knowledge, not birth. Sage Javal of an unknown class became a Brahman (Chhandogya Upanishad); Vishwamitra, a Kshatriya by birth, became a Brahman (Mahabharata); sage Matang, an outcaste by birth, became a Brahman. Vashishta was born of a prostitute, Vyasa of a fisherwoman, and Parasra of a Chandala woman, and yet all of them had the qualities of the highest Brahman. Their birth or Jati did not matter. Introduction of a fifth Varna to create three classes among the Hindus was a political ploy or a tool of the British to separate a large chunk of the poor and the uneducated for conversions. The irony is that while the British did not use the fifth Varna in their official and judicial documents, some respondents used the same term for getting reservations in the *Indra Sawhney case.*

---

[321] Ambedkar: Vol. 7 of his works: 174
[322] Ibid.

Caste—Occupation Nexus—Traditional Occupations

There were no permanent occupations as discussed in the earlier chapters. Ghurye stated that as caste professions in the past met the needs of most and provided some of the finest handicraft, many traditional professions continued to flourish in the villages. Cultivation, administration, and service in combat forces were always open to all castes. Martial races were a colonial innovation. Even the so-called Untouchables were weavers and others.[323] Some were even moneylenders. Colebrook observed in 1793, "Every profession with a few exceptions is open to every description of person; and the discouragement arising from religious prejudices is not greater than what exists in Great Britain from municipal and corporation laws." And Irwing stated, 'If we except the priesthood, caste has not necessarily any effect on the line of life in which a man embarks.'[324] O'Malley, census commissioner in 1932, denounced the common impression that every caste had a traditional occupation which its members invariably followed. It was a normal thing, he says, for one son at least in a family to succeed to his father's craft, provided it was sufficient for a living and he was not educated enough for a higher calling. This gave the boy 'an inalienable right to follow a particular calling and . . . an inherent skill exercised generally with the simplest of tools'.[325] Karanth in 1996 found it impossible to deduce a person's caste from his occupation because a 'carpenter was no longer from a carpenter caste nor was the blacksmith from a blacksmith caste.'[326] So there are other examples.

Distinction between the Shudras and the Vaishyas disappeared early. One of the Buddhist scriptures records, "Even Kshatriyas, Brahmans and Vaishyas will rise earlier and go to bed later than their Sudra master who has amassed wealth, grain, silver and gold. They will work at any occupation ordered by their Sudra master, become amiable toward him and flatter him."[327] In this sense Shudras were better off than people of other Varnas. It was wealth and political power that created occupations, not caste. The situation was no different during the colonial regime. The State included only those castes or Jatis in census reports during the British regime which were

---

[323]   Ghurye, 1961: 241-280
[324]   Colebrook and Irwin: as quoted by Desika Char, 1993: 27
[325]   O'Malley, 1932: 122-123
[326]   Khanna, 1962: 55-56
[327]   Yamazaki, 1997

important from view of numbers or of most importance in the provinces. Waterfield cautioned that "it must not be supposed that even a majority of any particular caste now follows the occupation according to which they are arranged". Therefore, he said, 'occupational differentiation' did not provide the 'key to caste distinction'. In fact, this 'most usable measure' of caste—occupation nexus 'flew in the face of recognition that caste titles rarely indicated true occupation'.[328] Daily observation showed even Brahmins were engaged in the menial profession of Shudras. A few years ago, the magazine *Outlook* found Brahmins in the national capital, Delhi, working as sweepers in Sulabhs (latrines). Middleton was a census superintendent in the 1920s. He admitted in a biting criticism of the colonial government:

> I had intended pointing out that there is a very wide revolt against classification of occupational castes; that these castes have been largely manufactured and almost entirely preserved as separate by the British Government. Our land records and official documents have added iron bonds to the old rigidity of caste . . . we pigeon-holed every one by caste and if we could not find a true caste for them, labeled them with the name of a hereditary occupation. We deplore the caste system and its effects on social and economic problems, but we are largely responsible for the system which we deplore . . . If the government would ignore caste it would gradually be replaced by something very different among the lower castes.[329]

The appalling machinations of the colonial rulers in construction of caste—occupation nexus could not have been better brought to light. As caste and occupation nexus did not exist, backward classes could not be backward because of 'generations' and 'centuries' of nexus between the two. This most usable tool to seek 'historical compensation' was based on fragile grounds. Sir Denzel Ibbetson was a highly regarded anthropologist administrator. He found that in Punjab and North-West Frontier the term 'Rajput' was not a matter of blood or a fixed 'ethnological fact'. It was a matter of 'fluid representation of *status*' which was often claimed by 'men in power'. Caste indicated 'distinction of occupation and political resources' between those who ruled and those who were ruled, and not the

---

[328]   Quoted by Dirks, 2001: 204-205

[329]   Middleton, 1921: as quoted by Ghurye, 2008: 43: *Caste in History*. Ed. Banerjee-Dube

'higher and lower types and races'. He thought 'rank, purity and hierarchy' were marginal features and caste prone to 'continual subtle change'. As caste varied from locality to locality, he rejected the notion that caste was 'static . . . with its tyrannical rigidity'.[330] Ibbetson found flexibility of function in people with caste names like 'Rajputs, Jats, Meos, Gujar and Thakur' and wrote 'a Machhi is a Machhi so long as he catches fish and, a Jat directly he lays hold of a plough.'[331] Rigidity was attributed or imparted not only to castes in the twentieth century, but also to unrelated Varnas. It adversely affected the judicial decisions.

Shail Mayaram, writing in 2008 specifically about Meos, a backward community in Rajasthan, says in general context, 'Castes in pre-colonial period were highly mobile, especially those belonging to middle sections of social hierarchy.' Depending upon the context, Meos were Sudra for 'Patwari and Qanungo' in the eighteenth century, but were 'Kshatriya' for others 'including the Brahmins'. She quotes Bhatnagar, Dube and Dube to distinguish between Rajputization and Sanskritization and says the former signifies a 'highly mobile social process', which enabled one to claim 'military-political power' and the 'right to cultivate land as well as to rule'. 'Legitimization and self-invention' of such ideologies was 'unparalleled in traditional Indian' and could be claimed by "all castes all over India from peasants and lower caste Sudras to warriors and tribal chiefs and even the local raja who had recently converted to Islam".[332] Giving reference of Peabody, Shail Mayaram brings out that 'rebellion' (by low castes) was not only common but was a 'defining feature of Hindu polity'. There was ambivalence and fluidity implicit in the categories of Kshatriya and Sudra in the pre-colonial period. Many groups identified as Shudra manufactured the Kshatriyas status and claimed the right to rule while the earlier Kshatriyas were often reduced to Shudra.[333]

Quoting from *A Glossary of Punjab Tribes and Castes*, historian Ram Swarup brings out that during the Muslim period many Rajputs were degraded to the Scheduled Castes and Scheduled Tribes status, but continued to retain the Rajput *gotra* of parihara and parimara. According to G. W. Briggs, 'Many chamars, though included among the lowest castes, still carry the names and *gotra* of Rajput clans like Banaudhiya, Ujjaini, Chandhariya,

---

[330]   Susan Bayly, 2008: 205
[331]   Ibid.: 207
[332]   Shail Mayaram, 2008: 109-111: *Caste in History*: 52-55. Ed. Banerjee-Dube
[333]   Mayaram, 2008: 128: *The Shudra Right to Rule: Caste in History*. Ed. Banerjee-Dube

Sarwariya, Kanaujiya, Chauhan, Chadel, Saksena, Sakarwar, Bhardarauiya, and Bundela.' Dr K. S. Lal also cites similar instances in his recent work *Growth of Scheduled Tribes and Castes in Medieval India*. Then, could all Rajputs be called forward and all chamars backward and discriminated for centuries? Ambedkar also found common *gotras* between Marathas and Mahars. At the same time, the Constitution provides reservations for existing discrimination and its effect on the present generation, not for the supposition that one's alleged ancestors and their subsequent generations might have badly treated someone else's alleged ancestors and their subsequent generations continuously for thousands of years, of which, in any case, no one has cited any verifiable proof, genetic or otherwise.

The whole idea of caste—occupation nexus was a conniving twist to what Harold Gould said in connection with pre-industrial societies in Europe. He described ascription-related backwardness where *occupation and individual* was one. In India, some brainy chap converted it into *caste and occupation* was one. The other type of backwardness, which Gould described as 'achievement related backwardness', depended upon education, merit, etc. and was an attribute of modern societies. In today's India, even the original ascription-oriented backwardness between individual and occupation is not relevant. In fact, no individuals or all members of a caste, even a family, are condemned to follow one occupation, traditional or other. The evidence shows they never were.

Purity and Pollution and Untouchableness and Untouchability

There is increasing realization among the modern historians and sociologists that purity and pollution and social acceptability, including untouchability, depend more on activities, morals, and behavior than physical activity. Peter Robb from University of London states that though one may think that 'racial elements' like 'otherness' were unequivocally present in untouchability as 'matters of body', in reality, they might be 'concerned more fundamentally with conduct, than with the physical characteristics'.[334] Many European theories, too, give pre-eminence to moral difference than the physical ones. Behavior and traits are more important to regard someone impure and polluted than one's physical appearances. For

---

[334] Peter Robb, 1995: The Concept of Race in South Asia: 9, 10

example, 'the idea of Jati does not seem racial when it evokes the oneness of creation'.[335] The concept of purity and pollution was not confined to Hindus. Purity is at the heart of Shinto's understanding of good and evil. Impurity in Shinto refers to anything which separates us from *kami* and from *musubi* the creative and harmonizing powers. A recent book describes:

> *Purity impurity*: Shaucha-ashaucha as: purity and its opposite, pollution, are a fundamental part of Hindu culture. While they imply a strong sense of physical cleanliness, their more important meanings extend to social, ceremonial, mental, emotional, psychic and *spiritual* contamination. Freedom from all forms of contamination is a key to Hindu spirituality, and is one of the yamas. *Physical purity* requires a clean and well ordered environment, yogic purging of the internal organs and frequent cleansing with water. *Mental purity* derives from *meditation,* right living and right thinking. *Emotional purity* depends on control of the mind, clearing the subconscious and keeping good company. *Spiritual purity* is achieved through following the yamas and *niyamas*, study of the Vedas and other scriptures, pilgrimage, meditation, japa, tapas and ahimsa. *Ritual purity* requires the observance of certain prayashchittas, or penances for defilement derived from foreign travel, contact with base people or places, conversion to other faiths, contact with bodily wastes, attending a funeral, etc.[336]

Unless we go back to the basics of the old religion, remove the alien interpretations of last many centuries, and correct our notions despite aberrations having sunk in the society, the incongruities that have crept in the social structure cannot be corrected, There have been studies to analyze whether people like 'Mlecchas' Abihars, Shudra, 'Raksasa', and many more like them who took part on both sides in the Mahabharata war were Aryans or from other races. At the end, the author acknowledges that although distinctiveness of various groups of 'outsiders' may 'loosely' be termed tribal groups or foreigners, 'in general the divergence was in culture and language.' And that "these distinctions were recognized not as much as means of

---

[335]   Ibid.
[336]   Reproduced from Internet. Purity impurity: Hindu—Hinduism Dictionary on Purity impurity

excluding such groups but rather as a preliminary to their absorption within the Aryan political and cultural framework".[337] There were even marriages with these groups. They were not outcastes as interpreted by the colonial rulers and accepted by the Indian intelligentsia captivated by the blessings of the British Raj. Now even the racial theory is rejected.

Conclusion

Thus, there is enough evidence to challenge the assumptions that four Varnas were watertight compartments and society was divisible into four rigid compartments in which Jatis were sub-castes of Varnas. In fact, there was enough mobility both upward and downward and those who were rich and powerful once became poor and backward at other times and the vice versa. Panchama was constructed from Shudras and just four nondescript tribes to give a new twist to the Hindu social structure. When a fifth Varna failed to impress, Risley invented a separate class of untouchables or *Acchyuts* in 1901 on racial basis despite ten years of resistance from his staff and failure to give them different racial identity. *Acchyuts* or untouchables were persons, not castes. Physical segregation was confined to scavengers involved in lifting human night soil. In the 1931 census, the population of untouchables was increased for political reasons, by relaxing the strict criteria created to find untouchability. There were traditional occupations, but no one was obliged to follow them generation after generation and century after century. In fact, due to migration and mobility it is difficult to follow even half a dozen past generations of any particular people, even in the rural areas. Caste—occupation nexus was a myth. There were no *middle castes* on the ground; there were only economic middle classes. When these notions spilled over to the post-independence era, they were made to masquerade as *essences* of the Hindu social structure. They affected even the judicial process. Therefore, the whole scheme of social justice needs a re-look.

[337]   John Brockington, 1995: 108 Concept of Race in Mahabharta and Ramayana in *The Concept of Race in South Asia*: Ed. Peter Rob

CHAPTER 7

THE MANDAL CASE JUDGMENT
CASE FOR REVIEW

The Second Backward Classes Commission was appointed in 1978 to *define* socially and educationally backward classes of citizens, to recommend steps for their advancement, and to make provision for reservations for any backward class of citizens, which was inadequately represented in the services under the State.[338] The Constitution describes Other Backward Classes in Article 15(4) as any socially and educationally backward classes and in Article 16(4) as any backward class of citizens. The issue was whether the two different expressions in the two articles pertained to the same or different people. The Mandal Commission explained the reason for different nomenclatures in both the articles by quoting Pandit Nehru, who clarified before the Select Committee that "this departure was made to bring the language of Article 15(4) in line with that of Article 340 which provides that a Backward Classes Commission may be set up for uplift of socially and educationally backward classes".[339] Therefore, despite their different nomenclature, Articles 15(4) and 16(4), according to Nehru as well as the commission, applied to the same people, whether you called them socially and educationally backward classes or backward class of citizens.

Nehru echoed the sentiments of the entire Constituent Assembly, when he stated, "We want to put an end to . . . all those infinite divisions that have grown up in our social life . . . we may call them by any name you like, the caste system or religious division etc . . ."[340] According to the commission, when Ambedkar stated in the Constituent Assembly that classes were nothing 'but a collection of castes', he meant that castes and classes were the

---

[338] *A.I.R.* Supreme Court 1993: 507: 12
[339] Mandal Commission's Report: 29: 7.6
[340] Ibid.: Chapter IV

same or identical. However, it failed to state that Ambedkar also qualified that classes were 'open' and castes 'closed' and therefore opposite to each other or antonyms. It also forgot that throughout his life Ambedkar had fought for annihilation of caste, not its perpetuation. Therefore, it cannot be presumed that Ambedkar wanted to promote a caste-ridden society by equating the constitutional expression classes with castes.

Middle Classes and Shudras

In 1930, when the Starte Committee divided *Backward Classes* into 'Depressed Classes, Aboriginal and Hilly Tribes and Backward Classes (including wandering tribes)', it used the term Backward Classes in two places. The first category called *Backward Classes* included all the three categories; the second category referred to as Backward Classes now comprised of Backward Hindus, who had appeared in the beginning of the twentieth century apart from depressed classes. To clarify it, the Committee renamed the second group as *Other Backward Classes* and *Intermediate Classes*, but did not explain intermediate *between* which backward classes. The Committee did not include the forward castes in this classification.

Seeing the ambiguity, Marc Galanter pointed out in 1984 that the term 'Backward Classes' never acquired a definite meaning at all-India level, nor any attempt was made to define the term or employ it on the national level. Its double usage continued in the wider sense to mean all the three groups and in the restricted sense 'as equivalent to Other Backward Classes'.[341] In 1992, the majority judgment, too, quoted Marc Galanter on the threefold division of *backward classes*, but called the Starte Committee simply as committee. According to the judgment, the committee divided *Backward Classes* into 'Depressed Classes, Aboriginal and Hilly Tribes and Other Backward Classes (including wandering tribes)' to avoid 'overlap in the expression Depressed Classes'.[342] Overlap means to partly cover, to have some common characteristics, or not be separate. It is difficult to say why the court used the words 'to *avoid* overlap'. Whether it was to clarify that the three types of backward classes were separate in the nature of their backwardness, or whether it was to refute the judgment of the Allahabad High Court quoted by the Mandal Commission, in which

---

[341]   Galanter, 1984
[342]   *A.I.R.* Supreme Court 1993: 548: 74

the court depicted socially and educationally backward classes of citizens comparable to Scheduled Castes and Scheduled Tribes because of their inclusion in Article 15(4), is difficult to say.[343] The refutation was more likely, because Scheduled Castes had been given reservations since 1936 in educational institutions and services, in addition to reserved seats in the legislature. Scheduled Tribes, though identified during the colonial rule, were treated after the independence in the same manner.

In 1951, the Supreme Court denied reservations to Other Backward Classes on the basis of caste and religion. They were restored to when the Constitution was amended in the same year and Article 15(4) inserted to provide special provisions for socially and educationally backward classes. Up to 1992, the courts had treated other backward classes, socially and educationally backward classes and backward class of citizens in Article 16(4) as one category. The confusion occurred when, in order to accommodate a non-existent firth Varna of Panchama, some respondents in 1991 converted the threefold classification of *Backward Classes* into threefold classification of Hindu community. They transformed upper three Varnas into a single group of twice born castes; created a new undefined middle group under the name of Shudra; and turned Depressed Classes, who had previously gone by the name of Shudras, into outcastes and Panchama. Neither the petitioners objected to Panchama, or the State, or the court. Scheduled Tribes were left out unspecified.

After 1947 when the Central Government enacted Article 340 to 'investigate the conditions of socially and educationally backward classes' and recommend 'steps' to improve their condition, it did not mention term like Shudra, not even Scheduled Castes and Scheduled Tribes. Similarly, when Ambedkar added the word 'backward' before 'class of citizens' in the Draft Article 10(3) and its successor Article 16(4), he also did not call backward class of citizens Shudra or include Scheduled Castes and Scheduled tribes in the said Article. He and the members of the Drafting Committee would not have refrained from doing so if OBCs were indeed Shudra, especially when Ambedkar had fought all his life for their uplift. In fact, Nehru took pains to show that despite the difference in their nomenclature, socially and educationally backward classes and backward class of citizens meant the same. When the crucial threefold division of backward classes was converted into threefold division of Hindu community in which backward classes of citizen or Other Backward Classes were placed between three

---

[343] Mandal Commission's Report: Para 7.40

upper Varnas as a single group and the Scheduled Castes now described as Panchama, that the problem occurred. Panchama was not mentioned in the Hindu Law enacted by the British in 1837 or had any scriptural and legal sanction. Terms Panchama and outcastes, which appeared in the nineteenth century, were imposed on Hindu social structure, as discussed in the previous chapter.

The issues now were: What was the structure of Hindu society? What was the definition of Shudra and who were the Shudras? What was the definition of backward class of citizens in Article 16(4)? Were they the same as other backward classes, which had been coming down since colonial times and converted under Article 15(4) into socially and educationally backward classes in 1951, and under Article 340, before that? If they were different, who were they? What was the status of Scheduled Castes and Scheduled Tribes? The answers become important when on the basis of the Mandal Commission's Report the court accepted some of the worst affected among the untouchables as examples of Shudras and the court accepted. (Infra)

After accepting backward class of citizens as socially backward and Shudra, the majority judgment clarified in 1992 that 'insisting upon educational backwardness in these may not be quite appropriate'. The idea was to distinguish socially backward classes from socially and educationally backward classes. Therefore, there were three unresolved issues. *First*, who were the newly described socially backward class of citizens and how were they different from the socially and educationally backward classes in terms of their social identity? If they differed, how did they differ? *Second*, why did the parliament include Scheduled Castes and Scheduled Tribes in Article 15(4) when earlier the Constituent Assembly did not do so in Article 16(4)? Were these additions merely to extend extra benefit to these categories or for some other purpose? Or else, why were Scheduled Castes and Scheduled Tribes not initially included under Article 16(4)? Was it because they differed in their backwardness from Other Backward Classes? *Finally*, on what grounds was crucial threefold division of backward classes converted into threefold division of Hindu society, when the court itself stated that the committee divided *backward classes* into three categories, without bringing in the forward castes? Only the State can answer, or some day, perhaps, the court itself.

Since the *Balaji* case in the 1960s, despite the difference in the nomenclature, the Supreme Court had not distinguished between the backward classes under Articles 15(4) and 16(4). As in the case of Nehru, it, too, used the term backward class of citizens in the sense of socially and educationally backward classes. In 1992, the majority judgment quoted Palekar, J. who on behalf of the Constitution Bench ruled in the *Janki Prasad Parimoo* case, "However, it is now settled that the expression 'backward class of citizens' in Art. 16(4) mean the same thing as the expression 'any socially any educationally backward class of citizens in Article 15(4)'. In order to qualify for being called a 'backward class of citizen' he must be a member of a socially and educationally backward class. It is the *social and educational backwardness* of a class which is material for purposes of Articles 15(4) and 16(4)"[344] (emphasis added).

In 1992, the Supreme Court overruled the judgment of Justice Palekar:

> "In our respectful opinion, however, the said assumption had no basis. The Clause (4) of Article 16(4) does not contain the qualifying words social and educational as they do in clause (4) of Article 15. The reason is obvious: backward *class* of citizens in Article 16(4) *takes in* Scheduled Castes, Scheduled Tribes, and *all* Other Backward Classes of citizens, including the socially and educationally backward classes."[345] Later, it stated that "the Shudras, Scheduled Castes and the Scheduled Tribes and *other similar backward classes* among Muslims and Christians had practically no entry into the administrative apparatus, it was this imbalance which was sought to be redressed by providing reservations in favor of such backward classes"[346] (emphasis added). It further says, "We are accordingly, of the opinion that the backwardness contemplated by Article 16(4) is mainly social backwardness. It would not be correct to say that backwardness under Article 16(4) should be both social and educational." [347]

Its reason for giving preference to social backwardness was the weightage given to it by the Mandal Commission. The criteria of *social backwardness* used by the commission were: castes and classes whom others thought were *socially and educationally backward*; (*not* socially backward), castes and classes which depended upon manual labor; castes and classes where

---

[344]   *A.I.R.* Supreme Court 1993: 556: 85
[345]   Ibid.
[346]   *A.I.R.* Supreme Court 1993: 557: 56
[347]   Ibid

there was early marriage in regard to State marriages; and finally, castes and classes where participation of females in work was at least 25% above the State average.[348] These criteria could identify any social and educationally backwardness in any caste or community due to any reason and were not Shudra specific. The commission did not call them socially backward classes, as did the court. Despite the weightage given by the commission, comparison of percentages with State averages does not make Shudras. Therefore, the Shudra identity of backward class of citizens in caste terms remained obscure.

This was also departure from the Starte Committee's Report, Nehru's equation of backward class of citizens and socially and educationally backward classes; the manner of enactment of Article 16(4) described below; and the previous judgments of the Supreme Court equating backward class of citizens with socially and educationally backward classes. Even the Mandal Commission was appointed to investigate the condition of socially and educationally backward classes.[349] Could it be, because the earlier discussed 'community' of 'Other Hindu', created by the British in the nineteenth century and called Shudra, was the source of all the three categories of Scheduled Castes, Scheduled Tribes and Other Backward Classes, but culled out at different points of time from the huge category? It is likely, because, as stated by the court earlier, backward class of citizens included Scheduled Castes, Scheduled Tribes, and *all* other backward classes of citizens, including the socially and educationally backward classes and that reservations were provided for the Shudras, Scheduled Castes and the Scheduled Tribes and *other similar backward classes* among Muslims and Christians. It also means that not only 'all other backward classes including socially and educationally backward classes were Shudra, but also SC and ST. Then who were outcastes and Panchama, if there were actually any?

The problem is, while framing Article 16(4) and its precursor draft article 10(3) of the Constitution, as passed by the Constituent Assembly, the word 'backward' was not present with class of citizens. Dr. Ambedkar 'on his own' added it later, but he, too, left it undefined for the Supreme Court to decide its meaning.[350] It is inexplicable why the members of the Drafting Committee and Dr. Ambedkar fell shy of calling it Shudra, if they thought the word backward meant it to be so. (Infra) The next question is who are

---

[348]   Ibid: 510: 16 A Social; 17: 11.24 Weightage
[349]   A'I'R Supreme Court 1993: 507: 12
[350]   A'I'R' Supreme Court 1993: 701, 702 Dr. Ambedkar's Speech

all other backward classes other than socially and educationally backward classes included above by the court? Again, there is no answer. Could *all* include the category of socio-economic backwardness or backwardness due to economic reasons mentioned in the Directing Principles and other sources? The answer must, again, come from the State. It is the right of the ordinary citizens to seek information or clarification from the State, though the final arbitrator would still remain the Apex Court. The writer, too, is an ordinary citizen, not an expert.

In 2006, The Government clarified in *The Central Educational Institutions (Reservation in Admission) Act, 2006 (No. 5 of 2007) Section 2(g)*, "Other Backward Classes means the class or classes of citizens who are socially and educationally backward, and are so determined by the Central Government."[351] It looks strange that the State had to clarify that after nearly 60 years of the enactment of Article 15(4) and so many Apex Court judgments, but even now it said nothing about backward class of citizens in Article 16(4) or their Shudra identity. Was ir because the Government thought all the three were the same? In fact, in 1992 the court had not only ruled that educational backwardness was not necessary under Article 16 (4),[352] but also had confirmed that 'certain classes which may not qualify for Article 15(4) may qualify for Article 16(4)' and, if repetition or misprint is ignored, perhaps, vice versa.[353] Its clarification that social backwardness would lead to educational backwardness and both would lead to poverty, is true, but that is not the subject of discussion. Important thing is that educational backwardness is not obligatory and with it, perhaps, also poverty in identifying backward class of citizens. In that case, reservations could be given under Article 16(4) on the basis of only social backwardness, which means *only* on account of being Shudra or Shudra *caste*. It actually happened, when the court ruled that caste could be the determinative factor both initially and at the end. (Page 166)

The submission is, if backward class of citizens under Article 16(4) differ from socially and educationally backward classes in Article 15(4) in which educational backwardness is mandatory, then there should have been at least two lists of Backward Classes from the beginning: one for the socially backward classes other than SC and ST and the other for

---

[351] Quoted by the Chief Justice of India in Writ Petition (civil) 265 of 2006 in Ashok Kumar Thakur v. Union of India case 2006: Para 18 of the judgment 2008

[352] *A.I.R.* Supreme Court 1993. 557

[353] Ibid.: 556, 557

socially and educationally backward classes. The two lists do not exist in reality. The Mandal Commission produced only one list and so has the National Commission for Other Backward Classes (Appendix 1). How the Government understood and implemented this vital direction is for it to explain. One list could be possible, if all the backward classes other than SC and ST, whether under Article 15(4) or 16(4), were initially socially and educationally backward and after getting requisite education remained socially and economically backward. Scheduled Castes and Scheduled Tribes would then be additions for added benefits, by the Parliament in Article 15(4) and by the Supreme Court in Article 16(4). Concurring on the point of 'width' of Article 16(4), an otherwise dissenting judgment agreed with the majority, but also added a new dimension:

> We have held that two expressions in Articles 16(4) and 15(4) do not mean the same thing. The classes to be identified under Article 16(4) cannot be confined to social and educational backwardness. The definition therein is much wider and is not limited as under Article 15(4). It is thus, evident that the identification of the 'backward classes' under Article 16(4) cannot be based only on the criteria of social and educational backward. Other classes which could have been identified on the basis of occupation, economic standards, environment, backward areas, residence etc, etc, have been left out of consideration. The identification done by Mandal is thus violative.[354]

While concurring with the majority judgment, the learned judge clarifies that the backward class of citizens under Article 16(4) could not be restricted to socially and educationally backward, and besides including Scheduled Castes and Scheduled Tribes, the identification could have also been done 'on the basis of occupation, economic standards, environment, backward areas, residence etc.' Later, when it stresses upon the 'means test' and the importance of economic standards, it opens the road for the entry of socioeconomic backwardness. Therefore, due to the word *any* in both the Articles 16(4) and 15(4), economic backwardness assumes quasi-legitimacy on its own. This could also mean that these articles in the form of socially and educationally backward classes and backward class of citizens, in reality, might have been enacted to remove the economic, educational and social

---

[354] *A.I.R.* Supreme Court 1993: Justice Kuldip Singh: 720: 619 (i)

backwardness described as socio-economic inequalities in the constitution, and give assured occupation in services under the State for a limited period, but unfortunately, the caste lobbies hijacked them by calling them Shudra. The significant thing is that despite the clarification in 2006 that Other Backward Classes and socially and educationally backward classes meant the same thing, in 2008 the Government did not call these classes Shudra. The court, too, refrained to go into their social identity. It only said, "the interpretation of the term 'socially and educationally backward' and its constituent classes was left for future generations to decide,"[355]

According to Ambedkar, the original Draft article 10(3), the precursor of Article 16(4), was put in place to give reservations to 'any class of citizens' who had 'so far had no look' in the administration and 'although theoretically' it was good to 'have the principle that there shall be equality of opportunity there must at the same time be a pro vision made for the entry of certain communities, which have so far been *outside the administration*' (emphasis added).[356] In this statement, there is no hint of any sinister social disability like that of Shudra under Article 16(4). Ambedkar introduced the word 'backward' in Article 16(4) only to restrict the number of the eligible among those, who were inadequately represented in services, but when he declined to define 'backward' and left it wide open, the only reason could be that he did not want to restrict it to a particular section of society and to a particular type of backwardness like that of Shudra. Caste and tribe related backwardness had already been covered and the word Shudra had not been even mentioned in the Drafting Committee. Only economic backwardness was left. When objections were raised in the Drafting Committee, Ambedkar expressed his optimism that the states would act in a reasonable way and if not, the Supreme Court would decide the meaning of the word 'backward'. He then hoped that the Constituent Assembly would 'accept the amendments he had accepted'.[357] It appears from the judgment of Justice Thommen, which quoted Ambedkar, that the Constituent Assembly accepted the change *without* a formal amendment.

Thus, the primary intention of the Constituent Assembly before enacting Article 16(4) was to provide reservations to all classes inadequately

---

[355]   Ibid.: Para 2

[356]   *A.I.R.* Supreme Court 1993: Dr Ambedkar's Speech in Constituent Assembly: 701-702

[357]   *A.I.R.* Supreme Court 1993: 701-703: Speech of Dr Ambedkar quote by Justice T.K. Thommen

represented in services under the State, irrespective of their caste and religion. Even later, the open-ended words *'any backward'* covered every type of backwardness, including the economic and educational backwardness or socioeconomic backwardness that was rampant due to centuries of foreign oppression. The addition of 'socially' before 'backward' in 1992 limited its wideness. The tragedy is that the courts ignored the primary issue of inadequate representation in services, for which Article 16(4) was primarily framed, stressed upon the word 'backward', converted caste into class, let loose caste lobbies and left different courts to interpret the article differently.

The word 'socially' before the word 'backward' in Article 16(4), was added in 1992. As there was no going back to the parliament at this time, it raised a constitutional dilemma. In 2010 a case was referred to a Constitution Bench to decide on the powers of the Supreme Court on amending the Constitution *on its own*. To the best of my knowledge, no decision has come so far. In a more recent case in 2011 a two-judge Bench of the Supreme Court ruled, "This court by judicial order cannot amend the statute or the Constitution."[358] Whether the addition of 'socially' before 'backward', which conveyed an entirely different meaning, was an amendment of the Constitution or an interpretation is for the apex court to decide. In the case of non-Hindus, the Mandal Commission recommended reservation for the former untouchables and those in hereditary occupations like in the case of Hindus, but without taking cognizance of the internal structure of their societies (infra). This has become an added issue in view of reservation for the Muslim community as a whole in some states.

Educational Backwardness

Educational backwardness of socially and educationally backward classes was defined for the first time in 2006, when the question of reservation in postgraduate education institutions cropped up. In 2008 Chief Justice Balakrishnan ruled in the *Ashok Kumar Thakur case*, 'The contention that educational standard of matriculation or (10+2) should be the benchmark to find out whether any class is educationally backward is rejected.'[359] Justice R. V. Raveendran concurred. Justice Passayat, speaking for himself and Justice Thakur, ruled that while determining backwardness,

---

[358] *Times of India*: 10 March 2011
[359] Judgment 2008: Chief Justice

'*graduation* (not technical graduation or professional) shall be the standard test yardstick for measuring backwardness'.[360] In plain words, it should mean that graduation should be the measure of *cessation* of educational backwardness rather than of its continuation. Justice Dalveer Bhandari went a step further. 'Once a candidate graduates from a university, the said candidate is *educationally forward* and is ineligible for special benefits under Article 15(5) of the constitution for post graduate and any further studies thereafter'[361] (emphasis added in all). The Court, however, upheld the constitutionality of 93rd amendment and Article 15(5) and with that included graduates among the educationally backward.

Socially Backward

Though the Mandal Commission's criteria of comparison of social, educational, and economic backwardness with the State averages could not prove the Varna status of castes or identify them as Shudras, they could certainly identify social backwardness due to economic, educational, and low occupation. The criteria such as opinion of backward classes themselves and opinion of others were subjective and tainted by the lure of reservations, while personal opinion of the Commission had no detectable measure and no appraisal. The Commission, in fact, admitted the political nature of castes when it said that what caste had lost over the years on the ritual front, it had more than gained on the political front.[362] The majority judgment, too, admitted that there was no reason for Other Backward Classes to be situated similarly to Scheduled Castes or Scheduled Tribes, but considering the difficulties involved in the 'ascertainment of backwardness' "it must be left to the Commission/Authority appointed to identify the backward classes" so that it can *"evolve proper and relevant criteria and test to weigh the several groups, castes, classes and sections of people against that criteria"*[363] (emphasis added). Wrongly identified classes, the Court said, could be questioned in the court. With the highest respect, it was a blank check signed and ready for misuse

---

[360] Ibid.: Justice Passayat
[361] Ibid.: Justice Dalveer Bhandari: Judgment 2008
[362] *A.I.R.* Supreme Court 1993: 510-512: 16, 17 and 14
[363] Ibid.: 561: 88

and it was misused. The National Commission of Backward Classes does not even mention Shudras, not to speak of defining and identifying them.[364]

Confusion of Shudra and Panchama

In Chapter IV of its Report in Para 4.9 to 4.12, the Mandal Commission quotes Srinivas and describes four categories of Shudras. It then cites examples of OBCs from the South, where untouchability was always more severe. Its illustrations like 'the Shanar, the toddy tappers of Madras, contaminates a Brahmin if he approaches the latter within twenty four paces'...Tiyan must keep himself at a distance of thirty six steps from the Brahmin...a Mahar, one of the untouchables, might not spit on the road lest a pure-caste Hindu should be polluted by touching it with his foot and finally, purada vannanas, one of worst affected among even the scheduled castes, could be examples of Scheduled Castes, but not of socially and educationally backward classes or backward class of citizens like Lingyats, Vokkilogas, Reddys and host of others in the South or like Yadavs, Gujjars, Kurmis and Koeris in the North Yet it overwhelmed the judiciary. Justice Ratnavel Pandian wrote in his concurring judgment, "Beyond the four Varnas, Hinduism recognizes a community by name of Panchama (untouchables) though Shudras are recognized as being the lowest rung of the hierarchical race."[365]

This observation gave an unnatural orientation to a social structure that had existed for thousands of years without the aid of a fifth Varna of Panchama and a hierarchical race. Another reason for adoption of the term 'Panchama' by the Court could be the statement of the council from Bihar supported by some other counsel which was quoted earlier. According to him, "backward castes in Article 16(4) meant and means only the members of Shudra caste which is located between the three upper castes (Brahmins, Kshatriyas and Vaishyas) and the outcastes (Panchama) referred to as Scheduled Castes" and "Article 16(4) was conceived only for these middle castes, i.e. castes categorized as Shudras in the caste system and for none else".[366] The council did not mention the position of Scheduled Tribes and considered poverty, lack of education and accompanying disabilities irrelevant. He advocated reservation on the grounds of *only* caste, read

---

[364] Appendix 1
[365] *A.I.R.* Supreme Court 1993: 592: 138
[366] Ibid.: 543: 63

as Shudra. The dilemma worsened when to support its contention the Commission quoted J. R. Kumble from his book *Rise and Awakening of Depressed Classes in India* published in 1936:

> In this (Tinnevelly) there is a class *of unseeable called puruda vannana*. They are not allowed to come out during day time because their sight is considered to be pollution. Some of these people, who wash the clothes of other exterior castes working between midnight and daybreak, were with difficulty persuaded to leave their houses to interview[367] (emphasis added)

The Commission, thus, reaffirmed the Shudra identity of puruda vannana and with this of all the depressed classes or the Scheduled Castes by saying, "The above account will show us as to how every important facet of a Shudra's personal, social and economic activity was severely influenced by his low caste status. Mythology and scriptures were also pressed into service to establish the inherent superiority of the Brahmin and the low social ranking of the Shudra."[368] Thus, the Commission acknowledged that even the lowest among the untouchables were Shudra and therefore there could be nothing like Panchama. This observation produced a devastating psychological effect on the Court, which Justice Pandian echoed by stating:

> Does not the very mention of the caste named 'puruda vannana' indicate that the people belonging to that community were so backward, *both socially as well as educationally beyond comprehension* . . . Does not the very fact that those people were treated with contempt and disgrace as if they were vermin in the human form freeze our blood . . . When people placed at the basic level in the hierarchical caste system are living like mutes . . . can it be said by any stretch of imagination that caste can never be the primary criterion in identifying the social, economic and educational backwardness[369] (emphasis added).

The observation of the honorable judge would have been valid if the Court was dealing with the people like Mahars and especially puruda

---

367   *Judgments Today*: 318: 104 and Mandal Report: 20: 4.12
368   Mandal Commission's Report: Chapter IV Para 4.20: Page 20
369   *A.I.R.* Supreme Court 1993: 608: 226

vannana or if the socially and educationally backward classes or backward class of citizens had been the same or similar to them, but they were not. The Commission was not appointed to identify the untouchable, the unapproachable, or worse, the unseeable, who already enjoyed reservations. When the majority judgment concurred with the Commission and decreed, "In Chapter IV the Commission deals with inter-relationship between social backwardness and caste. It describes how fourth caste, Shudra, were kept in a state of intellectual subjugation and the historical injustices perpetrated upon them",[370] not only the concurring judge, but also the majority opinions put the seal of Shudras on the social identity of the worst affected among the untouchables. If depressed classes or Scheduled Castes were Shudras, there could be no exterior castes and no Panchama. The disabilities of Other Backward Classes were different from those of the Scheduled Castes. The former were poor, illiterate and engaged in the lower, but not demeaning occupations, traditional or otherwise, and were socially backward because of these factors. Even Scheduled Tribes had different reasons for backwardness.

This also brings in non-Shudra economically, educationally, occupationally, and socially backward classes. The majority judgment apparently supported reservation for them when it clarified that while identification of backward classes could be done "with reference to castes along with other occupational groups, communities and classes", it was not the only method. It ruled that 'there may be some groups or classes in which caste may not be relevant at all', such as 'agricultural laborers, rickshaw pullers/drivers, street hawkers etc,' who could also 'qualify for being designated as Backward Classes'.[371] Therefore, it was surprising that in just the preceding paragraph, the Court denied 10 percent reservations to socially and educationally backward classes from forward castes, which were equally poor and illiterate and engaged in same or similar occupations, just because they were alleged to be from the upper castes. Justice Pandian agreed with the Court's reasoning for the denial when he cited from the majority judgment, 'a person's income and extent of property held cannot entitle one to reservation'.[372] With the highest respect, this could not be relevant in those who could not provide even two square meals for themselves and their children. There was nothing like only economic grounds. Most of the poor were also educationally backward and socially

---

[370]   Ibid.: 508: 3.2
[371]   *A.I.R.* Supreme Court 1993: 562: 90-91 and para 121(b)
[372]   Ibid.: Para 115

disadvantaged—socially, educationally and economically backward. The constitution does not distinguish between castes and religions, except in the case of Scheduled Castes.

The majority of the Intermediate Castes, which drumbeat their Shudra title in the twenty-first century had, in fact, lived for centuries in harmony with the upper castes.[373] Yadavs, Gujjars, Lingyats, and Reddys had little to do with untouchability, even impurity and pollution. If they were Shudras, they were Shudras either in the Puranic sense where every non-Brahmin was a Shudra or they were the 'new' tax-paying Shudras which consisted of downgraded Vaishyas, foreign elements, recipient of land grants, and who were described by the historians as 'tormentors of Brahmans'. They became the victims of foreign aggressions of Huns, Muslims, and the British, who plundered the country and, barring Muslims, generally went back. A dissenting judgment in 1992 argued against the Shudra identity of Other Backward Classes:

> But the same (Shudra identity) cannot be accepted for other backward classes, as it would be distortion of constitutional interpretation by importing a concept which was deliberately and purposely avoided. Insistence, for claiming reservations for the remaining or for all others who were in so called broad category of Shudras not because they (OBCs) were really backward without any regard to social and economic conditions, would be unfair to history and unfair to society. What is constitutionally provided has to be adhered to in spirit but not on assumption that all amongst Hindus who fell in the broader category of Shudra were subjected to same treatment as untouchables in India or Negroes in America. History, social or political, does not bear it out.[374]

Enough has been already said on hereditary occupations. One last observation made on the 1992 judgment should end the argument. Prof. M. N. Srinivas, in the introduction of his book *Caste: Its Twentieth Century Avatar*, politely pointed out in 1996 that 'the view expressed in Mandal judgment on close nexus between caste, occupation and social backwardness' was 'somewhat out of date' and that there was an increasing 'disjunction between the caste and traditional occupation' and that it was 'true not only

---

[373] Mandal Commission's Report: Dissenting Note of L.R. Niak
[374] J.T. 1992 (6): Justice R.M. Sahay: 508-509/J.: 737: 664

of urban areas but also of more prosperous villages'. He concluded with a warning, 'In the changing caste situation in rural and urban India, such a static view is not in tune with facts on the ground.'[375]

Adequate/Inadequate Representation in Services

Adequate or inadequate representation of each caste in services was neither objectively determined by the Mandal Commission nor scrutinized by the Court, nor later by the National Commission for Other backward Classes.[376] The Court ruled that 'whether a caste or a class is adequately represented in services under the State is a matter within the subjective satisfaction of the State' because of the words in the article 'in opinion of the State'. This opinion, it said, 'could be formed on the basis of any material in the possession of the State or collected by it'. It justified its contention by saying, 'The executive is supposed to know the existing conditions in the society, drawn as it is from among the representatives of the people in Parliament/Legislature.'[377] The Commission did not show any material in its report by which the executive formed or could form its opinion that each of the 3,743 castes it selected was inadequately represented in services under the State and hundreds of others it rejected were adequately represented. To leave representation in services, which was the primary reason for enacting Article 16(4), to the subjective satisfaction of the politicians, with respect, might be expediency, but where the future of more than a billion people is at stake it cannot be left to a commission or a state, which shows no measure and no method to determine it. The Government was obliged to show to the Supreme Court and the nation how some castes were inadequately represented in services under the State, and how those it left out were adequately represented, for reservation curtailed the freedom of non-beneficiaries.

Leaving the crucial issue of determining 'backward class of citizens' to the commission/authority because of *difficulty in ascertainment of backwardness* and another crucial issue of determining 'inadequate representation in services' to political executives because *they represent the people* without judicial scrutiny, with respect, could not be the ideal way of dealing with a

---

[375]   Srinivas, 1996: Introduction: xxxiii
[376]   Appendix 1
[377]   *A.I.R.* Supreme Court 1993: 561-562: 89

case with such far-reaching consequences. Risley's prophecy that the 'regime of caste would not permit the sentiment of unity and solidarity' required to develop 'a common nationality among the people of India' has ultimately come true.[378] He had made certain that 'nationality would be unable to release the tenacious grip of caste feeling'.[379] In post-independence India, too, Ambedkar's vision of annihilation of caste remained a cry in wilderness. The same happened to the constitutional mandate of creating a casteless society. Caste has already taken a firm hold on the Indian politics, and the result has been disastrous. In a recent revelation, a former United States Ambassador to India blamed Indian National Congress for 'crass political opportunism' and its preparedness to 'stoop to old caste/religious-based politics after the carnage of 26/11 by the militants from Pakistani soil'.[380] Parochial politics has changed the rules and with them the Indian National Congress. To hold on to power, the politicians in the present time keep dividing the society in the pursuit of vote banks.

Articles 15(4) and 16(4)—A Point of View

Clause (1) of Article 15 says, "The State shall not discriminate against *any* citizen on grounds only of religion, caste, sex, place of birth or any of them." The focus is on citizen or *individual* rights. The stress is on citizen as individual.

Similarly, Clause (2) of Article 16, which is a fundamental right, states, "No citizen shall, on grounds *only* of religion, race, caste, sex, descent, place of birth, residence or any of them be discriminated against in respect of any employment or office under the State." Again the stress is on citizen as individual, but there is no mention of the word class/classes in both the clauses. Thus, in both the articles cited above, there is no prohibition on special provisions/reservation for backward class/classes. The bar in clause (4) of each article is on instituting special provisions 'on grounds only of religion, caste, sex, place of birth or any of them.'

The problem arose in Article 15(4), which deals with 'advancement of *any* socially and educationally backward classes of citizens, or for the Scheduled Castes and the Scheduled Tribes,' because, to quote Chief Justice

---

[378] Risley: quoted by Dirks, 2001: 224
[379] Ibid.: 226
[380] *Times of India*, 12 October 2010

K.G. Balakrishnan in 2008, "The interpretation of the term 'socially and educationally backward', and its constituent classes, was left for future generations to decide."[381] They are still to decide. This rendered the words, 'backward class of citizens' and 'socially and educationally backward classes', open to different views and misapplication and that is what exactly happened in both the cases.

The Mandal Commission never conducted any survey on the basis of classes, not to speak of individuals and families. If it did survey, they were only castes and when it recommended reservation under Article 16(4), it was only for Shudras, which were never defined by any commission or by any court, and which find no place in the articles. This was unacceptable, if not unconstitutional. The word *only* was included in clauses (4) of article 15 and 16 to prevent reservation on account of only *whole* castes, religions etc, not their backward class/classes of citizens or their families. Where the Constitution intended relief for backward castes and tribes, it clearly stated Scheduled Castes and Scheduled Tribes. Where the Constitution and its makers intended relief in terms of vast spread poverty or socioeconomic backwardness to individuals or families of all communities, irrespective of their religion and caste, they stated classes. As caste cannot be equated with class, the matter remains unresolved. What happened in the Supreme Court in 1992 has been discussed above.

K. M. Munshi was a prominent member of the Drafting Committee of the Constitution. He emphasized during the Constituent Assembly debates that although there was paramount need for the highest efficiency in administration, the word backward class was used in Article 16(4) because of the conditions prevailing in several provinces of our country. "We want to see that backward classes, classes who are really backward should be given scope in State services, for the State services give a status and an opportunity to serve the country", and "this opportunity should be extended to *every* community, even among the backward people. That being so, we have to find out some generic term and the word backward class was the best possible term."[382] The stipulation '*even among* the backward people' tells the true intention of the constitution makers. The word 'generic' is applicable to *all*, not specific to any caste, class, or community. Confusion was created by multiple terms like backward class of citizens, socially and educationally

---

[381] Judgmwnt 2008: Chied Justice: Para2
[382] Ibid.: 520: 28

backward classes and other backward classes for the same people. Obsession with caste and community only increased it.

The Constituent Assembly intended to cover all communities and sections and sub-sections of the society, not one community or certain castes. It recognized that education was the primary requirement for getting into services. In fact, one of the members stated in the Constituent Assembly, 'The backward classes of people as understood in South India are those classes of people who are educationally backward.'[383] There was no reason to include caste, religion or Shudra, when every individual, even one without allegiance to any caste or any religion, was entitled.

In 1991, the petitioners had challenged the methodologies and the validity of the Mandal Commission Report, but the Special Bench refused to entertain these objections for two reasons. *First,* 'these details can be gone into before the Five Judge Bench later'. *Second,* "the Mandal Commission Report has not been accepted by the Government in its fullness nor has the Government accepted the list of Other Backward Classes prepared by it in its entirety". The Court clarified that it was not ruling on the validity of the Report, but on 'the validity of the impugned Office Memorandum issued on *the basis of the Report*"[384] (emphasis added). It created a piquant situation, for if the validity of the Report, which was the basis of the Office Memorandum, was doubtful, how could the *Memorandum* with such far-reaching consequences be valid on factual and legal grounds? The minority views recommended appointment of another commission.[385]

The identity of forward castes, too, is unclear. The Mandal Commission's 17.58 percent of the total population of forward castes was a hotchpotch of 5.2 percent Brahmins, 3 percent Rajputs, 2.21 percent Marathas, 1 percent Jats, 2.95 percent Vaishya-Banias, etc., less than 2 percent Kyastha and 2 percent nondescript and undeterminable Other Forward Castes, which were added to round off the total.[386] The Commission did not clarify the meaning of forward castes. Most Rajputs are from lower castes or Vratya Kshatriyas; Marathas were Shudras before and have been again since the death of Shivaji. Jats are Shudra in some states fighting for the same status in central lists, and 2 percent 'others' have no identity. Brahmins, Banias and Kyasthas with less than 10 percent population are the only etceteras which,

---

383   Ibid.
384   Ibid.
385   Ibid.: 579: 118
386   *A.I.R.* Supreme Court 1993: 513

so far, have not claimed backwardness. Recently, even the poor Brahmins have asked for special treatment. Justice Chinnappa Reddy was perhaps the only judge who tried to interpret what he called 'superior castes'. He says,

> Any view of the caste system, class or cursory, will at once reveal the firm links which the caste system has with *economic power*. Land and learning, two of the primary sources of economic power in India, have till recently been the monopoly of the superior castes. Occupational skills were practiced by the middle castes and in the economic system prevailing till now they could rank in the system next only to the caste constituting the landlord or learned gentry.[387]

It means that all those who have economic power, whether derived through land, learning, or occupational skills or, if we may add, commerce, industry, trade, and politics, irrespective of their caste and religion, should be called superior castes or rather *classes*; those who are educated, depend upon occupational skills, and are economically self-sufficient would be Middle or Intermediate *classes*. Low *classes* then would be those who lack economic power, are illiterate, in low occupations, and whose social backwardness would be due to poverty or socioeconomic inequality and illiteracy. Although this would produce different backward classes from the present caste related backwardness, the Constitution, prima facie, admits this definition and the present realities demand it.

Reservations for Minorities

Barring in Scheduled Castes and possibly in Scheduled Tribes, the Constitution is caste and religion blind, but its intended *non*-religious and non-caste character was compromised when the Mandal Commission recommended reservations for socially and educationally backward classes for Hindus on their dubious Shudra 'caste' identity and for non-Hindus on the similarly affected sections. The Supreme Court ruled, 'The concept of castes is not confined to the Hindus'[388] and similar identifications could also be done in the case of Christians. However, it restricted its application with

---

[387] *Judgements Today*, 1992: 450: 469
[388] *A.I.R.* Supreme Court 1993: 554-555: 83

its caveat "*provided* all groups, denominations, etc. are considered separately and all the available groups, sections, and classes of society considered independently in whichever order one proceeds.'[389] The caveat was breached after many years, when the Misra Commission in 2004, and the Sachar Committee in 2006, recommended reservations for a whole community, instead of its available groups etc.

70 percent of Indian Christians are indiscriminately called Dalit Christians. When the Sachar Committee on Muslim Affairs reported that only 9 percent of Indian Christians have Scheduled Caste status, with a further 32.8 percent having Scheduled Tribe status and 24.8 percent belong to other disadvantaged sections they were unhappy, because the committee had not treated all of them as *Dalits*. Obviously, 70 percent Christians could not have been untouchable scores of years after conversion.[390] While 'the Protestant churches had most consistently repudiated the caste system, rejecting it as a Hindu construct and made the greatest attempt to establish a casteless community, 'the Roman Catholic Church . . . chose to work within the established social system', but the Syrian Orthodox Churches projected all 70 percent as *one caste* to seek reservations.[391] This not only contravened the above direction of the Supreme Court, but also ignored that fifty-two percent of the total population of minority communities, including Christians, had already been included among the other backward class and the Indian Christians have one of the highest, if not the highest literacy rate, work participation, and sex ratio among the various religious communities in India.[392]

About converts to Christianity, Joseph Tharamangalam, a reputed professor of sociology, writes, "(T)he dichotomy between Christian egalitarianism and Hindu hierarchy is highly exaggerated if not an altogether false one. In the first place, Christianity has historically not only been the religion of highly *inegalitarian* societies (feudal, sexists, slaves, racists) but has also provided legitimations for these." The sects and movements among Christians committed to egalitarian social organizations such as 'Levelers, the Diggers and the Anabaptists were generally regarded as marginal and deviant'. Syrian Christians 'despise their Dalit workers and serve them only in outer veranda' though they are 'more considerate toward the same Dalits

---

[389] Ibid.
[390] http://en.wikipedia.org/wiki/Dalit_Christian
[391] Ibid.
[392] 2001 Census of India; also http://en.wikipedia.org/wiki/Christianity_in_India

if they are government servants or schoolteachers'.[393] This was written in 1996 in the book *Caste: Its Twentieth Century Avatar* edited by Prof. M. N. Srinivas. Inclusion of 52 percent of the community among the Other Backward Classes was an attempt to correct internal inequalities cited above. No figures are available or cited to know the present position.

Writing about the *Muslim societies*, Zarina Bhatty stated in 1996 that inequalities in Islamic societies have been a subject of study by social anthropologists only for the last twenty to twenty-five years. Though the Muslim clergy disliked the term caste and there were Koranic injunctions of creating male and female equally, 'there are no records to suggest that the egalitarian ideal was ever practiced in any Muslim society'. Caliph Omar distributed spoils of war 'in proportion to the length of time since a person's conversion to Islam'. The social status still depends on the date of conversion to Islam, and 'Nau-Muslims (New Muslims) are treated to a lower social status by Muslims of long standing'.[394]

She divided the community into *Ashrafs,* which were referred to as 'oonchi zat' (high caste) and were further composed of 'Ahl-e-Kalam (the religious intelligentsia), Ahl-e-Tegh (the warriors) and Ahl-e-Murad' or those that cater to the comforts and pleasures of the higher income groups.[395] *Non-Ashrafs* were 'neechi zat' (low caste). Marriages among the two, she said, were inconceivable. The impure *zats* (Jats or Jatis) were Mirasis (singers), Nais (barbers), and Dhobi (laundryman).[396] A 'fairly elaborate system of social stratification' existed since 'the beginning of Muslim rule in India'.[397] Bhatti acknowledges that post-1947 politico-economic environment shows movement toward a 'class-oriented stratification' among the general population as well as among the Muslims.[398] Thus, she not only recognizes internal disparities but also distinguishes caste from class and admits improvement in the community.

Similarly, in 1992 Justice P. B. Sawant distinguished between two main divisions among the Muslim community as Ashraf and Ajlaf. Ashraf meant 'noble' and comprised foreigners and 'high caste' Hindu converts, while Ajlaf meant 'Wretches' or 'mean people'. They were also called 'Kamina

---

[393]   J. Tharamangalam, 1996: 285-286
[394]   Zarina Bhatty, 1996: 246-248
[395]   Ashraf, 1932: quoted by Bhatty: 246
[396]   Ibid.: 249-250
[397]   Ibid.
[398]   Ibid.: 248

or Itar, base or Rasil' and included 'all other Mohammedans including occupational groups and converts of lower ranks'.[399] The same situation, he implied, exists even now. Another reason for poverty and illiteracy after the partition is attributed to the migration of the rich and influential Muslims to Pakistan and staying back of the poor among the community in India.[400]

According to Andre Beteille, quoted in one of the judgments in *Indra Sawhney* case, reservation under Article 16(4) meant for backward classes should have meant for certain *really* backward sections of backward classes which are not adequately represented in the State services. The same should have been with reservation in educational institutions for socially and educationally backward classes. The reason was that all sections, families and individual of a caste were not similarly situated, but the commissions and the committees appointed by the Governments embarked upon reservation for whole castes and communities due to political reasons. These, according to Prof. Beteille, only benefited the economically and educationally middle sections of such communities. His remarks, "Reservations for Scheduled Castes and Scheduled Tribes are, for all their limitations, directed basically towards the goal of greater equality overall. Reservations for the Other Backward Classes and for religious minorities, whatever advantage they may have, are directed basically toward a balance of power. The former are in tune with the spirit of the Constitution; the latter must lead sooner or later to what Justice Gajendragadkar has called fraud on the Constitution,"[401] are valid even today.

The French social scientist Robert Deliege too echoed the same in 1999, "The Backward Classes often use the poverty and oppression of some sections of population as an *alibi* to entrench their political dominance further" and "the demand of extension of quota in their favor is *not* motivated by a concern for justice in compensation for centuries of oppression; *it is part of power struggle*"[402] (emphasis added). Appreciable number of upper and middle classes have also appeared among the Scheduled castes and the Scheduled Tribes during the last 22 years, but they refuse to give up the tag. On the contrary, they bully the governments by bringing in compensatory discrimination and keep their low classes quiet by shouting 'Dalits in danger.'

---

[399] *Judgements Today*, 1992 (6) Supreme Court: 453: 475

[400] A.A. Engineer, 2001. *Muslim Middle Class and Its Role*. Mumbai, India: Center for Study of Society and Secularism

[401] *A.I.R.* Supreme Court 1993: 714: 587

[402] R. Deliege, 1999: 195

An excerpt from Ranganath Misra Commission's Report is reproduced: "As the Constitution does not specifically refer to it (economic backwardness) in Articles 15 and 16, (and) in *Indira Sawhney* case, the Supreme Court had observed, 'It is, therefore, clear that economic criterion by itself will not identify the backward classes under Article 16(4), the economic backwardness of the backward classes under Article 16(4) has to be on account of their *social and educational backwardness.*' Hence, no reservation of posts in services under the State, based exclusively on economic criterion, would be valid under clause (1) of Article 16 of the Constitution"[403] (emphasis added). This time a former chief justice of India, who presided over the constitution bench which first heard the Mandal case, while presiding over a commission after retirement, brings out that the word 'backward' in Article 16(4) meant both *social and educational backwardness*, but even he does not tell what the term really means. The key word is *classes*, not castes or communities, which may have both forward and backward classes.

The world has gone far beyond the colonial period, beyond even 1992. George Bernard Shaw's remark that his tailor was the wisest man, because every time he went to him he took his new measurements, is no less applicable to society. It too, needs periodic re-assessment.

Summary and Conclusion

Depressed classes, Backward and Aboriginal Tribes, and Other Backward Classes were three different categories or had three different types of backwardness. The word Shudra had been used in different ways, but in general perception it applied to the lowest castes or the Scheduled Castes. Panchama, as shown earlier, was a construction of the colonial period. Even the Mandal Commission called the lowest among the depressed classes Shudra and the Court agreed. Similarly, there was no caste—occupation nexus, and no one was obliged to follow the same occupation for centuries and generations. Varnas were not watertight compartments and class and caste could not be equated.

The significance of the word *any* in both the Articles 15(4) and 16(4) was overlooked. *Any* was a generic term which also included socioeconomically backward classes mentioned in the directing principles of the Constitution, but had been unjustly eclipsed by equating classes with castes. Similarly,

---

[403]   http://www.minorityaffairs.gov.in/sites/upload_files/moma/files/pdfs/volume-1.pdf

family has been the functional unit of social stratification for interaction and mobility for thousands of years and the most suitable unit for dispensation of social justice to all sections of society.

Finally, the individual representation in services of 3,743 castes forming backward class of citizens other than Scheduled Castes and Scheduled Tribes *was never determined or shown to have been determined*, defeating the very reason for enacting Article 16(4) of the constitution. A collective figure has no significance for the purposes of social benefits. This puts the legal veracity of backward class of citizens in Article 16(4) itself in jeopardy. Unfortunately, instead of facing it, there is trend to rationalize it.

The majority judgment had not only accepted the title of Shudra for Scheduled Castes like Mahar and puruda vannana, but had also enlarged its ambit to include socially and educationally backward, on the pretext of calling them socially backward classes. Both were not the same in the manner of their backwardness. If they were, the latter would have been included among the Scheduled Cases. The acceptance of contentious terms like outcastes and Panchama in Para 2 of the judgment created further problems.

Constructs

The British made many *constructs* to divide Hindu society. Some of them are as follows:

1. Caste derived from *casta* was the first construct. It converted Varnas into primary castes and Jatis into sub-castes.
2. Division of Varnas into watertight compartments was the second.
3. Varnas were four. The attempt to create a fifth Varna of Panchama was the third construct. Other constructs were outcastes, exterior castes, out of pail, pariah. All were divisive and invented for perpetuation and political reasons.
4. Traditional occupations formed an important part of rural economy, but no one was obliged to continue in one occupation. Caste—occupation nexus was constructed for sinister purposes.
5. Everyone, king or saint, was once-born Shudra at birth. Twice-born status was applicable to individuals and came with education and in the past also study of Vedas. The British constructed once-born and twice-born *castes* which had no sanction in Hindu religion. People were once-born or twice-born, not Jatis.

6. Purity and pollution existed for centuries and varied in different parts of the country and in different situations. Risley constructed a single uniform class of untouchables on racial basis in 1901, despite finding no support from his own staff for ten years.

7. Terms sufficient and insufficient Hinduisation and tribal religions were constructs in the British-created Hindu Law to separate a large chunk of population from the parent community.

8. Perhaps, the most diabolical *construct* of colonial time was the fabrication of the *community* of "Other Hindu" by indiscriminately including almost 97 percent population of South India and almost 83 percent population in the rest of the country under the label of Shudra. Though it might not have existed under the title of 'Other Hindu' in 1931 census due to discontinuation of recording of Varnas, it's composition of thousands of castes would have been known. The British extracted 14 percent population from it and called it Scheduled Castes. Post-independence India took out 7.5 percent population of Scheduled Tribes. The Mandal Commission 'culled out' another 52 percent, but called it Shudra.

The term Shudra had different meanings. British anthropologists denied even the existence of Shudra. Ambedkar said that large numbers of contemporary backward classes are not Shudra and the Aryan Shudras were Kshatriyas. Then there were new taxpaying Shudras, who were described as tormentors of Brahmins. Asprishya Shudras were also Shudra. So were those who were denied entry to temples, schools etc. Other Backward Classes might have been poor, illiterate and in low occupations, but they were not engaged in demeaning occupations. Therefore, Shudra or not, the backward class of citizens, or backward classes other than Scheduled Castes, were never shunned by Brahmins in taking water or food from their hands, or denied temple entry, or had to walk at a certain distance from a Brahmin, or barred from leaving their houses before sunset, as shown in classification and examples of Shudra quoted in Para 4.9 to 4.12 of Chapter IV of the Commission's Report. On the other hand, Risley quoted Sir Denzil Ibbetson, who wrote in 1891:

> Setting aside the priests and traders on the one hand, the artisans, and the menials on the other, we have the great body of agriculturists who constitute by far the largest portion of population. The great body of people lives by husbandry and

cattle forming, and so far their occupation is one and the same. But they are also the owners and occupiers of lands. The holders of more or less compact tribal territories; they are overlords as well as villains; and hence springs the cardinal distinction between the occupation of ruling and the occupation of the ruled. [404]

Thus, the only practical solution would be to discard all contentious issues, stick to poverty and illiteracy which lead to low occupations, and in combination to low position in society. Even here it would be desirable to make distinction between those who are below the poverty line and those above. Reservation can be made for limited period for the first category and for the others some form of affirmative action. Special provisions in Articles 15(4) do not mean reservation.

The removal of socio-economic backwardness due to poverty, illiteracy and low occupations is intrinsic in the Indian constitution. It was recognized in the debates in the constituent assembly, in many Supreme Court judgments and by the colonial rulers even in 1931. Therefore, it would not be unreasonable to say that Articles 15(4) and 16(4) were enacted to remove socio-economic inequalities among backward classes of people from all sections of society, but were hijacked by caste lobbies. The present problems would not have occurred if the Drafting Committee had defined 'backward' in Article 16(4) and the Parliament had not left the definition of socially and educationally backward classes to future generations in 1951. Socio-economic inequalities will be discussed in the next chapter.

---

[404]   Ibbetson as quoted by Risley: 1969: 411-412

CHAPTER 8

SOCIOECONOMIC INEQUALITY

It has been argued that major economic and other problems of pre-independence era were a result of colonization and disruption of Indian society by the British, but the roots of persisting poverty, illiteracy and present backwardness in post-dependence India lie in poor quality of political leadership and its elitist roots. Recent publication of data has shown that the average wealth of members of parliament runs into tens of millions. Money values have replaced ethical and moral values and corruption is rampant and unending. The old cultural values, family structure in villages and the traditional Indian value system have been put at the periphery of the society for the observation of only the marginalized people. The gap has widened not only between castes and groups, but has also increased amongst economic blocks and regions.

In 2007, when a Constitution Bench of the Supreme Court was constituted in the case of *Ashok Kumar Thakur case* v. *Union of India* to decide on the constitutionality of the 93rd Amendment and reservation in institutions of higher education under Article 15(5), the petitioners raised a number of contentious issues like inadmissibility of reservations on the basis of caste; the identification of socially and educationally backward classes/backward class of citizens and their social identity; obligation of judicial review; and some others. An odd intervener brought in inadmissibility of terms like Panchama. The Court, however, ruled only on the most critical legal issue: "We hold that the determination of SEBCs is done not solely based on caste and hence, the identification of SEBCs is not violative of Article 15(1) of the Constitution."[405] The other issues raised by a two-judge Bench and included in the Introduction remained unanswered. On the issue of bypassing Article 15(1), though the five-judge Constitution Bench took refuge in a technical excuse by saying identification was 'not solely based

---

[405] Judgment 2008: Chief Justice K.G. Balakrishnan: Para 142

on caste', it, nevertheless, provided an ample insight into the four decades of judicial thinking by extensively quoting from the previous judgments of the Supreme Court.

The reader would have noticed a number of terms for Other Backward Classes. To clarify, the Chief Justice quoted a 2006 Government's definition in which it was stated that Other Backward Classes meant the same thing as socially and educationally backward classes,[406] but nothing was said about backward class of citizens in Article 16(4). It was presumed that the same definition was also applicable to them. Although the Parliament had amended the Constitution and added Clause 4 in Article 15 to make special provisions for uplift of socially and educationally backward *classes* in 1951, the rejection of reservations on the basis of caste and religion by a seven judges Bench of the Apex Court was still on the anvil. Unable to circumvent this decision, the various Benches of the Supreme Court after 1951 started accepting caste on the pretext that reservation were given not on the basis of only caste but also because of the associated factors such as poverty, illiteracy, and low occupation, or because caste became a class, when it was backward as a whole. This conditional acceptance was in itself recognition of the fact that caste and class were not synonymous and no caste alone was admissible for reservation under Article 15(4) and 16(4). To entitle reservations and special provisions, other reasons were also needed and those reasons were provided by the terms socially and educationally backward classes and backward class of citizens respectively. The issue now was that if the other reason or reasons were common between two castes, could reservations be given to one caste because it was allegedly low, and not given to the other because it was presumed to be not low, for if it was given to the former and denied to the latter, other factors being equal, it would mean giving reservation *only* on account of caste and would contravene Articles 15(1) or 16(2), as the case may be. Perhaps, that was the reason why Chief Justice K.G. Balakrishnan found 'considerable disagreement' in the previous judgments of the Supreme Court in the 'category of disadvantaged sections.'[407]

---

[406] Judgment of the Supreme Court in Ashok Kumar Thakur v. Union of India Case No. 265/2006 placed on website supremecourtofindia.com http://www.judis.nic.in/supremecourt/CaseRes1.aspx Judgment Information System. As there were no pages in original judgment on the Internet, only Paragraphs are quoted. Later published in A.I.R. Supreme Court 2008 Supplement: 1. Also in Supreme Today 2008, Vol. 3, Vikas Books Unlimited

[407] Judgment 2008 ofChief.Justice K.G. Balakrishnan.: Para 1

In the case of *Balaji and others* v. *State of Mysore*, the learned chief justice continued, "it was observed that though in relation to Hindus, caste may be a relevant factor to consider while determining social backwardness of groups or classes of citizens, it cannot be made the *sole or dominant* test".[408] On the contrary, "in *Indra Sawhney's* case, which is a Nine Judges Bench decision, it was held that the caste could be a beginning point and a *determinative* factor in identifying the socially and educationally backward classes of citizens"[409] (emphasis added). Thus, according to *Balaji case*, unless there are additional factors like poverty, illiteracy and low occupations, not only castes, but also classes of citizens could not be called socially or socially and educationally backward. On the other hand, according to the Mandal case judgment, despite other factors being equal, caste could be a beginning point as well as the determinative or decisive or conclusive factor in identifying socially and educationally backward classes. This must be, because in the Balaji case the Supreme Court did not call socially and educationally backward classes Shudras, while in the Mandal case the Court did.

This brings up, *first*, to the definition of Shudra; *second*, was Shudra Jati or Varna; *third*, what is the meaning of backward class of citizens; *fourth*, if backward class of citizens were Shudra and the Mandal Commission could site even 'unseeables' as their examples, why were both not Shudra? Where was the need to bring in Panchama? *Finally*, other factors being equal, would giving reservation on the basis of *only* Shudra not contravene Articles 15(4) or 16(4), as the case may be? Thus, the problem ultimately boils down to the meaning of 'Shudra,' exclusion of an artificially imposed term Panchama, clarifying the social identity of other backward classes, the socially and educationally backward classes and backward class of citizens, which the Supreme Court had regarded as the same till 1992. Unless these issues are resolved, there can be no permanent solution. Panchama cannot be imposed on Hindu social structure, as it was shown in the previous chapters.

To recapitulate a few of the points discussed earlier: till 1947 the word 'Shudra' was used by the courts only for depressed classes or Scheduled Castes. The *Hindu Law* adopted by free India did not distinguish between depressed classes and Shudra. In the Hindu social structure coming down for ages there was nothing lower than Shudra. The constitution and its makers avoided the term completely. The courts equated backward classes

---

[408] Ibid: Para 109
[409] Ibid.

with backward castes, if the latter were backward as a whole, but failed to explain how heterogeneous structures like castes or caste clusters with a number of divisions, hundreds of thousands, or millions of families could be homogeneous and similarly situated? Finally what was the definition of caste? Till this date, there is no concrete answer. The Governments avoid these issues and reservations continue unabated on the basis of an unexplained caste structure.

The Chief Justice continued, "The main attack against the Act was that the socially and educationally backward classes of citizens were not properly identified and the delegation of power to identify the socially and educationally backward classes of citizens to the Central Government itself is illegal and the delegation of such powers by itself without laying down any guidelines is arbitrarily illegal."[410] The objection was well conceived, for we neither knew the meaning of Shudra in the manner it was used judicially, nor the meaning of socially backward, nor have a cogent reason for equation of class with caste. The Constitution provides reservation for backward *classes*, which are homogeneous groups or have identical families or individuals, not for castes which are heterogeneous. The presumption that a number of heterogeneous castes, when combined, would make a homogeneous class is totally false. Socially backward or socially unacceptable due to some objectionable traits, occupations, activities, or behavior are different from those who are socially backward only because of poverty, illiteracy, and low occupations. In the common notion, the Scheduled Castes are socially backward in the former sense, while the socially and educationally backward classes are socially, educationally and economically backward due to poverty and illiteracy. Owing to the word *any* backward class of citizens in the Article 16(4) and 'any' before socially and educationally backward classes in Article 15(4), it would not be unreasonable to argue that after conceding reservations to castes and tribes, reservations were intended on economic grounds, which lead to illiteracy, low occupations and social backwardness, found among people in every caste, religious community, sex and region. Only their extent differs.

In 1992, when the majority judgment agreed with the judgment in the *Chiterlekha* that reservations could be given on the basis of non-traditional occupations-cum-income to backward classes like Rickshaw pullers/drivers, agricultural laborers, street hawkers etc and said that caste may not be relevant in every case, it literally accepted reservations to socially

---

[410] Judgment 2008: Chief.Justice.: Para 105, 106

and educationally backward classes on the basis of poverty, illiteracy, low occupations and resultant social backwardness."[411] Therefore, the denial of reservations on similar grounds to the poor and uneducated from the alleged forward castes amounted to unequal treatment, if not discrimination. To give reservations to whole caste and communities has harmed the really backward, even within the backward classes. If the reservations can be legally and constitutionally given and withdrawn on the basis of their affected parts or groups in the case of Scheduled Castes and Scheduled Tribes, why the same cannot be done for the whole population, without bringing in caste and religion? This will improve the lot of not only the poor and the illiterate, but also open up more avenues for the needy. Giving reservations to whole castes and communities, even classes of people, is illogical, because there is disparity at the family levels. All barbers and milk sellers are not equally situated. Thus, it would be more logical to identify backward classes and then give reservations to their really backward families, whether in educational institutions or in services under the State. Others, if needed, can be helped otherwise. The same would apply for discontinuation of reservations.

The State Lists of Other Backward Classes obtained before 13 August 1990,[412] which the Government adopted in lieu of Mandal Lists of backward class of citizens under Article 16(4) in 1992 with the permission of the court, had not been prepared with one ideology. Out of the 13 states available for analysis in 1984, economic criteria were employed in *five*; occupation, border, and poor areas in *one* each and in the rest of the *seven* cases the criteria could not be detected.[413] This literally meant reservation on economic grounds. The Court was conscious of it when it stated that acceptance of lists as on 13 August 1990 'does not mean that those lists are meant to be sacrosanct' and whenever the State Governments make changes they would intimate them to the Central Government for 'additions or deletions'.[414] The Guidelines of the National Commission on Backward Classes quoted in Appendix 1 do not indicate when and how or if at all anything was done. In fact, the Registrar General of India complained in 1997 that different states

---

[411] *A.I.R.* Supreme Court 1993: 562: 91
[412] *A.I.R.* Supreme Court 1993: 581: 119-121
[413] Galanter, 1984: Pages 83-84 and Table 20
[414] *A.I.R.* Supreme Court 1993: 581-583: 119-120

used different criteria for identification of backward classes. He specially mentioned Punjab for using only economic criteria.[415]

Other backward classes are not a single homogeneous ostracized category which has come down unchanged from the Vedic times. In fact, there is no such category. Ambedkar had described them as a broad-based compilation of a miscellaneous and heterogeneous collection of tribes and groups which had nothing in common and to whom it would be wrong to call Shudra. According to the Mandal commission, these large collections of people comprised of 52 percent of India's total population, though *National Sample Survey Organisation* in Times of India of November 01, 2006 estimated their population at 41 percent. This has not been authenticated.

The National Commission of Backward Classes under the Ministry of Social Justice and Empowerment, too, defined Other Backward Classes (OBCs) as people who are *economically and socially backward* other than SC, ST, and FC.[416] FC means forward castes. At another place in 2014, it called them educationally and socially backward. If true, these non-Shudra social identities not only make their Shudra identity irrelevant, but also make the whole identification process spurious. The only essential thing is that a fair number among them, by whatever name we call them, are still poor and illiterate and because of that they are in lower occupations and socially disadvantaged. Those who have recovered or reached certain stage of improvement can be helped by an appropriate Affirmative Action, if necessary.

In July 2006 a commission was appointed under the chairmanship of Maj. Gen. (Retired) S. R. Sinha, to cater to the Economically Backward Classes.[417] Its term expired on 31 July 2010. Though its findings are not known, it seems that the concept of caste-unrelated socioeconomic backwardness finally dawned on the Government,[418] but such was the influence of caste lobbies that the governments and the courts overlooked for over six decades that Articles 15(4) and 16(4) might have been enacted to remove the type of backwardness to which the State has awakened only now. Caught up in the midst of castes and communities, the State and the courts ignored the family and the individual, which are the pragmatic units for dispensing social justice in every society, even among the Scheduled castes and the Scheduled Tribes.

---

[415]   *Times of India*, 27 June 1997
[416]   http://en.wikipedia.org/wiki/Other_Backward_Classes
[417]   http://www.jagranjosh.com/current-affairs/commission-for-economically-backward-classes-submitted-report-1286621728-1 and *The Hindu*, Monday, 24 July 2006
[418]   *The Hindu*: July 25, 2006

Case for Socioeconomic Backwardness

Socioeconomic backwardness was also recognized during the colonial period. As a member of the Franchise Commission in 1932, when Dr Ambedkar asked G. S. Pal of the United Provinces Backward Classes League whether the List of Backward Classes he gave him was of "backward communities who were touchable and educationally and economically backward" or "those who were untouchable and also educationally and economically backward", he was conscious of the same two categories.[419] Pal called the latter as untouchables and said, 'All the listed communities belonged to non-Dwijas or degenerate or *Sudra* classes of Hindus.'[420] Thus, the untouchables and educationally and economically backward and a stratum above were the same as those who were called depressed classes or 'Sudra class of Hindus' which were designated as Scheduled Castes in 1936. Backward Hindus or Other Backward Classes were not depressed classes. They were the touchable and educationally and economically backwards, which after independence and in Article 15(4) and 16(4) of the constitution were called socially and educationally backward classes and backward class of citizens respectively. Nehru described the latter as educationally and economically backward while Ambedkar described them as backward on the economic plane (infra). Scheduled Tribes were somewhere in between, but more akin to the latter than the former.

Similarly, when J. J. Hutton, the census commissioner for the 1931 census, found that his 'elaborate attempts' to identify 'untouchable groups' based on four criteria of 'purity and pollution', two criteria based on being debarred from 'public conveniences' and 'use of Hindu temples', and the seventh criterion based an 'unequal treatment meted to the similarly qualified' could not apply to all the poor and the illiterate, he devised two tests 8 and 9 to *exclude* them from the former group. Those tests were as follows:

a. Test No. 8. Whether the caste or class is merely depressed on account of its own ignorance, illiteracy or poverty and but for that would be subject to *no* social disability.

---

[419]   Galanter, 1984: 127; also 1931 Census Report: 472
[420]   *A.I.R.* Supreme Court 1993: 549: 75 also ibid.

b. Test No. 9. Whether it is depressed on account of the occupation
    followed, and whether but for that occupation it would be subject
    to *no* disability.[421] (Emphasis added)

Backward Hindus or Other Backward Classes were those who, but for
poverty, illiteracy, low occupation, and lower position in society, had no
other disability. There were plenty of poor and illiterate among the Hindus,
the Muslims, the Christians, and the other non-Hindu communities in
whom the criterion of social disability due to impurity and pollution did
not apply. The British did not include them among the depressed classes or
Scheduled Castes and so did not free India after 1947. Post-independence
political terms like Dalits for Scheduled Castes added to the confusion.

K. M. Munshi, a senior member of the Drafting Committee of the
Constitution, stated in the Constituent Assembly that besides Scheduled
Tribes and Scheduled Castes, there were "other backward classes who are
economically, educationally and socially backward. We need not, therefore
define to restrict the scope of the word 'backward' to a particular community.
Whoever is backward will be covered".[422] In this category, caste, religion,
creed, region, or any other reason did not apply. No member, including Dr.
Ambedkar, contradicted that statement or brought in caste or community.
As Scheduled Castes and Scheduled Tribes were separately covered, Article
16(4) and later Article 15(4) were enacted for 'economically, educationally
and socially backward'.[423] The State might have left the interpretation of
socially and educationally backward classes to the future generations, but
during the introduction of clause 4 of Article 15, Pandit Jawaharlal Nehru
unmistakably emphasized their concept and scope before the Constituent
Assembly by saying that 'the removal of *socioeconomic inequalities* was the
highest priority':

> But you have to distinguish between backward classes which are
> *specially* mentioned in the Constitution, that have to be helped to
> be made to grow and not think of them in terms of this community
> or that. Only if you think of them in terms of the community you
> bring in *communalism*. But if you deal with backward classes *as
> such*, whatever religion or anything else they may happen to belong

---

[421] Galanter, 1984: 127-129 and 1931 Census Report
[422] *A.I.R.* Supreme Court 1993: 520: 28
[423] Ibid.: Debates in Constituent Assembly

to, then it becomes our duty to help them toward educational,
social and economic advance[424] (emphasis added).

Nehru clearly meant that, unlike Scheduled Castes and Scheduled
Tribes, in Article 15(4) the Constitution intended reservations for that type
of backward classes which was found among all communities equally and
not only in 'this community or that', and therefore, the criteria chosen to
identify them should be such which were applicable to all. Considering the
importance given to socioeconomic inequality by Nehru, such common
criteria could be only poverty and accompanying illiteracy, which together
lead to lower occupations and in combination to social backwardness - the
economically and socially backward classes and the aim of the constitution
makers was their 'educational, social and economic advance.'

The First National Commission for Backward Classes had refused
reservations on the basis of caste, and the Central Government had urged
the State in 1960 to use economic criteria. It was the States that fudged
up the criteria and the Second Central Backward Classes Commission
completed the process. Removal of poverty and compulsory education
would have done more than reservations. Nehru, Ambedkar, and other
Constitution makers could not have imagined that any post-independence
commission in India would introduce the word Shudra, which is relevant
only to one community, brings in *communalism*, and defeat the original
idea of 'educational, social and economic advance' of all communities as
such, without making distinction on grounds of religion, caste, sex, region,
or any other parochial reason. To do otherwise would have defeated the
purpose of the said articles. Nehru was a keen student of history. There was
no reason for him to give socioeconomic inequalities the name of Shudra,
when his aim was to cover the whole of the Indian population. Nehru's goal,
the learned Chief Justice concedes, was a "casteless and classless society".
Ambedkar went even further when he advocated annihilation of caste. He
stated in the Constituent Assembly:

> We must begin by acknowledging the fact that there is complete
> absence of two things in Indian Society. One of these is equality.
> On the social plane, we have in India a society based on the
> principle of graded inequality which means elevation for some
> and degradation for others. On the economic plane, we have a

---

[424] *Judgements Today*, 1992: quoted by Justice P.B. Sawant: Pages 648-649: Para 413

society in which there are some who have immense wealth as against many who live in abject poverty.[425]

Inequality on the social plain was redressed with the identification of Scheduled Castes and, to a lesser extent, the Scheduled Tribes. The inequality on the economic plane was the same which Nehru described as socioeconomic inequality and had come down for hundreds of years due to foreign oppression. It was still continuing when India got its freedom in 1947. After independence, the State enacted Article 340 to appoint a commission and to remove inequality in educational institutions. Draft Article 10(3) and Article 16(4) were enacted to facilitate representation in services under the State. Therefore, when the Constitution used the word classes, it was in terms of classification of Marx and not castes or tribes. It would have been illogical to repeat Articles 341 and 342 in one form or the other. Economic inequality was relevant to vast majority of Indians and affected a much larger population than that on the 'social plane'. Mere inclusion of Scheduled Castes and Scheduled Tribes in Article 15(4) could not impart their or similar backwardness on the socially and educationally backward classes.

The Supreme Court might not have been bound by the opinions expressed in the Constituent Assembly, but the opinions quoted above were of the Prime Minister and the two most prominent members of the Drafting Committee of the Constituent Assembly. They could not be taken lightly. Realizing this, the Court recorded several past judgments in which the Supreme Court had wanted to ascertain the 'original intent' of the constitution makers.[426] In one form or the other, most of the judgments of Supreme Court quoted below gave the highest priority to the removal of poverty and illiteracy. Only uncertainty with caste masked this intention, and they tended to return to caste to a variable extent.

The next question was: Did the Indian Constitution, too, support the concept of socioeconomic backwardness? Describing the 'core of the Indian Constitutional philosophy' *in Part 111 of 'Fundamental Rights' and Part 1V dealing with 'Directive Principles of State Policy'*, Justice Ratnavel Pandian refers to two types of backwardness in his concurring judgment. The *first* arose out of 'historic injustice and inequalities, either inherited or artificially

---

[425] Judgment 2008: C.J.: Para 3
[426] *A.I.R.* Supreme Court 1993: 551: 78

created' and the *second* out of '*social and economic inequality*'.[427] There is no third. The former was covered in the form of Scheduled Castes in 1936. Even Scheduled Tribes, who were covered after 1947, had no stigma. The other category was of social and economic inequality or of socially, economically, and educationally backward classes. Thus, the Indian Constitution does support the concept of economic or socioeconomic backwardness and its relief. Articles 15(4) and 16(4) were enacted to achieve this constitutional purpose. The uncertainty returned in 1992 when the Court in its majority judgments added an additional category of outcastes or Panchama, which did not belong even to the age old caste system. With the utmost respect, there was certain dichotomy in the Mandal case judgment. If on the one hand it separated backward class of citizens other than SC and ST and called them Shudras, on the other hand it agreed with the Mandal Commission that even the worst affected Scheduled Castes like puruda vannana, whom it had described as outcastes and Panchama in Para 2 of the judgment, were the example of the same *Shudras*. Both could not be equated. In fact, the first category, despite a name different from socially and educationally backward classes due to reasons discussed earlier, was none other than the same category, described in the 'core philosophy' as category of 'social and economic inequality'. The category of 'historic injustice and inequalities, either inherited or artificially created' comprised of only Scheduled Castes. Scheduled Tribes did not have similar disabilities. Post-independence rhetoric and politics further fudged up the already distorted ancient social structure.

Justice Pandian blamed '*social ostracism*', undignified social status, and sub-human living conditions for the miserable condition of those 'living below the poverty line' and says that the only solution is "to achieve equal status and equal opportunity" through "constitutional justice so that all the citizens of this country *irrespective* of their religion, race, caste, sex, place of birth or any of them may achieve the goal of an egalitarian society".[428] Social ostracism, which was a procedure under Athenian democracy to expel any citizen from city state, is not relevant by any stretch of imagination to Other Backward Classes like Yadavs, Lingyats, and hundreds of others, not even Scheduled Castes. Therefore, but for it, the statement of Justice Pandian could be truer for the category of socioeconomic backwardness, which is still rampant in most parts of the country. People living below the poverty line, in

---

[427] J.T.: 294: 11
[428] Judgements Today, 1992 (6) S.C.: 292: 4

sub-human living conditions and without an opportunity to get reasonable occupation due to illiteracy or lack of opportunity, irrespective of their religion, race, caste, sex, place of birth or any of them, were reasons enough in themselves to seek redress. Such was the intensity of the propaganda after the independence that even habitually somber Apex Court could not view socially and educationally backward classes from a neutral perspective. Caste psychosis has crippled the nation. The governments and the courts, even the people at large, have been conditioned to 'historic' injustice and inequalities inflicted by the non-existing invading Aryans upon the equally non-existing 'foreign' Dravidians and the local Aborigines so much that they completely ignore even now the eventful period of past millennium or more, which reduced the Indians to abject poverty, ignorance, loss of power, bonded labor, and exploitation.

On the issue of equality, the Chief Justice Balakrishnan quotes from the 1948 Universal Declaration of Human Rights. Its Preamble speaks of 'the equal and inalienable rights of all members of the human family' . . . and of 'the equal rights of men and women' and comments that "reservation is one of the many tools that are used to preserve and promote the essence of equality, so that disadvantaged groups can be brought to the forefront of civil life".[429] The Universal Declaration of Human Rights was concerned with equality between all people. It did not distinguish between different religions and upper and lower castes. The disadvantaged could be from any section of society and so the advantaged. Disadvantaged have no one description.

At the concluding address of the Constituent Assembly when President Rajendra Prasad asserted "that it will be our endeavor to end poverty and squalor and its companions, hunger and disease; to abolish distinction and exploitation and to ensure decent conditions of living" and hoped that in this "we shall have the unstinted service and co-operation of all our people and the sympathy and support of all the communities",[430] he did not distinguish between poverty and hunger among adherents of this religion or that or this caste or the other and this region or that. Therefore, the criteria for identification had to be the same for all communities, castes, and regions and the aim, too, the same—the removal of social and economic inequality. Education was provided through Article 15(4) and assured appointments in services under the State for a limited period through Article 16(4).

---

[429]   Chief Justice: 2008. Para 4-6
[430]   Ibid.: Para 7

Reservation may be a tool to remove inequality, but once that inequality is removed at family level, its continuation means denial of 'equal rights of men and women' not only of those whose right to equality was appropriated temporarily, but also of those who still linger far behind and get restricted access to measures meant specifically for them. Continuation of reservations for more than sixty years has made a mockery of the dictum. "The claim to equality before the law is in substantial sense the most fundamental of the rights of man."[431]

In 1960, when the Central Government left the identification of socially and educationally backward classes to the respective States with the advice to use *economic criteria*, once again it confirmed the original intention of the Constitution makers in enacting Articles 15(4) and 16(4), but politics intervened and the States ignored the original intention.[432] The word 'backward' lost its universal character to the detriment of poorer sections. Even religion, which was assiduously evaded by Nehru, Ambedkar, and the Constitution, is being surreptitiously introduced as a basis for backwardness. It appears we are being dragged towards proportional representation, which divided the country in 1947 and was assiduously rejected by the constitution makers. Compulsory education till fourteen years of age is the only welcome step toward educating the poor.

Central Government's Views in 2007

The Solicitor General's remark in *Ashok Kumar Thakur* case in 2007, "centuries of calculated oppression and habitual submission has reduced a considerable section of our community to a life of serfdom,"[433] repeats the same old story. The composition, occupation and the status of members of castes have been changing for ages even in the case of the lowest castes. Joan Mencher gives the example of *chamars* who are one of the lowest in the supposed caste 'hierarchy' and says that the "present day chamars are scattered over wide areas of Northern India and are recruited from a number of tribes and local castes. Only a small number of chamars are working with skins of dead animals and most of them have shifted to agriculture labor".[434]

---

[431]   Judgment 2008: Chief Justice: Para 4
[432]   Tata Institute's Report in Mandal Commission's Report
[433]   Judgment 2008: Para 60
[434]   Joan Mencher, 1991: 96-97

In 1936, the British excluded *Backward Hindus*, the future Scheduled Tribes, Muslims, Christians and Sikhs, etc. from the *Scheduled* Castes because they suffered from no 'calculated oppression and habitual submission'. Muslims had ruled India for centuries and Christians had benefitted from the British rule. Where was the question of their being oppressed? The poverty and illiteracy of some sections due to internal factors, was another issue.

The admission by the Solicitor General that backward classes were '*nothing* but collection of certain castes' almost concedes that reservations were made only on the basis of castes. His contention that State Lists were operating for the purposes of both Articles 16(4) and 15(4) and because there had been no challenge it meant that the criteria of the Mandal Commission were 'more or less accepted' was, at best, half truth.[435] The Supreme Court gave no opinion on the validity of the Commission's Report or its lists of Backward Classes. On the contrary, the Government had to accept the pre-August 1990 lists with the permission of the Court. His assertion that "the National Commission held 236 public hearings at various places since its inception", recommended '297 for inclusion and rejected 288 requests' after examining the applications and taking note of '*ethnographic history* of the concerned castes/sub-groups/communities', is, again, a ploy. He does not reveal the 'ethnographic history' of both—the included and the excluded castes. Nor does he explain on which new ethnic history the Commission included Jats and some others among the OBCs in some States in the year 2000, when their previous ethnographic history qualified them to be among the forward castes in 1980 and again in 1992. Nor does he reveal the ethnic history of a minority community which entitled it to reservations as a whole. Nor does the Solicitor General mention the reasons for *exclusion* of Marathas from the Central List of SEBCs, when even Ambedkar stated that after the death of Shivaji they were reduced to Shudras. The ethnographic histories of 3,743 castes comprising the socially and educationally backward classes were never produced before the Court; perhaps they never existed. In fact, no caste once included among the backward classes was excluded from the list in more than last sixty years.

Mentally, the Solicitor General was still under the British rule when he stated "that large sections of the country are socially and educationally backward; that this problem is not new but is age old; that such backwardness arose because of certain peculiarities of the caste system which proceeded on the assumption that in many castes the choice of occupation of its members

---

[435] Ibid.: Para 60

was pre-determined and that members of particular castes were prohibited from engaging themselves in occupations other than those certain occupations which were considered to be degrading and impure and considered fit only for those castes".[436] There was no predetermination of caste and no prohibition to change of occupation. Carpenters and milkmen carrying on the same occupations did not become degraded and impure, nor the carpet makers. Their backwardness was due to poverty and illiteracy. One can agree with the Solicitor General when he says, "Education can be a liberating capability but access to it is made difficult, if not impossible, by such inherited characteristics as lower social status, rural origin, informal work status and gender or combination of these."[437] These factors were not new and were not peculiar to any particular caste and community. Lack of access to education was due to siphoning off of billions of rupees, which could have altered the face of the country, incompetence of governments, politicization of backward castes, and the failure to implement constitutional intentions like abolition of caste.

An Additional Solicitor General's argument in 2007 that judicial scrutiny was unnecessary, as 'the constitutionality of quotas has been repeatedly affirmed' and the Indian law and the Indian Constitution do not 'compel" *the* courts to review 'suspect classification', the Courts are obliged to accept even the 'suspect identification', was amazing.[438] The issue was not of constitutionality of quota but of its veracity. The Constitution might or might not compel, but it also does not prohibit scrutiny, especially of a suspect classification. If even the suspect identifications are to prevail, then why not exclude the provision of judicial scrutiny altogether? To quote the Chief Justice of Australia from the majority judgment itself: "In difficult cases the Governments leave decisions to courts not only due to political expediency and to pursue a safe course, but also because the people accept the Courts as the appropriate means when Governments decide not to attempt to solve the disputes by the political process."[439] Why the learned advocate and the Government it was representing were scared of facing the truth, it is for the State to say. The view that the Supreme Court is bound by the Government's *suspect identification*, because the 'political executive is co-equal of judiciary' and 'know its people well', might be acceptable in an ideal society, but was the Mandal Commission's identification above suspicion

---

[436] Ibid.: 60
[437] Ibid.
[438] Ibid., 2008: C.J.: Para 61
[439] *A.I.R.* Supreme Court 1993: 519: 26A, quoted in the majority judgment

even in the eyes of the Court? Errors, too, could occur in any 'exercise of such magnitude and complexity' and could be righted, 'if pointed out', but, with respect, was the detection and correction of errors in the lists of backward classes, which were not accepted even by the Supreme Court in 1992, not the ultimate plea of the petitioners in 2007?

It can also be argued that having dealt with caste and tribe-related backwardness separately, Articles 15(4) and Articles 16(4) of the Constitution were enacted to remove the widespread poverty and illiteracy rampant in the society and to empower the Indian people, irrespective of their religion, caste, sex, and region. The British accepted caste-based reservations in the form of Scheduled Castes as an exception. They identified, but did not give backward status to future Scheduled Tribes. In the case of Other Backward Classes, the Indian Constitution had to be amended to entitle them to special provisions, but as socially and educationally backward *classes* and not as castes or communities. When the case came up before the Supreme Court in 1991, the colonial anthropology and Dumont's Homo Hierarchichus still ruled the roost, but by 2008, enough new material had emerged to challenge the old perceptions. Therefore, when the *Ashok Kumar Thakur* case came up before the Constitution Bench in 2007-2008, it was surprising that the main petitioners did not challenge the 1992 judgment on perceptual grounds. This brings us to the very important matter of how the Supreme Court viewed this issue prior to 1992.

Previous Judgments

In Champakam Dorairajan, a seven-judge Bench of the Supreme Court "struck down the Government Order on the ground that founded on the basis of religion and castes, it is opposed to the Constitution and is in violation of the fundamental rights guaranteed to the citizens".[440] Constitutionally and factually, this 1951 judgment is still the landmark judgment. The problems started when classes in Articles 15 and 16 were equated with castes on one pretext or the other. Few sociologists and historians would agree with the notion that caste is a homogeneous endogamous social unit in which there is no mobility and that a barber remains a barber even if he has acquired wealth. In fact, every caste has differently placed segments, members, and families, and even the lowest castes are not obliged to follow any particular

---

[440] Judgment 2008: Chief Justice: Para 106-121

occupation. If they were, there would have been no Phule, no Ambedkar, no 'Dalit' President of India, no 'Chamar' lady Speaker of the Lower House of Parliament, and thousands of others in present times, and in the past, no Valmiki and scores of similar highly learned saints and rulers or ruling dynasties, which came from the families of supposedly low origin.

In 2008, the Chief Justice quoted various counsels who reported from the previous judgments that the problem of determining who are socially backward classes is undoubtedly very complex; distinction between caste and class is indispensable in order to find a *new* basis for ascertaining social and educational backwardness in place of caste; classification of socially and educationally backward classes should be made on the basis of economic condition and occupation; under no circumstance, a class can be equated to a caste though the caste of an individual or group of individuals may be a relevant factor in putting him in a particular class; and finally, if caste *as a whole* is socially and educationally backward, reservation can be made in favor of such a caste. This shows the hesitation in the quoted judgments, even in the conditional equation of caste with class.

In a subsequent decision, in *Triloki Nath (II)*, the Supreme Court observed that the expression 'backward class' is not synonymous with 'backward caste', and in another case it stated that 'the Government should not proceed on the basis that once a class is considered as a backward class it should continue to be backward class for all times'. The Supreme Court states from the famous case of *M. R. Balaji & Ors*:

> State of Mysore issued an order that *all* the communities except the Brahmin community would fall within the definition of socially and educationally backward class and Scheduled Castes and Scheduled Tribes and 75 percent of the seats in educational institutions were reserved for them. It was held that the classes of citizens who are 'deplorably poor *automatically* become socially backward' and 'the occupation of citizens and the place of their habitation also result in social backwardness'. However, it was held that 'the classification of socially backward citizens on the basis of their caste *alone* is not permissible under Article 15(4) . . . *The Problem of determining who are socially backward classes is undoubtedly very complex . . . it will need an elaborate investigation and collection of data and examining the said data in a rational and scientific way*'[441] (emphasis added).

---

[441] Judgment 2008: Chief Justice (C.J.). Para 109

The perception of the State of Mysore that except for Brahmins *all* communities would fall under socially and educationally backward classes and Scheduled Castes and Scheduled Tribes was interesting. It was an indirect endorsement of the Puranic notion that, but for Brahmins, by which it meant the learned, the rest all would be Shudras in Kaliyug and, therefore, both forward and backward classes would have to be found among the same Shudras and *not* that all Shudras would be backward. It once again brings up the definition of Shudra. Another important observation was that 'classes of citizens who are deplorably poor automatically become socially backward'. If this stresses the importance of abject poverty in causing social backwardness, it also hints at the futility to identify every type of social backwardness in terms of impurity and pollution. What was required was continuous 'elaborate investigation' and scientific research to justify the presence and persistence of backwardness and need to continue corrective measures only where they might be needed. Despite the above direction of the Supreme Court, none of the States and the Central Governments went into any sophisticated investigations of the Hindu social structure after independence, or collected any data to analyze it in a systematic way. At least, the 2008 judgment does not mention any. Nor any data is available in public domain. On the contrary, the State of Tamil Nadu claimed 88 percent of its population as backward and provided 69 percent reservation in educational institutions and services under the State on caste basis, without explaining the rationale behind it. Even the meaning of social backwardness remains unclear. In *K. C. Vasantha Kumar and Another* v. *State of Karnataka* Desai, J. observed:

> It is said, 'look at the caste, its traditional functions, its position in relation to upper castes by the standard of purity and pollution, pure and not so pure occupation, once these questions are satisfactorily answered without anything more, those who belong to that caste must be labeled socially and educationally backward'. This over-simplified approach ignored a very realistic situation existing in each caste that *every such caste, whose members claim to be socially and educationally backward, had an economically well-placed segment* [442] *(emphasis added).*

---

[442]   Ibid.: Para 118

Justice Desai's recognition that *every* caste has a well-defined economically advanced segment tells the factual story of how the society has always functioned. The same disparity is seen in education and occupations. Only the percentages vary. The same applies to minority communities. In an oft quoted judgment, Chinnappa Reddy, J. observed:

> *Poverty,* the *economic factor* brands all backwardness just as the erect posture brands the homo sapiens and distinguishes him from all other animals, in the eyes of the beholder from Mars. But, whether his racial stock is Caucasian, Mongoloid, Negroid, etc., further investigation will have to be made . . . In India, the matter is further aggravated, complicated and pitilessly tyrannized by the ubiquitous caste system . . . It is a notorious fact that there is an upper crust of rural society consisting of the superior castes, generally the priestly, the landlord and the merchant castes, there is a bottom strata consisting of the 'out-castes' of Indian Rural Society, namely the Scheduled Castes, and, in between the highest and the lowest, there are large segments of population who because of the low gradation of the caste to which they belong in the rural society[443] (emphasis added).

One more judgment admits poverty to be the principle cause of backwardness. One more judgment uses the expression 'out-castes' and racial configuration of India's population into Aryan Dravidians and Aborigines and Caucasians, Mongoloids, and Negroid, which had plagued the nation for more than one and a half century. Luckily, with better knowledge the racial notions have been finally rejected. The assumption of a hierarchically based middle 'strata' was invented to defend the 19th century expression 'outcastes'. Yet, the British administrators and the Indian sociologists often reported that each caste considered itself superior to the other, especially in the so-called middle strata. The merchant and landlord strata are a fact, but their composition keeps changing. Sanskritization and Rajputization of lower castes and appearance of new tax-paying Shudras has been occurring for centuries. Landlords are mostly agriculturists and the merchants are from all sections of society. Even the rich Shudras had servants from the upper castes.[444]

---

[443] Ibid.: Para 119
[444] Yamasaki, 1997: 25

One of the main arguments of the court in the Mandal case was that as 'caste, occupation, poverty and social backwardness were intertwined in our society' one could take a caste, "apply the criteria of backwardness evolved by it . . . and determine whether it qualifies or not. If it does qualify, what emerges is a backward class. The concept of caste in this behalf was *not* confined among Hindus".[445] With the highest respect, even if these criteria were applied, what would emerge would be backward *castes*, not backward classes. With plenty of mobility at the level of families, composition even of the the lowest castes keep changing. Mere caste name does not entitle reservations. The absence of nexus between caste and occupation has been amply discussed in previous chapters. The Chief Justice continues:

> In *R. Chitralekha*' it was laid down by the Supreme Court that classification of socially and educationally backward classes should be made on the basis of *economic* condition and *occupation*. Suba Rao, J. (as he then was), speaking for the majority, held that a classification of backward classes based on economic conditions and occupations is not bad in law and does not offend Article 15(4). It was also held that '*under no circumstance* a class can be equated to a caste . . . though the caste of an individual or group of individuals may be a relevant factor in putting him in a particular class'.[446] (Emphasis added)

It was an oft-repeated admission by the highest court in the land that the economic condition mattered the most, for upon economic conditions and education depend the occupations and on all of them, the social status. A judgment now also says reservation on the basis of economic conditions and occupation is not bad in law and that under no circumstances a class can be equated with class, but yet allows a caste to become a relevant factor without indicating that factor. A particular class is a vague term usually used for economic classes. The difficulty is the unexplained 'relevant factor', which instead of being an exception has become the rule to justify caste-based reservations. Like in *P. Rajendran* v. *State of Madras*, where the Apex Court held that the 'backward class' in Article 16(4) *cannot* be read as 'backward caste',[447] in Pradip Tandon's case, too, it was stated in Para 17:

---

[445] *A.I.R.* Supreme Court 1993: 554: 83
[446] Judgment 2008: Chief Justice: Para 111
[447] Ibid., 2008: 121

The expression 'classes of citizens' indicate a *homogenous* section of the people who are grouped together because of certain likenesses and common *traits* and who are identifiable by some common attributes. *The* homogeneity *of the class of citizens is social and educational backwardness.* Neither caste nor religion nor place of birth will be the uniform element of common attributes to make them a class of citizens[448] (emphasis added).

It was an important and realistic statement. Classes are homogeneous. Castes are not homogeneous sections of people. 'Common traits' and 'attributes' do make 'homogeneous' *classes* of citizens, but not a collection of differently placed people within castes and communities alone or in combination. Each must be treated separately and redress provided at the functional level of stratification. On the question of the meaning of social backwardness, the Chief Justice states from the judgment in the *Indira Sawhney* case:

And in *Indra Sawhney's case* (supra), the majority held that the ideal and wise method would be to mark out various occupations which on the lower level in many cases amongst Hindus would be their caste itself and find out their social acceptability and educational standard, weigh them in the balance of economic conditions and, the result would be backward class of citizens needing a genuine protective umbrella. And after having adopted occupation as the starting point, the next point should be to ascertain their *social acceptability.* A person carrying on *scavenging becomes an untouchable* whereas others who were as law (probably 'low') in the social strata as untouchables became *depressed* (? Nehru's *stratum higher* than the untouchables but, nonetheless, depressed.) The Court has cautioned that the backwardness should be *traditional.* Mere educational or social backwardness would not have been sufficient as it would enlarge the field thus frustrating the very purpose of the constitutional goal. It was pointed out that *after* applying these tests, the economic criteria or the means-test should be applied *since poverty is the prime*

---

[448] Ibid.: Para 12

cause of all backwardness as it *generates* social and educational backwardness.[449] (Emphasis added)

If we go by the last part of the judgment first, it clearly and unambiguously brings out that in the eyes of even the 1992 judgment poverty was not only *the prime cause* of all backwardness but it also *generated* social and educational backwardness. This observation of a nine judges Bench supported by many judgments quoted above should be enough to state that poverty or socioeconomic backwardness was and remains the principle cause of backwardness or depression in Indian society. Social unacceptability of scavengers in the form of untouchability was understandable, but how to find those who, though not untouchable, were still as low as them. Occupations, too, largely depend upon economic and educational status. How occupations were misused as castes by the British Government was shown in the statement of census superintendent Middleton in Chapter 6. Applying some of the worst scenes in South India to the whole country was unacceptable. Marc Galanter points out that in 1931 Franchise Commission had to reconcile a South scene where there was 'unproblematic untouchability and a North in which it could be doubted whether the same phenomenon ever existed.' Ultimately, Duskin remarked even in the case of Scheduled Castes that "hundreds of various castes listed form any kind of unity through a common relationship their members have with government".[450] The question whether caste-based reservation infringes Article 15(1) is answered by Chief Justice Balakrishnan by quoting Justice Jeevan Reddy, who further quoted Chief Justice Wanchoo in the *P. Rajendran* v. *State of Madras* case:

> The contention is that the list of socially and educationally backward classes for whom reservation is made under Rule 5 is nothing but a list of certain castes. Therefore, reservation in favour of certain castes based only on caste considerations violates Article 15(1), which prohibits discrimination on the ground of caste only. Now if the reservation in question had been based only on caste and had not taken into account the social and educational backwardness of the caste in question, it would be violative of Article 15(1). But it must not be forgotten

---

[449] Judgment 2008: Chief Justice: Para 121
[450] Galanter, 1984: 14 and 130; Khanna, 2002: 90-92

that a caste is also a class of citizens and if the caste *as a whole* is socially and educationally backward reservation can be made in favour of such a caste on the ground that it is a socially and educationally backward class of citizens within the meaning of Article 15(4). *As it was found that members of these castes as a whole were educationally and socially backward, the list which had been coming on from as far back as 1906 was finally adopted for purposes of Article 15(4)*[451] *(emphasis added)*

The *first* problem is that no one clarifies the meaning of caste. If caste is a social class, it has to be homogeneous. *Second*, no caste or Jati is socially and educationally backward 'as a whole'. Each one has economically, educationally, occupationally, and socially differently placed segments, families, and individuals. These make them diverse and not homogeneous. *Third*, the commissions or the courts do not explain how a caste or caste cluster spread over large areas with populations often of millions could be identified as backward as a whole on analyzing two villages in a district. Merely laying down the theoretical parameters, with respect, is not enough. We do not even know the grounds on which the 1906 List was made. Therefore, it is difficult to digest that just because the list was made by our late masters of fair skin when these Articles could not be imagined, the same lists would remain relevant for the purposes of Article 15(4) and 16(4) for all times to come.

From being an educated Scheduled Caste family and after having known privations, Chief Justice Balakrishnan was fully cognizant of the situation. Realizing the relevance of objections, he quoted Chinnappa Reddy, J. in *K. C. Vasantha Kumar*, "One cannot quarrel with the statement that social science *research* and *not judicial impressionism* should form the basis of examination, by courts, of the sensitive question of reservation for backward classes"[452] (emphasis added). Social sciences research is an ongoing process, not a one-time affair. The nation cannot stick to made-up concepts of caste and social justice of colonial times, which have been fed to scores of generations for the last two centuries. Justice Arijit Pasayat, speaking for himself, and Justice Thakur, too, echoed the Chief Justice from the case of *Thomas* which had warned that "social science research, *not* judicial impressionism, will alone tell the whole truth". And "a constant process of

---

451   Judgment 2008: Chief Justice.: Para 120
452   Judgment in Ashok Kumar Thakur case, 2008: C.J.: Para: 160

objective re-evaluation of progress registered by the 'underdog' categories is essential lest a once deserving 'reservation' should be *degraded* into reverse discrimination"[453] (emphasis added). In the previously quoted *Balaji* case, too, the Supreme Court had warned that determining socially backward classes was a complex problem which would need proper evaluation with the upgrading of knowledge. Fortunately, there is enough new knowledge available and cited to merit a re-look at the entire issue of social justice.

The conflicting observations of the Supreme Court show how difficult it must have been for the judges to come to any definite conclusion after the independence. Historical accounts of the past societies were not available. Scanty records of some foreign travelers and historians were not good enough. The Muslim period was again not of much help. Europeans had their own versions. Then there were conflicting interests, religious expansionism, politics, and propaganda during the colonial regime. Post-independence India, too, adopted the colonial relics which plague the Hindu social structure and the 'Law of Caste' in the *Hindu Law* even today. Therefore, if the courts showed reluctance to go into the emerging racial, societal, historical, and social anthropological views, which have challenged the colonial time anthropology and racial theories, it was understandable. In 2008, the five-judge Constitution Bench was bound by the decision of the nine-judge Special Bench. Still Justice Dalveer Bhandari unmistakably expressed the anguish of the Bench by saying, "*Sawhney I has tied our hands*".[454] Justice Arijit Passayat and the concurring judge observed in a highly significant comment, 'The ultimate object is the eradication of castes and that is the foundation of reservations.'[455] If today it is difficult to eradicate castes, it is not because of the Constitution or its makers, but because the courts have converted classes into castes and the politics has overwhelmed social structure.

Graduation removes educational backwardness, but poverty and its resultant social backwardness take time to go. However, graduation does put a question mark on caste and religion-based admissions in post graduation institutions, where reservations are meant for socially and *educationally* backward classes, and which made Justice Bhandari to observe that graduation makes one educationally forward. To give a level playing field, a modified affirmative action would have better fulfilled the necessities

---

[453] Ibid.: Justice Dr Arijit Pasayat: Para: 54
[454] Judgment 2008: Justice Dalveer Bhandari: Para 434
[455] Judgment 2008: Justice Arijit Passayat

and hopes of the former educationally backward to go in for postgraduate studies or higher technical and professional education. Affirmative action does not mean reservation.

Summary

None of the pre-1992 judgments cited above mentions Panchama and Shudra. If these were so important, they would not have escaped the notice of the highly learned judiciary for more than forty years after the independence. On the contrary, almost every judgment referred to poverty as the most crucial element in backwardness, and most of them said that caste cannot be equated with class. There is enough evidence from the colonial period, in the speeches of Nehru, Ambedkar, K. M. Munshi, and others in the Constituent Assembly, the Directing Principles of the Constitution, and the Supreme Court judgments quoted in this chapter to show that besides the Scheduled Castes and the Scheduled Tribes there was a large section of population which was socially, educationally and economically backward and in which poverty, illiteracy, and lack of representation in the corridors of power were the critical factors. Some people called them Other Backward Classes, some socially and educationally backward classes, some socioeconomically backward classes, and some backward class of citizens. In 1931, it was recorded that these classes were poor, illiterate, and in low occupations and but for them suffered from no disability. Ambedkar said it was wrong to call them Shudras. However, the Mandal Commission still labeled the same backward classes Shudra, without defining the term. There was no reason to think it was correct.

Present Situation

Maybe it is time to discard the past and enter the present and the future. It has been said that castes are impossible to distinguish on the basis of general appearance. 'As there is no pure race, there is no pure caste.' In fact, there are no races at all and no pure castes. There is a sea change in the attitude of backward classes. In the pursuit of reservations and political gains, some politicians often indulge in puerile propaganda. "The claim that one is a Brahmin is absolutely untenable and untrue, just as the denunciation that one is a Shudra or Antyaja." Sedasivan further quotes M. A. Sherring, who stated, "It is very probable that originally all Hindus were not merely of the same race, but of the same family and in their earlier relationship were entirely free from those distinctions, which have separated them for many ages into numerous castes and tribes."[456] Racial theory of caste was a clever idea to divide a vibrant society. It prevailed, till it was recently shown that Indians have been a mixed population for millenniums. The way caste was used by the colonial rulers destroyed the creative and inventive talent of the majority of population. Its central role was its *structural* sense in which Jatis combined and still combine with each other to pursue economic and political power and create lateral mobility to represent the 'regional system of interdependence'. This has mostly benefited the dominant castes such as Yadavs and Jats in the North and Lingyats, Vokkilogas, and others in the South. They were included among the backward classes in the twentieth century. The result is that the lowest and the poorest sections of society have neither been able to combine nor get the intended benefits from the remedial measures.

Before 1947, the ruled were the agricultural labor and the large number of cultivators and tenants of past landowners. With post-independence land reforms, when the occupiers and tenants turned into owners of lands, it completely altered the rural scenario. These old and new landholders now form the most powerful lobby among the recently called Shudras. They are combining to form pressure groups and are the greatest exponent of their invented discrimination. Some of them relish their 'Shudra' status and deliberately use crass language to assert their humble origin. They are politically strong and socially high landholding dominant castes. Many of their children get their education abroad and are in prominent Government jobs, in business, and now also in politics. Yet they continue to be included among the backward and discriminated castes. The unorganized labor that forms over 90 percent of the labor force does not get even minimum wages and collateral benefits. In the rapidly increasing urban society, increased education and mobility have greatly diminished the traditional role of castes, but new upper 'castes' or groups have emerged on economic and occupational lines in both urban and rural areas. The religious minorities have many economically, educationally, and socially disadvantaged groups, but they are hardly identified and separated from the main community for social benefits.

---

[456]   M.A. Sherring, quoted by Sadashivan: 200: 288

Irrational reservations on the basis of whole castes have upset social relation, promoted economic disparity and retarded progress of the truly backward sections of society. Appearance of Sanskritized, Kshatrized, and Rajputized lower castes, Vratya Kshatriyas, and new tax-paying Shudras and increased mobility among various sections of society during the last hundreds of years, have made it impossible to know who should be called culturally forward and who backward. Even Rajputs are vratyas or from lower castes. Composition of poor and the backward has been changing for thousands of years. Rigidity was added to it during the last couple of centuries and a new 'caste system' emerged when the British took over. The political power has shifted, after the independence, to the better off among the so-called lower castes and among the non-Hindus, to their feudal sections. Service of humanity, love for the weak, and assertions of equality and human rights are often cloaks to hide bigotry. The latest entry in politics is civil society. No one knows its length, breadth or reach.

India is often described as a multi-racial, multi-lingual, multi-cultural, and multi religious society. In reality, it is a mixed population in which separate races cannot be isolated; different people's physical characteristic are a matter of environment and most of the languages and dialects have common origin. Cultures and social practices of different regions have both common and distinct features. Even the religions, which appeared in India of the past, have considerable common elements. Colonial Raj created two types of backwardness—one related to castes in the form of depressed classes and backward tribes and the other related to classes or those who were simply poor, illiterate, and in low occupation and but for that had no disability. The Constituent Assembly enacted Articles 341 and 342 to cover the specific categories of Scheduled Castes and Scheduled Tribes and Articles 15(4) and 16(4) to cover social and economic disparities in the general category, which comprised of rest of the population. Barring poverty and lack of education due to centuries of foreign domination, the second category had no specific disability and yet reservations were given on the basis of their castes.

The courts are as much bound to implement Articles 14, 15(1) and 16(2), which are essential and more *enduring* parts of the Fundamental Rights than clauses 4 of Articles 15 and 16 that were envisaged as temporary measures. Provided initially for ten years, there is no end to reservations even after sixty-three years. The result is that clauses (4) of both articles are becoming permanent and clauses (1) and (2), respectively, of Articles 15 and 16 more or less redundant. One inescapable conclusion from the study of backward classes is that multiple nomenclatures and absence of clear definitions create multiple confusions and make it difficult to find one's way. Reliance on commission/authority and political executive for determining backwardness and representation in services of each caste without a critical judicial review, with respect, proved to be an escape.

In spite of reservations since 1936, UICEF showed that 25 million Indian children have never gone to school; three out of five drop out and barely 31 percent reach to the level of 10th class. In 2004-2005, population below the poverty line was 27.5 percent. In 2009, it arose to 37.2 percent despite the expenditure of thousands of millions. The Human Development Index which was 122 in 1992 came down to 132 in 2007—08. The increase in absolute figures could be expected, but not the percentage populations. The benefits of reservations are either usurped by the upper and the middle echelons of backward classes or consumed by corruption. The elegantly named creamy layer, instead of remaining a plateau, has become a pyramid. The situation in some States of the country is alarming. Maoist rising in large inaccessible parts of the country is a warning to the nation. In urban areas, the increasingly restive proletariat is bound to rise in revolt. The complacency created by increase in GDP and increased foreign direct investment with no relief to the masses is hardly comforting, if not sickening. In recent years, there is fall even in GDP and the economy is in doldrums.

The Mandal Commission created surrogate backwardness and surrogate backward classes under the garb of Shudra when it cited the worst among the untouchable as examples of socially and educationally backward classes. Other Backward Classes had nothing to do with untouchability. Reservations on the basis of caste—occupation nexus had no basis. Judicial impressionism needs to be revisited in view of changed perceptions. The constitutional goal could not be different from what Nehru said during the introduction of Article 15(4): "Whatever religion or anything they (other backward classes) may belong to . . . our duty (is) to help them toward educational, social and economic advance." Any diversion, he said, would be *communalism*. Socioeconomic backwardness is common to all communities. Barring in some selected Scheduled Castes, social backwardness is a lot more intertwined in the economic and educational backwardness than the other way round.

The truth is that some dominant castes in the Janata Party Government appointed the Second Backward Classes Commission in 1978 to create vote banks and capture political and economic power. After the fall of Janata Party Government in 1979, when the new Central Government took over and found no consensus among the States, it kept the report in cold storage. After ten years, the V. P. Singh Government, comprising roughly the same or similar elements as in 1978, resurrected it to save a minority Government, but it instead caused cleavages in the society. The change in perceptions in sociology, history, and historiography in recent decades has heightened the need for a second look at the whole issue of social justice, including the British time 'Law of Caste' in *Hindu Law.*

Therefore, the nation and the courts have to ponder as to what to do: *when* there is no consensus on the meaning of caste; when castes do not form four watertight compartments and the fifth one is an outright construction of the nineteenth century; when caste has been more a political than a social unit for centuries; when caste or a Jati is an antithesis of class; when there is no nexus between caste and occupation; when no caste or religious community is backward or forward *as a whole* and when an entire caste or an entire religious community cannot become the medium of social benefits due to internal diversity. The Constitution provides social benefits only for their socially and educationally backward *classes* or backward *class* of citizens. It is established now that in contrast to political units like caste, family has been the functional unit of social stratification, mobility, economic dealings, and inter-caste and intra-caste relations for centuries. Therefore, social justice, too, should be rendered on the basis of backward classes, and *within* the backward classes on the basis of families and, where applicable, individuals. Backward classes can be found within all castes, communities, and groups. Articles 341 and 342 already provide reservations for groups and parts of castes and tribes and so should Article 15(4) and 16(4) in which parts and groups could be classes. The continuing increase in the financial limit of the 'creamy layer' has denied opportunities to the really deserving.

The next question is: Should reservations continue as such or be replaced by a suitable form of affirmative action as in it is in rest of the world? The country can no longer be held hostage to obsolete theories like compensatory discrimination. The need today is for more schools, more colleges, more medical units, more jobs, more opportunities for self-employment and for enforcement of minimum pays and perks even in temporary jobs like unorganized labor. The situation has changed since 1947 when only Government jobs were considered prestigious. Other occupations and earnings from self-employments, too, must be considered in discontinuing reservations. The social sciences are emerging out of the shadow of the colonial era. Now it is the turn of the society and the law.

With the change of Central Government in May 2014, one hopes that the whole gambit of backward classes would be given a fresh look, including the procedure for their identification and relief in consonance with Articles 15(1) and 16(2) on the one hand, and to meet the requirements of Articles 15(4) and 16(4) on the other. A further review would be needed by the highest court in the land not only of the aforesaid issues, but also of the definition of Shudra and the type of backwardness it covers.

It was reported on 25 June, 2014 that with an eye on the approaching assembly elections the Congress-NCP government of Maharashtra has approved 16 per cent reservation for Marathas and five per cent for Muslims in government jobs and education institutions. This has raised the quantum of the reservation in jobs and educational institutions in that State to 73 percent of total posts held. The provision would come into effect immediately.

This has not only contravened the 50 percent limit of reservations fixed by the Supreme Court, but, based on caste and religion, the order is also unconstitutional. As a similar matter is still pending before the court, the only lasting solution is a comprehensive review of the entire Indian social justice.

In the *Indra Sawhney* case the Supreme Court drew a distinction between equality and equality of opportunity. Equality of opportunity has been a matter of discussion in the Western countries since 1960. It is also mentioned by the Supreme Court in some other judgments in India. The Rajinder Sachar Committee was appointed to suggest setting up of an equality of opportunity commission, but, it was alleged to have restricted itself to one community. Therefore, its targeted population is still unclear. The subject has its controversies. The next chapter deals with that aspect.

CHAPTER 9

EQUALITY OF OPPORTUNITY

Rajinder Sachar Committee was appointed in 2005 by the Indian Prime Minister Manmohan Singh. It was commissioned to prepare a report on the latest social, economic and educational condition of the Muslim community of India. The Committee appointed two groups, one Expert Group to recommend constitution of *Equality of Opportunity Commission* and one Expert Group on proposed *Diversity Index.*

Prof. N. R. Madhva Menon, the Chairman of the Expert Group wrote in the Preamble of the Report that although equality of opportunity in matters of public employment was a guaranteed fundamental right of every citizen and all forms of discriminations on grounds only of religion, race, caste, sex, descent, place of birth, residence, or any of them in respect of any employment or office under the State were barred, there were a number of groups that were still disadvantaged in terms of accessing the basic necessities of life to live with dignity. They were either discriminated or disproportionately denied opportunities in the fields of education, employment, nutrition, and health for circumstances that were not of their creation or which they could not overcome. He further pointed out that many multicultural societies had experimented with diverse institutional mechanisms with varying degrees of success, but in India, there were not much success due to either 'institutional weakness or weakness of policies'. Therefore, the Committee decided to recommend the appointment of an Equality of Opportunity Commission in line with those which already exist in certain countries.[457]

In Article 16, clause 1 says that there shall be equality of opportunity for all matters relating to employment or appointment to any office under the State. Clause 2 says that no citizen shall, on grounds only of religion, race, caste, sex, descent, place of birth, residence or any one of them, be eligible for, or discriminated against in respect of, any employment or office

---

[457] http//minority affairsgov.in/newsite/reports

under the State. In clause 2, the bar is not only on discrimination, but also making a citizen or citizens eligible on grounds of only religion, race etc. This raises the question, what is the meaning of discrimination; general and legal. It cannot be simply subjective or imagined or a mere propaganda. In the Preamble, Prof. Menon also does not mention undue eligibility and how it determined equality of opportunity for all citizens from all sections of society, in matters not only relating to employment or appointment to any office under the State, but also others.

The Supreme Court had also raised the issue of constitutional assurance of 'equality before the law' and 'equality of status and opportunity' in 1992. The Court had observed, "Equality has been and is the single greatest craving of all human beings at all points of time . . . all religions and political schools of thought swear by it, including the Hindu religious thought, if one looks at it by ignoring the later crudities and distortion." The concept of equality before the law, it said, "contemplates minimizing the inequalities in income and eliminating the inequalities in status, facilities and opportunities not only among *individuals* but also among *groups of people* . . ."[458] (emphasis added). The Court observed that equality was fine as an ideological concept, but as it would be 'repugnant' to treat unequal as equal, there could not be equality between the unequal.' On principle, the observation was unexceptionable, but there was a lacuna. The Court in this statement did not indicate the level at which the inequality should be determined and removed or what was meant by 'groups of people'. It also did not use the terms castes and communities, whose boundaries are notional and hazy and in each one there are many differently placed groups and sub-groups. In this direction, the court also ignored the families and individual members of such 'groups', which are the actual victims of inequalities. In the West the groups may be documented for their different circumstances, but the endeavor is always to obtain equality of opportunity at individual levels in the entire community. No individual from any community or group is barred from approaching the Equality of Opportunity Commission.

The issue now was what was meant by 'equal' and 'unequal'. Inequalities between castes did not apply to inequalities between religions, or between the majority community and the minorities. Minorities are also not one group to be branded with one name or strike. Each one is different. Socioeconomically and educationally, some minorities are more than equal. Equality of opportunity in the West is based on the principle of *equalizing*

---

[458]   *A.I.R.* Supreme Court 1993: 502: 4

opportunities, but how to equalize opportunities in India, where groups like castes and communities are hazy and their population may be in tens of millions? Not only that, there are also considerable internal inequalities not only among sub-groups, but also their families and members in economic, educational, occupational and social fields. The census figures are not available or are deceptive for they do not show the internal circumstances of each chosen group, and the State in search of its political goals jumps to reservation for every group, caste and community as a whole.

The Equality of Opportunity Group's report contains some quotes from the previous *Supreme Court judgments*. Their gist is quoted. For details, the reader may refer to the original report:

1. *The equalizing measures will have to use the same tools by which inequality was introduced and perpetuated* . . . A mere formal declaration of the right would not make unequal equal. It is necessary to take positive measures to equip the disadvantaged and the handicapped to bring them to the level of the fortunate advantaged.

2. 'Equality before the law' is illustrated not only by Articles 15 to 18 but also by the several articles in Part IV and in particular Articles 38, 39, 39-A, 41 and 46. The concept of equality before the law contemplates minimizing the inequalities in income and eliminating the inequalities in status, facilities and opportunities not only amongst individuals but also amongst groups of people to protect them from social injustice and all forms of exploitation.[459]

3. The concept of equality under the Constitution is a dynamic concept. It takes within its sweep every process of equalization and protective discrimination. In a hierarchical society with an indelible feudal stamp and incurable actual inequality, it is absurd to suggest that progressive measures to eliminate *group* disabilities and promote collective equality are antagonistic to equality on the ground and that every individual is entitled to equality of opportunity based purely on merit judged by the marks obtained by him, for to do so would make the equality clause sterile and perpetuate existing inequalities . . . 'Equality of opportunity is not simply a matter of legal equality . . . or the absence of disabilities but on the presence of abilities.'[460]

---

[459]   The Supreme Court of India through J. Sawant in Indira Sawhney v. Union of India (1992), Supp 3 SCC 215

[460]   The Supreme Court of India speaking through J. Bhagwati J. in Dr Pradeep Jain and

4. The rule of classification is not a natural and logical corollary of the rule of equality but the rule of *differentiation* is inherent in the concept of equality. Equality means parity of treatment under parity of conditions . . . The question therefore is: On what basis can any citizen or class of citizens be excluded from his or their fair share of representation? The notion of equality of opportunity has meaning only when a limited good or, in the present context, a limited number of posts, should be allocated on grounds which do not a priori exclude any section of citizens of those that desire it . . . What then, is a priori exclusion? It means exclusion on grounds other than those appropriate or rational for the good (posts) in question. The notion requires not merely that there should be no exclusion from access on grounds other than those appropriate or rational for the good in question, but the grounds considered appropriate for the good should themselves be such that people from all sections of society have an equal chance of satisfying them.[461]

Two divergent views emerged. One view presumes a hierarchical society with an indelible feudal stamp and an incurable actual inequality and answers 'one cannot countenance' to a suggestion that "progressive measures to eliminate *group* disabilities and promote collective equality are antagonistic to equality on the ground that every individual is entitled to purely on merit judged by the marks obtained by him". The other opinion asks, "On what basis can any citizen or class of citizens be excluded from his or their fair share of representation?" And answers: "The grounds considered appropriate for the good should themselves be such that people from *all* sections of society have an equal chance of satisfying them." Census figures cannot be the same not only for groups, but also for their sub-group, families and individuals. The important thing is what is meant by equality of opportunity; what is the level at which it should be obtained and how? The Equality of Opportunity Group quotes Dr Ambedkar:

On the 26th of January 1950 we are going to enter a life of contradictions. In politics we will have equality and in social and economic life we will have inequality. In politics we will be recognizing the principle of one man one vote and one vote one

---

461   Others v. Union of India and Others (1984), 3 SCC 654 at pages 676-677
Expert Group's Report

value. In our social and economic life, we shall, by reason of our
social and economic structure, continue to deny the principle of
one man one value. How long shall we continue to live this life of
contradictions? How long shall we continue to deny equality in
our social and economic life? If we continue to deny it for long,
we will do so only by putting our political democracy in peril.[462]

Though his principal interest during all his life had been Scheduled
Castes, when Dr Ambedkar spoke in the Constituent Assembly, he sought
one man one value in economic and social life for the *whole* population. The
present Group was constituted to achieve equality in social and economic
life of hitherto unmentioned or less mentioned sections of society as groups,
but without citing the reasons for such inequality in relation to others and,
especially, gross inequalities often *within* the targeted group or groups
themselves. Census reports do not tell the reasons of inequality in relation
to others, or expose the unequal conditions within the targeted groups and
sections themselves. Therefore, true equality or inequality of opportunity
can only be determined and rectified at family or individual levels, which are
easily identifiable. That is the basis of Equality of Opportunity Commissions
throughout the world.

What is Equality of Opportunity

Equality of opportunity has been extensively studied in Western
countries, but there is no consensus on its definition or its scope or the
manner in which it should be applied. In fact, there are many contradictions.
The Western modules do not apply to India. In United States, the unequal
and discriminated classes are the Negroes or African Indians, the Red
Indians, and the migratory populations from Asian and other developing
countries which are called ethnic minorities. Ethnic minorities are only a
fraction of the main population. There are no discriminated groups within
the majority population of white Americans. A similar situation is seen in
Britain and other Western countries. In India, it is different. Scheduled
Castes are almost all from Hindu majority community; Scheduled Tribes
too are mostly Hindus, and out of the 52 percent of Other Backward
Classes 43.4 percent are Hindus and 8.6 percent are non-Hindus. The total

---

[462]   Ibid.

population of backward classes is a little more than 75 percent of the total population of India. Thus, in contrast to the Western countries, most of the existing *discriminated* classes (in fact castes) come from within the home country. There are no ethnic minorities imported from abroad.

The alleged backward and the discriminated in India would, thus, be the reverse of those in the West. In the Western countries, the most affected are those engaged in labor and other low occupations. All of them seek affirmative action, which in the United States means providing opportunities for disadvantaged groups such as ethnic minorities, women, or people with disabilities, usually in the fields of employment and education. Positive discrimination is a controversial term which is avoided in the West. In India, it means reservation. Its advocates insist that it is necessary to create equality of opportunities with the 'historically privileged groups' in the form of reservations, though such groups have never been convincingly determined. In the West, legal and political debate is mostly focused on adverse implications of positive discrimination and there is preference for affirmative action.

There is no agreement on the definition of equality or equality of opportunity. There is disagreement on whether equality can ever be attained through nature or through human endeavors or through coercive means. Americans understand *equal liberty* in a negative sense as *freedom* from unwarranted restraints on an individual's pursuit of happiness. Legal restraints are particularly suspect because of widespread belief that governments are necessary evil. In India, it is the opposite. We restrict opportunities of some in a positive sense, to give them to others.

Political philosophers in ancient and medieval history assumed that human beings were not only different but also unequal in their moral, political, and social values. 'Democracy was condemned, for it inverted' what they called 'the natural order by making rulers of those who should be subjects, and subjects of those who should be rulers'. Though such perceptions are obsolete, in some kingdoms and modern democracies like India the increasing hereditary successions to power and ugly display of might by small and big rulers have made equal liberty an unachievable ideal. We could just as well legalize hereditary democracies! Studies on equal opportunity or equality of opportunity on racial considerations first started in the United States and in some Western countries. They have been taken over recently by ethnic diversity, which is mostly acquired. Therefore, there is no precise definition of equality or of equality of opportunity. Formal definitions of equal opportunity require that all positions be open to all applicants equally, but in the substantive definitions of equality of opportunity, some form of affirmative action policies is inescapable. Some use equality as a descriptive term intended to provide a certain social environment in which no people are excluded from activities of society such as education, employment, or health care. 'Unfair opportunity' practices are measures which are taken by an organization to ensure fairness in the employment process. Affirmative Action is considered to be one.

Oxford Dictionary of POLITICS in 2011 defined equal opportunity as "equal access to the procedure under which some office or benefit not available to all is allocated, with stipulations about the fairness of the procedure in view of its purposes. For example, nineteenth-century reforms of the civil service in the United Kingdom introduced the allocation of positions by competitive examination, to replace patronage or family connection as determinants of success". However, it admits that equal opportunity can be misused to support situations which may be discriminatory, such as claims that higher education should be made available to all who want it irrespective of merit. This is characterized as a demand for *equality in distribution.* This can be achieved only if demands and supply are equal. Article 15(5) in India gives preference on the basis of equality in distribution in the form of discriminative reservation in postgraduate studies, but without creating enough resources. Equality of distribution is almost reverse of equality of opportunity for it snatches opportunity from those who deserve it to give to some who apparently do not deserve. This has also been described as 'equality of outcome'. It is also reflected in reservation in promotions.

Equal opportunity, the dictionary says, is an elastic notion because it requires deciding at what point in a process it is appropriate to measure it. A competitive examination may provide equal opportunity for candidates to be tested, but that does not mean they have had an equal opportunity to acquire the knowledge and skills required for success and hence may not be a true guide to talent. The equal accesses would then mean the *circumstances* in which individuals receive their education or *acquire* the skills to be tested or equal conditions 'in the period before the rationing' or a demand that, because those conditions have not in fact been equal, "the procedure takes account of the previous relative lack of resources or opportunities of some competitors by discriminating in their favor". These factors are individual sensitive and appropriate only at the entry level, not group centric or at subsequent levels. In the egalitarian sense, 'equality of opportunity affirms, promotes, or characterizes by belief the equal political, economic, social, and civil rights for all people', regardless of their race, religious beliefs, or gender. The goal is to give *all* persons an equal chance to education and employment. *Substantive* equality of opportunity requires affirmative action policies to *equalize access* to equal opportunity. In United States, equality of opportunity aims to improve the lives of individuals born in disadvantaged socioeconomic situations. They include areas such as early childhood care, education, extracurricular programs, substance abuse prevention, college access, and job training. Such measures are practically absent in India in respect of general population. We only know the unequally distributed reservations.

In Britain, the disadvantaged sections are seen in terms of *ethnic minorities*. *Unequal Chances* focuses on the experiences of the 'second generation' of the children of the immigrants—the children who are born and raised locally. Do these local-born immigrant children fare as well as the children from the majority population in getting ahead in life? Does the second generation compete on equal terms in the labor market with equally qualified members of the white majority population? In the case of European migrants to the USA, Canada, and Australia, optimists suggest that the *migrant* generation would experience disadvantages, but succeeding generations would come to compete on equal terms with the established majority population. The situation would be different with the children of Asian countries. Both these situation do not apply to India for there are no migratory populations. The problem in India is that no committee or commission goes into internal reasons of groups for disparities within them and in relation to others. The British and later the Indian State went into that in the case of Hindus, but they politicized and made a mess of it. Census figures are only figures. They cannot tell the causes of low representation in educational institutions and services. In India no figures are available to measure *intra group* disparities.

While equality in outcome requires that all persons should end up in the same conditions, equality of opportunity requires that persons should be equally placed with respect to opportunities, but *not outcome*. Distributive justice is *'suum cuique'*, meaning 'to each his or her due', but this does not explain how to determine what is due to a person. How should one interpret one's due? If distributive justice is applied in the sense of equality of outcome, what is the meaning of 'outcome' when it is to be applied to millions? The encyclopedia sums up by saying that the world 'is trying to come out from mere perceptions to actual implementation', where *'distributive justice cannot mean quotas or reservations.'* John Rawl's 'alternative distributive principle', which he calls the 'Difference Principle', is attractive, because it allows allocation that does not conform to strict equality so long as *the materially better off are the* 'least advantaged in society than they would be under strict equality.' This principal should also apply to those who have recovered. If social benefits are given to whole castes or whole religious communities or the lower limit of the creamy layer keeps rising, which have recently risen to Rs. 600,000 yearly, this principle will be violated and the most disadvantaged will get the least benefit. Feminist critiques of existing distributive principles note that States tend to ignore the particular circumstances of women, especially the fact that women often have primary responsibility for child-rearing. Some feminists therefore modify distributive principles to make them sensitive to the circumstances of women and to the fact that, on average, women spend less of their lifetimes in the market economy than men.

Reservation v. Affirmative Action

The Western modules do not apply to India in many ways, nor does India have its own cogent theory. There is a fundamental difference between the Western model of affirmative action and the Indian model of reservations. Reservations for backward classes mean the quota system while the affirmative action in United States has two objects: *first* to create equality of opportunity and the *second* to *reduce* inequality to build the society. "It is a coherent packet of measures, of a *temporary* character, aimed specially at correcting the position of members of a target group in one or more aspects of the social life, to obtain effective equality"[463] (emphasis added). In India, reduction of inequality within the groups is wanting. The unqualified 'quota system' has proven not only to be irrational by not promoting uniform progress but also has tended to acquire perpetuity. It has affected the non-beneficiaries adversely in areas of social mobility 'where the means of mobility are always scarce and competition intense'. Reservations are illegal in the United States and Great Britain, but the State encourages a holistic approach when 'analyzing an *individual's* candidacy for a position'.[464] The affirmative action policy includes social security and welfare programs, which enhance the living condition of citizens who may be socially and economically disadvantaged. Reservation and quotas were

---

463   British Encyclopedia
464   Wikipedia quoting Labor employment Law, Lawyer.com April 2012

initially a British idea in 1936, but was restricted to 14% of total population. Free India carried the same to a ridiculous extent. The Expert Group on Equality of Opportunity in India, too, concedes this, but still recommends affirmative action, by which it means reservation, on the basis of whole group or whole community, knowing well that it would undermine the rights of the poorly placed individuals and their families even in the same group, not to speak of other groups, for all members and families of various groups are not similarly situated.

Stanford University Encyclopedia on Philosophy, 2002, also differentiates between equality of opportunity among castes and others: "Equality of opportunity is a political ideal that is opposed to caste hierarchy but not to hierarchy per se. The background assumption is that a society contains a hierarchy of more and less desirable, or superior and inferior positions. Or there may be several such hierarchies." In a caste society, it says, the assignment of individuals to places in the social hierarchy is fixed by birth and the child acquires the social status of his or her parents. This is generally not true today. In other societies where equality of opportunity prevails, the assignment of individuals to places in the social hierarchy is determined by *some form of competitive process*, and all members of society are eligible to compete on equal terms. On its scope, it contends, "Equality of opportunity prevails in a society only when *all* worthy human capacities are encouraged, developed, and rewarded. The wider the range of worthy capacities and abilities, other things being equal, the greater is the extent to which it achieves equality of opportunity." In 2007, the same encyclopedia did not go far, by saying that equality was a contested concept and the people who praised it or disparaged it even disagreed on what they praised or disparaged. Sociological and economic analyses suggest that as the people disagree on how inequalities can be determined and measured and what their causes are, the "social and political philosophy is in general concerned mainly with the following questions: *what kind of equality,* if any, should be offered, *and to whom and when*" (emphasis added).[465] In India, where social identities have been mixed up by alien interpretations, it is difficult to answer. Society is no longer, if it ever was, the way it was interpreted in the colonial times, but impressions die hard. The world, at large, has gone far ahead. India cannot remain still.

---

[465]   Stanford University Encyclopedia—Politics, 2002 and republished 2007 on Equality of Opportunity

Indian Expert Group

The Indian Expert Group appointed on the recommendation of the Sachar Committee was alleged to have dealt only with the status of Muslims. SC, ST, OBCs, and other minorities and women were added later only to complete the formality. Answering its own question *why an Equal Opportunity Commission*, the Group says, 'Equality is a foundational value of our Republic which is secured by the Constitution through Fundamental Rights. It is strengthened by the Directive Principles of State Policy and widely shared in public policy and democratic arena, but inequalities remain the 'stark contemporary social reality'. Therefore, it argued, here was need to have EOC (Equality of Opportunity Commission) to *supplement* the existing policy of reservation, 're-envision and expand policies to address inequalities', and 'fine-tune, expand and reformulate the affirmative action policies'. The Group admits different reasons for inequalities in different communities and different social identities within every community, but it does not define 'stark inequalities' among the specific community or communities it was concerned with, or their internal inequalities, or differentiates between affirmative action and policy of reservations. It talks of supplementing reservation, but in fact, keeps switching from affirmative action to reservation and back and refrains from studying other communities—majority or minorities.

Finally, the Expert Group lays down the mandate of the EOC, which would extend to *particular* groups, deserving candidates, *any* citizen of India, public and private sectors, education, and employment. The object of Equal Opportunity Commission, it says, would be to remove unfair discrimination, to enforce constitutionally guaranteed right to equality, to bring about equality of status and opportunity, to do away with entrenched attitudes and conventional mindsets through social engineering and legal and democratic institutions by acknowledging group identities and opting for incremental and consensual change to create a balance between liberty and freedom and equalization of opportunities for disadvantaged people. Its scope, the Group admits, may even overlap with the other commissions. It does not elucidate the *'particular groups'* or identify disadvantaged people. The only hope it offers is when it says, *'any citizen of India'*.

In a report published in the *Times of India*, Abantika Ghosh, TNN, quotes from an article, published on the website of the Centre for Advanced Study of India (CASI), University of Pennsylvania, in which Rakesh Basant, professor of economics at the Indian Institute of Management, Ahmedabad, and a former member of the Sachar Committee, complained that the main recommendations like creation of an Equal Opportunities Commission (EOC), based on the lines of the UK Race Relations Act, which was not community-specific, was recast to make it sound Muslim-centric. Basant says, 'The UPA (United Progressive Alliance—the ruling coalition) has not only picked up recommendations in isolation but has also highlighted the community-specific programs and its implementation in its election manifesto and other communications' and that 'mainstreaming would require a significant change in the nature of politics'.[466]

Subodh Ghildiyal wrote in *Times of India* about the ongoing tussle between the Minority Affairs Ministry and the ministries of social justice, tribal affairs, higher education in HRD, and the EOC encroaching on the panels for SCs, STs, OBCs, women, and children.[467] The argument that the Equal Opportunities Committee should have been constituted under the auspices of a general ministry like Human Resource Development Ministry or the Welfare and Social Justice Ministry has merit. Even Women and Child-Welfare do not come under the Minority Affairs Ministry. Among the minorities, too, only Muslims were covered.

The Group has a point when it says that six decades ago the 'world knew India only as a poor nation', but the awareness of unprecedented wealth has heightened our sensitivity to 'disproportionately distributed poverty and deprivation'. Poverty alleviation and other universalized measures have not redressed the specific 'disproportionate inequalities', and in its view, the 'pursuit of universalistic goods' can often conceal the growth of 'particularistic evils', which, too, must be monitored. In another remark, the Group recognizes the *inter-group inequalities* but omits to mention *intra-group inequalities* and fails to clarify what it understands by group, disproportionate inequalities, and particularistic evils in relation to various communities. It also fails to address the rights of individuals in the same community and of the individuals and families with identical problems of other communities that it did not analyze. It admits that reservation for equalizing opportunities for identified discriminated groups does not automatically bring about equalization in a heterogeneous society. 'Deprivation and exclusion are complex processes' and need an 'affirmative action agenda' *in addition* to the 'reservation strategy' available to *certain* deprived groups. Luckily, it cautions that "we have now arrived at a stage

---

[466] *Times of India* and posted on Internet on 3 July 2011, at 1.53 a.m. IST
[467] Subodh Ghildiyal, *TNN*, 17 June 2009, 1.42 a.m. IST

where group membership *alone*—while continuing to be relevant and even important, may not be relevant. Sub-groups may emerge within any given group that can legitimately claim to be disadvantaged not only vis-à-vis society as a whole but also in comparison to other members of their own larger group". This was a vital and welcome statement, for sub-groups already exist. Throughout this book, the stress has been on differentiation within the groups and sub-groups and ultimately the identification of a functional unit of social stratification in society as a whole, which would equally apply to all communities.

The Group stresses upon the need for 'fresh thinking' due to the existence of more than one axis of disadvantage in the society. For example, people uprooted from their original environment due to the demands of 'development' in the form of dams, large industrial projects, or special economic zones also need redress. Although strictly speaking they do not come under inequalities and unequal opportunities, their need is urgent, even immediate. The Equality of Opportunity Group understands equality of opportunity in two ways. The formal approach involves openness of opportunity without direct discrimination. The Constitution no doubt provides this minimal guarantee, but 'inherent in the Constitutional Right to Equality is a *substantive* understanding of equality of opportunity', which 'involves creation of *level playing fields* by neutralizing the effect of circumstances on achievement of key objectives'. This approach, the Group says, puts a positive obligation on the State to control 'direct as well as indirect discrimination' and 'take into account the burden of history', but as always without explaining what it means by equal opportunity, direct and indirect discrimination, deprivation, and burden of history and how these terms were applicable to the community or communities it was dealing with. Census figure are deceptive, for they do no cover sub-groups.

The Group admits that the concept of equality of opportunity, its 'careful examination', and 'attractiveness', too, can to be 'used and misused' in a variety of ways. The idea of equality of opportunity has a much wider appeal than the idea of equality itself. As equality of opportunity may or may not lead to equal outcomes, the Group suggests a fair race at the end of which some participants get rewards, others don't. 'Unequal rewards are morally acceptable—even desirable—as long as everyone had an equal chance in the race, and as long as the unequal rewards are due only to unequal ability or effort.' This crucial statement negates continuous reservations for generations after generations and in promotions for selected community or communities.

The Group distinguishes between equal opportunity and equality of opportunity to see which is closer to the letter and spirit of the Indian Constitution. A substantive approach to equality of opportunity differs from a formal approach in three fundamental but related ways. A substantive approach, the Group says, goes beyond the absence of direct discrimination and includes within the scope of equality of opportunity 'a mandate to eliminate *indirect* discrimination'. Then it embarks on a risky adventure when it states that indirect societal discrimination no longer 'ends with numerical equality or standard of proportional equality or even the premise of an intended behavior', but also takes 'into account the private inequalities of wealth, of education and other circumstances'. Equality is fundamental to the Constitution. Equality of opportunity like affirmative action is temporary and a means to achieve equality. Its misuse by foraying into private fields will end into reverse discrimination.

The Group, again, lands into a contentious field when it recommends an integrated, forward-looking strategy to assess inequality, *size* of the group, or individual inequalities in each community and, especially, to measure 'indirect discrimination' and '*intended behavior*'. This must be to impress its political masters, for it does not show the parameters or the method to quantify an outrageous *indirect* discrimination, and even more audacious *intended behavior*? The fact is that the Group borrowed these expressions from somewhere, without knowing what they meant and by which sophisticated means they could be determined. It is not without reason that in the western world there is disquiet in even perception of equality of opportunity, not to speak of its implementation. India cannot construct another monolith-like caste, which it cannot even define. The highly learned Group must be aware of it. Perhaps, it had no choice, but to conform to the given mandate.

Finally, the Group defines equal opportunity and equal opportunity practice. By *denial of equal opportunity*, the Group means, "any action, conduct, or measures resulting in or likely to result in discrimination or deprivation, and includes any action of taking away existing resources or opportunities for livelihood, occupation or employment or any other rights and entitlements". The Committee does not explain why it could not apply the same yardsticks to all communities, when it earlier talks of 'a person or all persons'. Deprived persons are not confined to any particular community or section of society. In the Committee's opinion, equality of opportunity means a *level playing field* to the oppressed *classes* combined with affirmative action. The Committee does not define oppressed classes, or demonstrate the criteria by which it determined particular section or sections of society as oppressed. Are such sections defined in the Constitution as oppressed? What about the constitutional rights of those who, after a hard work of whole life, gather just enough to provide themselves and their children a reasonable life, a chance to get education and medical treatment, a decent and livable house, and a retired life reasonably free of wants? Why should they be deprived? Would that not be a direct denial of equality of opportunity?

The perceptions have changed since then. Relative differences in census figures do not indicate discrimination or level of deprivation. Deprivation should be due to *current* societal action and for the EOC's intervention, the Committee clarifies, "discrimination must be systemic, i.e. non-random; cannot be an accidental chance event; must be the result of human actions— not an act of God or nature and finally, must produce real differences in that it must set apart or distinguish in an unjustifiable manner a particular group (or groups) from other groups". Did the Committee apply these parameters to all communities equally across the board before declaring any particular community discriminated? Are such results available? Deprivation is only relevant where the minimum threshold conditions for a decent and dignified human life are not met due to collective action. Even an identifiable sub-group within a large group could suffer from deprivation. Inequality of opportunity can only make sense provided there is a specific contrast class, within the community or outside, as in the case of severe malnutrition or complete absence of primary schooling. Even here the causes of deprivation may be internal or external. The solutions would be different. The diversities are not only between majority and minorities, but also between and within each of them, whether majority or minority. These too need to be considered in the incentive system. And yet the basic equality cannot be dispensed with in the search of still a hypothetical equality of opportunity which may not even be determinable between groups. Finally, when should the measures end so that one can revert to basic equality? Or would they also become irreversible like reservations.[468]

A prestigious daily *The Hindu* reported on 27 August 2010 that Sachar Committee's Report which included Prof. Mahadev Menon Group's recommendations and covered many important bases was presented to the Prime Minister. The Report spoke of covering all groups of public and private sectors and proposed that "the EOC should focus on advisory,

---

[468]   'An Unequal Opportunity Commission', http://www.thehindu.com/opinion/lead/
        an-unequal-opportunity-commission/article598378.ece

advocacy, and auditing functions rather than grievance redress".[469] The paper called the recommendations 'toothless' though some might say that the Commission showed wisdom in doing that in the present parochial and uncertain environment. Zee News.com reported on 29 June 2013, that EOC is going to be set up soon. It will now be for the next government to decide.

Report of the Expert Group on Proposed Diversity Index and the Modalities of Implementation

Biodiversity is everywhere, both on land and in water. It includes all organisms, from microscopic bacteria to more complex plants and animals. A diversity index is a mathematical measure of species diversity in a community. Diversity index is also statistic which is intended to measure the local members of a set consisting of various types of objects. Diversity indices can be used in many fields of study to assess the diversity of any population in which each member belongs to a unique group, type or species. It is used in ecology to measure biodiversity in an ecosystem, in demography to measure the distribution of population of various demographic groups, in economics to measure the distribution over sectors of economic activity in a region, and in information science to describe the complexity of a set of information. In man, so far the diversity index has been found to be of little value.[470]

According to Expert group Diversity also provides information about rarity or commonness in a community. In measuring human diversity, the diversity index measures the probability that any two residents, chosen at random, would be of different ethnicities. If all residents are of the same group, the index is 0. If half are from one group and half from other, it is 50. The idea is to measure the local residence of a set consisting of various types of objects. The question is: should diversity index in a particular locality not be related to the percentage population of different communities in that locality instead of basing it on absolute figures? An odd refusal of tenancy cannot be universalized to show discrimination. It demands trust.

---

[469]   Ibid.
[470]   Wikipedia at different sites and http://www.greenfacts.org/en/biodiversity/index. htm#1

Understanding diversity in the Indian social milieu is a complex task. The Expert Group felt that implementation of this new approach at the national level would be far more challenging as it would mean a paradigm shift in dealing with the problem of unequal access to sociopolitical space in the country. Nonetheless, it believed that it had made a beginning by building in the idea of a consensus across political parties. The objective of attaining 'unity in diversity', the Group stresses, would need "an understanding of the nature of diversity, the processes that generate it and if and to what disparity and inequity the diversity reflects. One can then attempt to identify the factors, institutions and vested interests responsible for that and design a system of redressal". The principle concerns, it says, would be to determine concentration or clustering of populations with similar socioeconomic, religious, and ethnic characteristics in geographical, social, political, and institutional spaces in recent years. Then it describes various ways it can be determined.

For a scientist, such studies on a wider basis may be important for recommending high-sounding solutions and for the politician to build up vote banks, but for the common man, these differences are not new. The reasons for diversity among human beings are not so much biological, not even ethnic, but mostly are due to trust deficit, conservative attitudes, and attempts to capture power by consciously combining with others or by dividing others. In India the conflict is also due to the inability to implement the Constitution and its Directing Principles, but one has to start from somewhere. To build confidence, the State can open a certain percentage of seats in all educational institutions, minority or majority, for people below the poverty line, irrespective of their religion or region or Article 30 or some other article. This can begin at local level and go on to the national. Reservations for whole communities are even more illogical than reservations for whole castes due to diverse socio-economic parameters. It is not surprising that diversity indices in human affairs have not proved a solution in most countries in which it has been evaluated. The Group, too, admits that to quantify diversity by proposing an index is fraught with serious problems that are well documented in literature. Poverty rates computed at national or state levels collected through census figures have only limited utility. They do not show internal diversities.

The Constitution, the Group says, has the principle of "equality in law", but there is also the second principle which is "equality in fact". It does not clarify who is to decide what is equality in *fact* and how does it differ from equality in law. Equality does not preclude diversity, which expressed in biological and social sense is not always an unwanted thing. Biology deals with genes, genetics and genetic variations, and society in mutual relations. One of the controversial but important aspects is debate over *mental traits*, which focuses on the confusion surrounding IQ, its connection with status, wealth, and power and the estimation of its heritability. Once it was believed that genetic diversity among groups would support the claims about race and class differences, the relative variation within and between geographical populations, and the effect of adaptation and migration, but this is now refuted. Eighty-five percent of total genetic variation among human beings is due to individual differences within populations and only 15 percent are between different populations or ethnic groups. (Chapter on Race and Class)

Why the Sachar Committee ultimately concerned itself only with the Muslim community would be difficult to know. But if it did, why did it take the whole community as one unit, when many of its members and advisers were known historians and sociologists from the same community? It was the non-Ashrafs or Ajlafs and similarly affected others that were really backward, discriminated, poor, and illiterate, not the whole community. It was these that were deprived of equality of opportunity, when relief was sought for the whole community.

On the social or sociological side, James A. Banks reported in 2004, "Racial, ethnic, cultural, and language diversity is increasing in nation-states throughout the world because of worldwide immigration. The deepening ethnic diversity within nation-states and the quest of different groups for cultural recognition and rights are challenging 'assimilationist' notions of citizenship and citizenship education. A delicate balance of unity and diversity should be essential goal of citizenship education in multicultural nation-states."[471] Diversity does not divide people into forward and backward classes or into advanced and discriminated races or ethnic groups or castes. It is the notion of otherness, non-acceptance of variety among the human beings, which divides. Diversity is the rule in nature, not homogeneity. It cannot be removed by force or coercion. The present unacceptable situation is due to non-acceptance of diversity and attempts to perpetuate. One monolith is other backward classes; another in offing is a whole religious community. In the West, the individual and his family remain the units for giving relief.

---

[471] Teaching for Social Justice, Diversity and Citizenship in a Global World: The Educational Forum, Vol. 68, Iss. 4, 2004, 296-305

> Legal meaning of equal opportunity in United States is: "a right guaranteed by both federal and many state laws against any discrimination in employment, education, housing or credit rights due to *a person's* race, color, sex (or sometimes sexual orientation), religion, national origin, age, or handicap. A person who believes he/she has not been granted equal opportunity or has been outright sexually harassed or discriminated against may bring a lawsuit under federal and most state laws, or file a complaint with the federal Equal Opportunity Employment Commission or an equal opportunity agency which can be approached by *anyone* and from *any* community, white or black."

The approach to EOC in United States is a right granted to a *person of any* race, color, sex, religion, origin or age and community or communities, while the approach to Equality of Opportunity Commission in 'secular' India is aimed to deny it to an overwhelming majority of the Indian population.

Other Views from Internet

One view states that equality of opportunity in the sense of identical opportunity for all individuals is impossible. "One child is born blind, another with sight. One child has parents deeply concerned about his welfare who provide a background of culture and understanding; another has dissolute, improvident parents. Children at birth clearly do not have identical opportunities in relation to abilities or environment."[472] This situation comes within what is described as *'category of circumstances'*. It makes no sense to hold any individual responsible for anything that falls in the category of circumstances. Such people simply cannot be equalized, but their disability can be remedied or compensated.

In another opinion, Dr Mark Cooray draws a distinction between *"equality of opportunity"* and *"equality of outcome"*.[473] No arbitrary obstacles, he says, should prevent people from achieving those public positions to

---

[472]   Milton and Rose Friedman, 1980: Free to Choose, New York, pp. 131-132. Document towards formulation of a policy for social equity

[473]   Mark Cooray: Equality of Opportunity and Equality of Outcome. From the Australian Achievement: From Bondage to Freedom. Also http://www.ourcivilisation.com/cooray/btof/chap20.htm

which their talents fit and which their values lead them to seek. Birth, nationality, color, religion, sex, or any other equivalent characteristic should not determine the public opportunities that are open to a person—only talent and achievement. People are different in their genetic and cultural characteristics and hence should be able to pursue in careers they want. Equality of opportunity and freedom, he says, are two facets of the same basic concept.[474]

He distinguishes equality of opportunity from the power to force others not to pursue their private interests or vocation in a certain way. Equality of opportunity means freedom to engage in a trade, but does not mean 'right to compel you to give another person an equal chance of pursuing your trade'. Equality of opportunity provides that all start the race of life at the same time. Equality of outcome attempts to ensure that everyone finishes at the same time. Equality of outcome was rejected even by the Indian Group. A quota system in promotions, for example, would mean a coercive equality of outcome, or worse, reverse discrimination. A *level playing field* demands that all have equal *initial* conditions and equal opportunities and then let individual choices and their effects dictate further outcomes. In other words, once the individuals have made the choices to lead their lives in one or another way starting from the initial equality, then justice would *not* demand further compensation even if the risks taken were to turn out badly. It also makes no sense to hold others responsible for anything that falls in the category of circumstances. To try to create Equality of Opportunity for one community makes no sense.

Stanford Encyclopedia concludes by saying that the slogan of equality of opportunity commands wide allegiance among the members of contemporary societies. Under scrutiny, equality of opportunity divides into several different ideals, some of them being opposed by rivals. It is controversial which of these ideals are morally acceptable and which, if any, should be coercively enforced as requirements of justice. "Debates about the seemingly banal norm of equality of opportunity reveal profound disagreements as to the nature of fair terms of cooperation in the modern world."[475]

Fred Argy from Australia goes into the reasons why some countries do well on equality of opportunity and some do not. Equality or equality of

---

[474]   Ibid.
[475]   http://www.science.uva.nl/~seop/archives/spr2007/entries/equal-opportunity/, *Stanford Encyclopedia of Philosophy*

opportunity or formal equality of opportunity (FEOP) often means 'little more than equality under the law'. Many Australians refer to substantive equality of opportunity (SEOP) as 'a situation in which everyone is able to develop their full potential, irrespective of the original circumstances of their birth and childhood'. FEOP is about ensuring that the best person wins at any point in time, while SEOP, being concerned with risk factors and handicaps in early childhood and teenage years, extends this focus beyond this. In FEOP, minimal intervention is expected by governments, while under SEOP, governments are expected 'to ensure that as children, the citizens are not unduly impeded by lack of parental wealth, status and power in achieving their full education potential' and as adult citizens, they 'are not impeded by location, inadequate access to secondary training or skill-enhancement and poor availability of health, housing, welfare or networking from achieving their full employment potential.' Increased mobility seen in some advanced countries facilitates this potential. He defines social mobility as 'the ease and frequency by which people move up the social hierarchy during *their lifetime* and *between generations*, irrespective of their different backgrounds and starting opportunities'. He attributes rate of social mobility to ability to adapt to new situations. While within the same generation income mobility depends upon rising 'from the lowest to one grade above,' in inter-generational mobility, which is more permanent and represents about 'two thirds of cross-sectional annual inequality', it is different. In the United States, the association of fathers' and sons' incomes is appreciably stronger and a child's economic background a better predictor of latter's earnings or school performance than in the Scandinavian countries, but despite being a 'world leader in economic liberalization and structural change' and 'less influenced by historical class distinctions and/ or hierarchies', social mobility in the United States is much lower between generations than social democratic countries such as Sweden, Norway, and the Netherlands. The missing link Argy attributes to political ideology on redistribution.[476]

The lower social mobility with high inequality in countries like United Kingdom, and the United States is due to greater inequality between generations. In the Nordic countries 'where income is distributed more evenly' between generations, the mobility is higher. Similar arguments apply to health and other public benefits. Despite the populations becoming

---

[476]   Fred Argy Australia: http://www.tai.org.au/documents/downloads/DP85.pdf: The Australia Institute The Discussion Paper Number 85 April 2006 ISSN 1322-5421

healthier 'as the economy expands, relative health outcomes do not necessarily narrow'. In Nordic and some European countries, *greater* Government involvement in reducing health inequalities has given poor families better access to medical care than in the United States where low-income children tend to suffer from more health problems both in childhood and as adults.[477]

In India where the differences in high and low incomes are colossal within one generation as well as between generations and dismal Government participation in educational and health institutions, there is inadequate social mobility not only in terms of income but also health and other welfare spheres. The opening of hundreds of well-equipped private hospitals has not improved medical treatment of the poor sections of society in the same manner as the thousands of private educational institutions have not given a large majority of them better education. Privatization is not a cure for all ills. Adequate governmental participation in a country like India is paramount.

Equality does not mean all people are physically and mentally equal. True equality implies that potentially everyone should have the same opportunities, that is to say that 'potentially the toddler could play professional basketball and potentially the six-year-old could become a future Einstein regardless of superficial characteristics'. Because these two people may not actually achieve their dreams, it does not mean they should be limited by what people perceive they are capable of. This is equality of *perception*, which means that 'all people should be allowed the same opportunities even if they aren't capable of realizing them'. This allows people to reach their own plateaus without unfair external pressures. However, when one attempts to use equality of outcome to *create* opportunity, one must take away opportunities from one person to give them to another, rather than allow both individuals to reach their own personal peaks.[478] Equality of outcome is unacceptable.

There is another view too. It says that if no one could start (or continue) life with any advantages, children would have to be separated from their parents at birth and 're-united with them, if at all, only when the environment had had its lasting and irreversible effect' and "taught precisely the same things, in precisely the same fashion, by teachers of precisely the same level

477   Ibid: Also Issue 10, August 2009, Fred Argy, Equality of Opportunity—Fred Argy [PDF, 65.3 kb] Updated 20: Equality, the Goal Not the Signpost. Posted on Internet on Sunday, 27 April 2008 in Sociology

478   http://anthologyoi.com/sociology/equality-of-outcome-equality-of-oportunity.html Anthropology of Ideas

of competence or more likely, incompetence. No parent would be permitted to leave anything to his children, and therefore one of the great motives for economic prudence would be vitiated". Equality of opportunity would then mean, if it means anything, 'equality of poverty, inhumanity and horror'. The writer further says that while giving people equal opportunities is impossible, giving at least the vast majority of people *a considerable level of opportunity* is not impossible.' And yet, 'often in the very name of equality of opportunity, we have created a society many of whose members have far fewer opportunities than they could and ought to have'. Therefore, the focus ought to be on 'increasing opportunity', not on increasing equality of opportunity, just as it should be on "*increasing* the material conditions of the members of society' and not to bring about '*the equality* of material conditions' among all members. Give the poor the opportunities that the rich have, but do not hold the rich and middle classes back 'in the name of a misguided ideal'[479] (emphasis provided).

The above references have been cited to give the reader an idea of how the world has been thinking about Equality of Opportunity. Like many other thoughts, this too is not a panacea for all the ills of the Indian society. India has to find its own medicine. Therefore, it is time to lay aside the ridiculous comparison of any minority in India with the erstwhile American Negroes or migrants from developing countries to the West. It would be worth the while to pause and ponder, if 90 percent of population becomes eligible for reservation, how will the State choose which group or its part should be given reservation and which not, especially, within the the present limit of 50 percent of total posts.

In an important observation, the Group on the formation of Equality of Opportunity Commission comments:

> EOCs or similar bodies are becoming the norm in democracies that are waking up to the challenge of diversity across the world. Their experience varies, as does their jurisprudence, yet there are many lessons to be learnt: *there is no alternative to recognizing social identities.* EOCs need to respond to the specificities of the challenge of equal opportunity in each country. (Emphasis added)

Hindus, Muslims, Christians and others are not single *social* specificities to be treated for social benefits as a whole. Each one is a conglomerate

---

[479]   24 February 2008—Posted by Blackadder, Equality of Opportunity

of many social identities, which cannot be neglected. Scheduled Castes are only a list of castes isolated from thousands of others. The Scheduled Tribes are a list of hundreds of tribes, again, isolated from many tribes. Both have populations of tens of millions and also their own neglected internal inequalities. Similarly, the Other Backward Classes, a residual category of all those among Hindus whom the British did not include among Scheduled Castes, now consist of thousands of castes and similarly backward sections from all communities. The population of some of them is equal to the population of small countries. 'Minorities' is a word borrowed in recent times from the West to manufacture a political conglomerate, in which different minorities have nothing common among them—not even politics. The Mandal Commission provided reservations for 52% of India's population, which included all religious communities, not for only one community. It was ignored for political reasons. There is no community wise quota. It is the eligibility that matters, not the population of any particular community. If eligible, there can be more reservations for the Muslims than the Hindus.

With the improved condition of backward classes, a new category of *below the poverty line* is increasingly coming into focus. It is time to define and separate it and cater to its members as a separate category, irrespective of their caste, religion, sex, or region. This is the only category that might require reservations for a specified period. The rest of the poor should be shifted to a modified form of affirmative action. In a class of barbers, for example, all barbers are not similarly situated or belong to any particular religion or community. Therefore, the really *backward* barbers have to be found at families and individuals levels for social benefits, irrespective of their caste, religion, sex, region or place of birth.

So far there is no scientific evidence of future births, not to speak of birth in the same castes, communities and occupations etc, to justify backwardness of backward classes for generation after generation and century after century. On the contrary, in the theory of rebirth, one can be a Brahmin in one birth and an untouchable in another; or born in one community in one and born in another community in another, or be rich in one birth and poor in another. Compensatory discrimination or reservation on the basis of birth in the same families or similar circumstances is a false idea. It restricts opportunities for the really backward.

In India the conflict is between rights of an individual and rights of a group. The *Times of India* dated September17, 2013 quotes Ayn Rand in 'A

Thought for Today': "The smallest minority on earth is the individual. Those who deny individual rights cannot be defenders of minorities."

Family is the basic or the smallest social group. The rest are aggregates, small or big, but generally heterogeneous economically, educationally, occupationally and socially, individually, or in combinations, and unfit for reservation or affirmative action as a whole. Family is the only social group that is relevant in present times.

APPENDIX 1

REPORT OF NATIONAL COMMISSION FOR BACKWARD CLASSES

Guidelines for Consideration of Requests for Inclusion and Complaints of Under Inclusion in the Central List of OBCs by National Commission for Backward Classes[480]

Initial Comment

1. If Other Backward Classes were identified because they were poor, illiterate, in lower occupation and because of them socially and educationally backward or economically, educationally and socially backward or backward class of citizens, there could be no objection.
2. If they were socially and educationally backward or backward class of citizen without taking caste into account, again, they could have been acceptable, for it would have meant the identification was made on socio-economic grounds and not because they were alleged to be Shudra.
3. The problem arose when the Court said reservations were meant only for Shudra, Scheduled Castes and Scheduled Tribes and similar classes among non-Hindus. Therefore, the National Commission was obliged to identify the backward class of citizens or the socially and educationally backward classes or other backward classes as Shudras. The Commission does not show how it was done, not even bring in the term Shudra in identification.

---

[480] Extracted from Official Websites of National Commission of Backward Classes 'ANNEXURE-VI Guidelines for Consideration of Requests for Inclusion and Complaints of Under-Inclusion in the Central List of Other Backward Classes': Re-confirmed 9.03.2014

Activities like farmers, agricultural labor, criminality, illiteracy and poverty are not the hallmarks of Shudras. Many others could be equally affected.

Criteria for identification were:

A. Social

1. Castes and communities *generally considered* as *socially backward:*
    (a) Castes and communities, which mainly depend on agricultural and/or other manual labour for their livelihood and are lacking any significant resource base.
    (b) Castes and communities, which, for their livelihood, mainly depend on *agricultural and/or other manual labour* for wage and are lacking any significant base.
    (c) Castes and communities, the women of which, as a general practice, are for their family's livelihood, engaged in agricultural and/or other manual labour, for wage.
    (d) Castes and communities, the children of which, as a general practice, are, for family's livelihood or for supplementing family's low income, mainly engaged in agricultural and/or manual labour.
    (e) Castes and communities, which in terms of caste system, are identified with traditional crafts or traditional or hereditary occupations considered to be lowly or undignified.
    (f) Castes and communities, which in terms of the caste system, are identified with *traditional or hereditary occupations considered to be 'unclean' or stigmatised.*
    (g) Nomadic and semi-nomadic castes and communities.

2. Denotified or Vimukta *Jati* castes and communities.

Explanation (by the Commission): The term refers to castes/communities which had been categorized as *Criminal Tribes* under the Criminal Tribes Act, 1924, Act No. VI of 1924 passed by the Indian Legislature and repealed by the Criminal Tribes (Repeal) Act, 1952, Act No. XXIV of 1952 subsequently referred to as *Denotified* or Vimukta Jatis (all emphasis added).

Comment: Essentially, the Commission includes castes and communities which are engaged in agricultural labor or other labor, those who were branded as criminal tribes by the British and with occupations which were *unclean' or stigmatized* or considered to be *lowly or undignified*. Such occupations are associated with Scheduled Castes. In the study conducted by Anthropological Survey of India 75% of agricultural labor was found to be from Scheduled Castes.

Farmers and cattle keepers like Ahirs, Yadavs, Kurmis, Lingyats, Vokkilogas and hundreds of other OBCs were never engaged in unclean, undignified, stigmatized or demeaning occupations. Classically they would have been Vaishyas. Hereditary or traditional occupations sustained millions and cannot be the source of discrimination. Then how did the commission distinguished between Scheduled Castes and Other Backward Classes?

Most of those branded as criminal tribes by the British are included among the Scheduled Tribes. The commission was appointed to identify Other Backward Classes. How did it differentiate between the two? The Commission was required to identify Shudras, which were equated with castes like puruda vannanas? There is no indication it even defined them, not to speak of identify them.

3. Castes and communities, having no representation or poor representation in the State Legislative Assembly and/or district-level Panchayati Raj institutions during the ten years preceding the date of the application (emphasis added).

Explanation: This is only an indicator of the presence of castes and communities in these bodies.

Comment: Poor representation in these bodies does not make them Shudra. There are a number of castes among OBCs, which are over-represented in legislatures and panchayats. Then who are they and why are they still among OBCs? Does representation in these bodies determine one's Shudra identity?

Educational

1. Castes and communities, whose literacy rate is at least 8 percent less than the State or district average

2. Castes and communities of which the proportion of matriculates is at least 20 percent less than the State or district average.
3. Castes and communities, of which the proportion of graduates is at least 20 percent less than the State or district average.

Comment: Educational backwardness is again an offshoot of poverty and lack of access to educational backwardness. Figures of 8 and 20 percent are arbitrary. They make one educationally backward. Shudra, if defined and identified, may be one category.

Economic

1. Castes and communities, a significant proportion of whose members *reside only in Kachha houses.*
2. Castes and communities, the share of whose members in number of cases and in extent of agricultural lands surrendered under the Agricultural Land Ceiling Act of the State, is nil or significantly low.
3. Castes and communities, *the share* of whose members in State Government posts and services of Groups A & B/Classes I & II, *is not equal to the population-equivalent proportion of the caste/ community* (emphasis added).

Comment: Again, these are signs of poverty, even abject poverty, which is rampant in all sections of society. They do not identify a person as Shudra (all emphasis added).

D. *Representation in Services*

In addition to the above, arising from Article 16(4), the following condition has also to be fulfilled: Castes and communities, which are not/ are inadequately represented in the Central Government posts & services of Group A & B. Each Group/Class should be taken separately.

The Commission's further statement that "till information regarding the position of each caste in the Government of India's services becomes readily available, it may be presumed that this factor is fulfilled by a caste/ community/sub-caste/synonym/sub-entry" derived "on the basis of their own observations and other relevant materials that may be available to it" is astounding (emphasis added).

Comment: This prima facie means that the primary condition of determining inadequate representation in services of the state separately in each of the 3743 castes identified, and adequate reservation in rest of hundreds of castes not included, was neither fulfilled by the Mandal Commission nor subsequently met by the National Commission. It makes reservations under Article 16(4) legally untenable.

APPENDIX 2

1931 CENSUS REPORT

Enlarged scanned version of actual Photostat Copy of Appendix 1 of Report

N.B.—*No attempt has been made here to deal with events that have taken place since 1931.*

This term for the Hindu castes hitherto known as "depressed" was originally suggested by the Census Superintendent for Assam and has been adopted in this report as the most satisfactory alternative to the unfortunate and depressing label "depressed class". It has been criticised as being the same term as 'outcaste' only of five instead of two syllables, and it must be admitted that 'exterior' is but old 'out' writ large. At the same time it is here submitted that outcaste, with an *e*, has not unnaturally attracted to its connotation the implications of the quite differently derived outcast, with no *e*. Outcaste correctly interpreted seems to mean no more than one who is outside the caste system and is therefore not admitted to Hindu society, but since in practice the exterior castes also contained those who had been cast out from the Hindu social body for some breach of caste rules 'outcaste' and 'outcast' were in some cases synonymous and the derogatory implications of obliquity attaching to the latter term have unjustly coloured the former, a taint which is not conveyed by the substitution of the word 'exterior', which may connote exclusion but not extrusion.

The instructions of the Government of India for the taking of this census concluded with the following enjoinder:

> "The Government of India also desire that attention should be paid to the collection of information conducive to a better knowledge of the backward and depressed classes and of the problem involved in their present and future welfare."

In that connection the following instructions were issued to the various Superintendents of Census Operations in India:

"For this purpose it will be necessary to have a list of castes to be included in depressed classes and all provinces are asked to frame a list applicable to the province. There are very great difficulties in framing a list of this kind and there are insuperable difficulties in framing a list of depressed classes which will be applicable to India as a whole."

A subsequent instruction ran as follows:

"I have explained depressed castes as castes, contact with whom entails purification on the part of high caste Hindus. *It is not intended that the term should have any reference to occupation as such* but to those castes which by reason of their traditional position in Hindu society are denied access to temples, for instance, or have to use separate wells or are not allowed to sit inside a school house but have to remain outside or which suffer similar social disabilities. These disabilities vary in different parts of India being much more severe in the south of India than elsewhere. At the same time the castes which belong to this class are generally known and can in most parts of India be listed for a definite area though perhaps the lists for India as a whole will not coincide."

The question of the preparation of lists for each province was discussed at a meeting of the Superintendents of Census Operations in January 1931 before the census took place. It was agreed that each province should make a list of castes who suffered disability on account of their low social position and on account of being debarred from temples, schools or wells. No specific definition of depressed castes was framed and no more precise instructions were issued to the Superintendents of Census Operations, because it was realised that conditions varied so much from province to province and from district to district, even, within some provinces that it would be unwise to tie down the Superintendents of Census Operations with too meticulous instructions. The general method of proceeding prescribed was that of local enquiry into what castes were held to be depressed and why and the framing of a list accordingly. It was decided that Muslims and Christians should be excluded from the term "depressed class" and that, generally speaking, hill and forest tribes, who had not become Hindu but whose religion was returned as Tribal, should also be excluded and in the numbers of the exterior castes given below these principles have been followed. A note on the depressed and backward classes in Assam submitted to the Franchise Committee by the Superintendent of Census Operations for that province affords a very clear example of the way in which these principles were intended to be applied and have been applied by Superintendents of Census Operations, and an extract from it is given towards the end of this appendix.

Comments

- Outcaste (with e) meant one who was excluded—excluded from taking part in rituals, but remained a part of Hindu society (not excluded from society as implied above). Even ritual exclusion is a thing of distant past.
- Outcast (without e) meant expelled or extruded from Hindu society for some heinous crime. Even a Brahman could be an outcast. Most of them used to be taken back after expiation.
- The word exterior caste was chosen for outcaste to avoid the taint attached to the similar sounding term outcast and because exterior meant 'external, outer, peripheral, but part of the same structure, society, organization or configuration.'
- Another reason to reject outcaste in 1931 could be, because the British had disapproved outcaste in 1902 as 'derogatory and unsuitable.' (See Panchama in Chapter 6).
- The outcastes were originally depressed classes or untouchable. The census does not tell why they were debarred from entry into temples, schools or use of wells. Many, including, Ambedkar and Risley, blamed beef eating or similar activities. To justify the term Shudra, the Mandal Commission cited some depressed classes from South India, as examples of backward class of citizens or socially and educationally backward classes. This could not be accepted.
- Occupations, hereditary or otherwise, were found insignificant in identification of depressed classes in 1931, not to speak of OBCs. If they were, there would not have been "insuperable difficulties' in identifying them. In 1992, it was claimed that other backward classes had to follow such occupations generation after generation. Could lower occupations not be the result, rather than the cause of backwardness? Could that cause not be intense poverty and illiteracy? Unfortunately, it was taken the other way round.

SELECT BIBLIOGRAPHY

Ambedkar, B.R. 1990: *Writings and Speeches of Dr. Babasaheb Ambedkar*, Vol. 7, Education Department, Government of Maharashtra

Ballhatchet Kenneth 1995. The Language of Historians and Morphology of History: In *The Concept of Race in South Asia*. Ed. Peter Robb Oxford University Press Delhi

Banerjee-Dube Ishita 2008: Introduction: Question of Caste. In *Caste in History*: Ed. Ishita Banerjee-Dube, Oxford University Press, New Delhi

Basham A.L. 1967. The Wonder That Was India: A Survey of the Indian Sub-Continent before the Coming of Muslims, Grove Press, New York

Bayly Susan 1995: Caste and 'Race' in the Colonial Ethnography of India: In *The Concept of Race in South Asia*. Ed. Peter Robb Oxford University Press Delhi

Beteille Andre 1991: Caste, Class and Power: Changing Patterns of Stratification in a Tanjore Village in *Social Stratification*. Editor Dipankar Gupta, Oxford University Press, Delhi

N.N. Bhattacharya N.N. 1996: 11 *Indian Religious Historiography*: Munshiram Manoharlal Publishers Pvt. Ltd. New Delhi

Bhatty Zarina 1996: Social Stratification among Muslims in India. In *Caste: Its Twentieth Century Avatar*. Ed. M.N. Srinivas, Viking—Penguin Books India, New Delhi

Charsley, Simon 1996. 'Untouchable'—What Is in a Name? *J. Royal Anthropological Institute*. (N.S.) 2, 1-23

Brockington John: 1995: concept of race in Mahabharta and Ramayana: In *The Concept of Race in South Asia*. Ed. Peter Robb Oxford University Press Delhi

Chattopadhyay B.D: 1996. Change through Continuity: In *Sociology and Ideology in India*. Ed. D.N. Jha, Munshiram Manoharlal Publishers Pvt. Ltd., New Delhi

Cohen Bernard S. 1996: Notes on the Study of Indian Society and Culture. In *Structure and Change in Indian Society*. Eds. Milton Singer and Bernard S. Cohen, Rawat Publications, Jaipur and New Delhi

Colebrook 1798: Encyclopedia Britannica: 465

Debi Chatterjee: 2004: Comparitive Study Of Ambedkar and Periyar. *Up Against caste* Rawat Publications Jaipur

Deliège Robert 1999: *Untouchables of India*: Berg Publishers, Oxford, UK

Desika Char S.V. 1993: Caste Religion and Country—A View of Ancient and Medieval India, Orient Longaman New Delhi

Dipankar Gupta 1991: Continuous Hierarchy and Discreet Castes: *Social Stratification*. Ed. Dipankar Gupta, Oxford University Press, New Delhi

Dubey Leela 1996. Caste and Women: *Caste: It's Twentieth Century Avatar*. Ed. M.N. Srinivas, Viking—Penguin Books India, New Delhi

Dumont Louis 1970; Homohierarchicus: An Essay on Caste System. Translated by Mark Stainsbury, University of Chicago Press, Chicago

Enthoven R.E. 1902: Census of India 1901, as quoted by Simon Charsley 1996. *J. Roy. Anthrop. Instit.* (N.S.) 2, 1-23

Galanter M. 1984. *Competing Equalities: Law and the Backward Classes in India*, University of California Press, Berkley

Galanter Marc 1996: Changing Legal Conceptions of Caste. *Structure and Change in Indian Society*. Eds. Milton Singer and Bernard S. Cohen, Rawat Publications, Jaipur and New Delhi

Geetha V. and Rajadurai S.V.: 1998: *Towards a Non-Brahmin Millennium*. Bombay: Popular Prakasham

Ghurye G.S. 1957. *Caste and Class*, Popular Book Depot, Bombay

Ghurye G.S. 1963. *Scheduled Tribes*, Popular Prakasham, Bombay

Ghurye G.S. 1991: Features of Caste System: *Social Stratification*. Ed. Dipankar Gupta, Oxford University Press, New Delhi

Ghurye G.S. 2008: Middleton Who Was One of Census Superintendents in 1921: Caste and British Rule, *Caste in History*. Ed. Ishita Banerjee-Dube, Oxford University Press, New Delhi

Gould, Harod A. 1987: Hindu Caste System. Vol. 1: The Sacralization of Social Order, Chanakya Publications, New Delhi

Gould, Harod A. 1988: *Caste Adaptation in Modernizing Indian Society*, Chanakya Publications, New Delhi

Gupta A.K. 1984. Caste Hierarchy and Social Change (A Study of Myth and Reality), Jyotsna Prakasham, New Delhi

Hellmann-Rajanayagam Dagmar 1995: Is There a Tamil Race: *The Concept of Race in South Asia*. Ed. Peter Robb

Holmstrom M. 1991: *Social Stratification*. Ed. Dipankar Gupta, Oxford University Press, New Delhi

Hunt J.J. Census Commissioner quoted in 1931 Census

Huxley Aldous 1983: Brave New World—Revisited; Foreword, http://www. harpercollins.com/ London

Jaffrelot Christopher 1995: The Ideas of Hindu Race in the Writings of Hindu Nationalist Ideologues in the 1920s and 1930s: A Concept between Two Cultures: *The Concept of Race in South Asia*. Ed. Peter Robb Oxford University Press Delhi

Jain Meenakshi 1996: Backward Caste and Social Change in U.P. and Bihar. *Caste: Its Twentieth Century Avatar*. Ed. M.N. Srinivas, Viking— Penguin Books India, New Delhi

James Legge: *A Record of Buddhistic Kingdoms*. This article also incorporates text from The Medical times and gazette, Volume 1, a publication from 1867 now in the public domain in the United States and Travels of Fa Hien: 1971 Oriental Publications New Delhi

Jayaram N. 1996: Caste and Hinduism. In *Caste: Its Twentieth Century Avatar*. Ed. M.N. Srinivas, Viking—Penguin Books India, New Delhi

Kalia, Aloke K. 1994: *The Ethnography of India*, Munshiram Manoharlal Publishers Pvt. Ltd., New Delhi

Karanth G.K. 1996: Caste in Contemporary India. *Caste: It's Twentieth Century Avatar*. Ed. M.N. Srinivas, Viking—Penguin Books India, New Delhi

Karkala John B.A. 1980. *Vedic Vision*, Arnold Heinmann, New Delhi

Karve Irawati 1961. *Hindu Society—An Interpretation*, Deccan College, Pune

Khanna L.M. 1962. *Incredible Story of Social Justice*, Aravli Books International (P) Ltd., New Delhi

Klass Morton 1993. *Caste*, Manohar Publishers, New Delhi

Kotani H. 1997: *Caste System, Untouchability and the Depressed*. Ed. H. Kotani Manohar, New Delhi

Ling Trevor 1992. Indian Social Analysis: From Varna to Class: In *Philosophy Science and Social Progress*. Eds. Suman Gupta and Hiltrud Rustau, People's Publishing House, New Delhi

Lorenzen D. 1982: Imperialism and the Historiography in India. *India: History and Thought (Essays in Honour of A.L. Basham)*. Ed. S.N. Mukherjee, Subarnekha, Calcutta

Mandal Commission's Report: Report of the Second Backward Classes Commission, 1980 published by different publishers. One was Alankar Daryaganj Delhi.

Mandelbaum David G. 1996: Family, Jati, Village. *Structure and Change in Indian Society*. Eds. Milton Singer and Bernard S. Cohen, Rawat Publications, Jaipur and New Delhi

Mason Phillip: 1970: *Patterns of Dominance*, Oxford University Press, London

Mencher Joan P. 1991: Caste System Upside Down, In *Social Stratification*. Ed. Dipankar Gupta, Oxford University Press, New Delhi

Milner Murray 1994. Status and Sacredness: A General Theory of Status Relation and an Analysis of Indian Cuture, Oxford University Press, Oxford

Mujumdar R.C. 1960: *The Classical Account of India*, Firma Mukhopadhyay, Calcutta

Naik L.R. 1991. Report of Second Backward Classes Commission (Mandal Report), Alankar, New Delhi

Nandi R.N. 1996: The Aryan Invasion of Indian Cities: Evidence and Assumption, In *Sociology and Ideology in India*. Ed. D.N. Jha, Munshiram Manoharlal Publishers Pvt. Ltd., New Delhi

Notes on Anthropology 1966: Published by Anthropological Society of Great Britain and Ireland originally in 1922-23

O'Malley L.S.S.1932—Curzon Press (London and Totowa, N.J Reprint 1974 Reprint of the 1932 ed. published by The University Press, Cambridge, Eng. I

Oldenberg Hermann 1916—Reprint 1991: *The Doctrine of Upanishads and the Early Buddhism*. Translated by Shridhar B. Shroti, Motilal Banarsidas Publishers Pvt. Ltd., New Delhi

Orenstein Henry 1996: Towards a Grammar of Deffilement in Hindu Sacred Law. *Structure and Change in Indian Society*, Eds. Milton Singer and Bernard S. Cohen. Rawat Publications, Jaipur and New Delhi

Padmanabh Samarenra 2008: Career of Caste in Colonial Census. *Caste in History*. Ed. Ishita Banerjee-Dube, Oxford University Press, New Delhi

Prabhu Pandharinath H. 1936—Reprint 1993. *Hindu Social Organisation, A study in socio-psychological ideologies*. Popular Prakasham, Bombay

Quigley Declan 1993: *The Interpretation of Caste*, Clarendon Press, Oxford, UK

Radhakrishnan S. 2004: The Dhammapada (Chapter XXVI: Brahminavaggo). *The Buddhism Omnibus*, Oxford University Press, New Delhi

Radhakrishnan P. 1996: Backward Class Movements in Tamil Nadu. In *Caste: Its Twentieth Century Avatar*. Ed. M.N. Srinivas, Viking—Penguin Books India, New Delhi

Rao S.R. 1991: Dawn and Devaluation of Indian Civilisation. Aditya Prakasham, Delhi Report on Casteism and Untouchability, 1955 Indian Conference of Social Work, 6/A Cooperage, Bombay

Risley Sir Herbert 1915—Reprint 1969. *The People of India*, Oriental Books Reprint Corporation, New Delhi

Robb Peter 1995: Introduction: *Concept of Race in South Asia*. Ed. Peter Robb: Oxford University Press Delhi

Roche Patrick A. 2008. Caste and the British Merchant Government, 1639-1749. *Caste in History*. Ed. Ishita Banerjee-Dube, Oxford University Press, New Delhi

Sadasivan S.N.L *A Social History of India*: APH Publishing, 01-Jan-2000 - India

Sarkar Sunil: 1997: *Writing Social history India*: Oxford University Press India and in Google books.

Shah A.M. 1996: The Judicial and Sociological View of Other Backward Classes, *Caste Its Twentieth Century Avatar*. Ed. M.N. Srinivas, Viking— Penguin Books India, New Delhi

Sharma R.S. 1982: The Age of Kali: A Period of Social Crisis. In *India: History and Thought*. Ed. S.N. Mukherjee, Subernekha, Calcutta

Sharma R.S. 1996: The State and Varna Formation in the Mid-Ganga Plain: An Ethno-archeological View, Manohar Delhi

Singh K.S. 1992: Ed. *People of India Vol. I: Introduction*, Anthropological Survey of India, Calcutta

Singh K.S. 1992. Ed. *People of India, Vol. II: Scheduled Castes*, Oxford University Press of India, New Delhi

Singh K.S. 1996: Manu and Contemporary Indian Ethnography, In *Society and Ideology in India*. Ed. D.N. Jha, Munshilal Manoharlal Publishers Pvt. Ltd., New Delhi

Smith Brian K. 1994: Classifying the Universe: The Ancient Indian Varna System and the Origin of Caste, Oxford University Press, New York

Spellman J.W. 1982: Development and Indian Cultural Values. In *India: History and Thought (Essays in Honour of A.L. Basham)*. Ed. S.N. Mukherjee, Subernekha, Calcutta

Srinivas M.N. 1962: *Varna and Caste*, Asia Publishing House, Bombay

Srinivas M.N. 1991: Varna and Caste. *Social Stratification*, Ed. Dipankar Gupta, Oxford University Press, New Delhi

Srinivas M.N. 1992: *On Living in a Revolution and Other Essays*, Oxford University Press, New Delhi

Srinivas M.N. 1996: Introduction. *Caste Its Twentieth Century Avatar*: Ed. M.N. Srinivas, Viking—Penguin Books India, New Delhi

Srinivas M.N. 1996: Mobility in the Caste System. *Structure and Change in Indian Society*. Eds. Milton Singer and Bernard S. Cohen, Rawat Publications, Jaipur and New Delhi

Stutley Margaret and James 1997: *A Dictionary of Hinduism*, Routledge and Paul Kugan, London and Henley

Thapar Romila 1986: *Situating Indian History*. Eds. Sabyasachi Bhattacharya and Romila Thapar, Oxford University Press, New Delhi

Thapar Romila 1996: Ideology and the Upanishads, *Society and Ideology in India*. Ed. D.N. Jha, Munshiram Manoharlal Publishers Pvt. Ltd., New Delhi

Tharamangalam Joseph 1996: Caste among Christians in India, *Caste Its Twentieth Century Avatar*, Viking—Penguin Books India, New Delhi

Varma Prativa 1980: *Philosophy of Mahabharata and Manusmriti* Classical Publications New Delhi

Walker Benjamin 1995: *Hindu World: An Encyclopedic Survey of Hinduism, Vol. II*, An Imprint of HarperCollins Publishers, Noida

Williams Durham 1991: *Co-Evolution: Gene, Culture and Human Diversity*, Stanford University Press, Palo Alto, CA

The World Dictionary 1991: World Book Inc. A Scott Fetzer Company, Chicago, London, Sydney, Tronto

Yadav J.N. 1992: *Yadavs through the Ages*, Vol. I, Sharada Publishing House, New Delhi

Yamazaki G. 1997: *Social Discrimination in Ancient India and Its Transition to Medieval Period*: Caste System, Untouchability and The Depressed Ed.: H. Kotani Manohar Delhi

Encyclopedias

British Encyclopedia and Ultimate Reference Book 2005
British Encyclopedia Students and Home Edition 2009
Stanford Encyclopedia 2002
Wikipedia—the Free Encyclopedia

Law Books

Gupte S.V. 1980. Hindu Law (With Supplement up to July 1981) All India Reporter Ltd., Nagpur Judgment (J.)

A.I.R. Supreme Court 1993, Vol. 80, Page 479 onwards in the case of *Indra Sawhney and Others* v. *Union of India* and Others

Judgment Today (J.T.) 1992 (6) Volume 6; Citation JT 1992 (6) S.C.; Published by Taxation Publishers (P) Ltd.

Judgment of the Supreme Court in Ashok Kumar Thakur v. *Union of India*, Case No. 265/2006: 2008: Original Judgment downloaded in 2008 from website supremecourtofindia.com Judgment Information System, http://www.judis.nic.in/supremecourt/CaseRes1.aspx. Later, the same judgment was published in *A.I.R.* Supreme Court 2008 Supplement: and became available sometimes in 2009—for information

INDEX

ABOUT THE AUTHOR

Dr. L. M. Khanna is a surgeon by profession. He became an Intervener in Person in 1991 in the famous *Indra Sawhney and Others vs. Union of India* case on the suggestion of a family friend who was a sitting judge of Delhi High Court and appeared before the nine judges Special Bench of Supreme Court in person. After about 15 minutes of submissions, when the Chief Justice saw disheveled papers in his hand and found that he was a surgeon and not a professor, he asked him to deposit his papers with the court master who would get them typed and circulate among the members of the Bench. In 1992, when the judgment was delivered he was delighted to hear in the open Court that Dr. (Col) Khanna was also of assistance. It was repeated in the judgment. However, the castigation of Hindu social structure by the court produced a sickening sensation. How could such a sick society survive for thousands of years? He got curious to find the truth. It was only when he met Prof. A. M. Shah, Head of the Department of Social Sciences Delhi University in 1996 and he introduced him to some excellent articles and suggested some books that he began to realize that there was also a version other than the one on which the court had relied upon. It seemed to contradict the much advertized notions of Hindu social structure, which were the relics of colonial rule and, in the absence of adequate resistance, adopted by the court. In 2002, he published a book. *Retirement from active profession later*, enhanced his interest in social justice and in 2008, he again appeared before the Supreme Court in the case of reservations in post-graduate education, but the court, bound by the decision in Indra Sawhney case, stuck to the constitutional provisions. The changed sociological and historical perceptions were, therefore, barely discussed. Gradually this book came into existence.